Precarious Worlds

Precarious Worlds

CONTESTED GEOGRAPHIES OF SOCIAL REPRODUCTION

EDITED BY

KATIE MEEHAN
KENDRA STRAUSS

THE UNIVERSITY OF GEORGIA PRESS
Athens & London

© 2015 by the University of Georgia Press
Athens, Georgia 30602
www.ugapress.org
All rights reserved
Set in 10/13 Minion Pro Regular by Graphic Composition, Inc.
Printed and bound by Sheridan Books, Inc.
The paper in this book meets the guidelines for
permanence and durability of the Committee on
Production Guidelines for Book Longevity of the
Council on Library Resources.

Most University of Georgia Press titles are
available from popular e-book vendors.

Printed in the United States of America
19 18 17 16 15 P 5 4 3 2 1

Library of Congress Cataloging-in-Publication Data

Precarious worlds (University of Georgia Press)
    Precarious worlds : contested geographies of social reproduction / edited by Katie Meehan and
Kendra Strauss.
        pages cm. — (Geographies of justice and social transformation)
    Includes bibliographical references and index.
    ISBN (invalid) 978-0-8203-4880-3 (ebook) — ISBN 978-0-8203-4881-0 (hardcover : alk.
paper) — ISBN 978-0-8203-4882-7 (pbk. : alk. paper) 1. Feminist economics. 2. Feminist
geography. 3. Labor. 4. Households—Economic aspects. 5. Economics—Sociological aspects.
I. Meehan, Katie. II. Strauss, Kendra, 1975– III. Title.
    HQ1381.P74 2015
    305.42—dc23

                                                                        2015007739

British Library Cataloging-in-Publication Data available

CONTENTS

FOREWORD

SUSAN BRAEDLEY AND MEG LUXTON

Social reproduction has become one of the most promising and exciting concepts for feminist-informed research and activism because of its rich potential to address women's oppression. Its perspective invites the recognition that all oppressions—of gender, race, class, sexuality, ability, and more—are connected.

A social reproduction perspective begins by posing three significant challenges to prevailing assumptions about human life and social organization:

1. The sex/gender divisions of labor that exist in most societies are not natural, or based on biological differences between women and men, but are historically and socially constructed and subject to change (Coontz and Henderson 1986; Connell 2002).
2. The activities involved in sustaining and reproducing daily life are not just biological or instinctive expressions of the way people naturally live in families, but constitute work that is determined by regional historical, political, economic, and social relations (Seccombe 1992; Seccombe 1993).
3. These labors are not just private activities involved in intimate kinship and family relations but work that is socially necessary and central to the production of both subsistence and wealth in any society. In the capitalist economies most of us live in, that labor is essential to the process of capital accumulation (Picchio 1992).

One of the most important insights of the global feminist movement has been the recognition that capitalist economies depend for their existence on the unpaid and/or undervalued care work that most women—and, to a lesser extent, men—do. Feminist scholars have shown that this work involved in social reproduction acts as a subsidy for the private profit making essential to capitalism. Feminist activists have called for collective responsibility and support for unpaid and low-waged care work, demanding, for example, paid leaves and quality socialized care for dependent people. Both have asked to what extent capitalism can be reformed to improve the lives of the world's peoples, instead of just its elites.

While most scholarship on social reproduction has focused on unpaid or undervalued care work, there has been a wealth of scholarship analyzing the relations through which social reproduction is accomplished—whether they are kin-based or affective relations of domestic labor in households, marketized relations, or those relations organized by states (Luxton 1980, 1983; MacDonald and Connelly 1983; Arat-Koç 1990; Luxton, Rosenberg, and Arat-Koç 1990; Doyal 1999; Armstrong and Kits 2004; Duffy 2005; Bezanson 2006a; Bezanson and Luxton 2006; Braedley 2006; Cameron 2006; Luxton 2006; Braedley 2010; Braedley and Luxton 2010; Luxton 2010; and Braedley 2012 are just a few examples). This work has begun to distinguish the full range of social reproduction, including not only unpaid domestic labor and low-waged precarious employment associated with cleaning, laundry, food preparation, and bodies, but also professionalized, well-paid work such as teaching or nursing. For example, there is an extensive literature on the role of education in social reproduction, inspired by the work of scholars like Bowles and Gintis (1976). There is also a significant feminist political economy vein of the literature on "care" and care work that draws upon conceptual framings of social reproduction (Folbre and Nelson 2000; Armstrong and Laxer 2006; and Baines 2006 are just a few examples).

Feminist political economists have begun to chart the relationship between social reproduction and international financial systems, global governance, and social reproduction. Bakker, for example, documents the relationship between the power of capital and social reproduction (Bakker 1998; Bakker 2002; Bakker and Gill 2003; Bakker and Silvey 2008). Mahon plots the relationship between international finance; supranational, national, and local governance; and child care provision (Mahon 2005; Mahon 2008; Mahon et al. 2012). Other related scholarship explores how the work of social reproduction is valued economically (Gardiner 1997; Luxton 1997; Folbre 2006), the class dynamics of elite conspicuous consumption and poverty (Naylor 2011), and the political implications of campaigns to measure and value all aspects of social reproduction, especially unpaid work in the home (Waring 1999).

Many questions remain. What is the relationship between the almost entirely feminized work involved in reproducing people, whether generationally or in the daily round of cleaning, cooking, teaching, creating, and caring, and the economic and political directions and conditions of life involved in people's daily existence? For example, what happens to working people and their households when a major source of employment, such as the auto industry, is restructured, as occurred in Canada and the United States after the 2008 financial crisis? What happens to the work of daily living when people are dispossessed of land and/or personal safety, or when they are wrenched away from their way of life? When economic crisis hits, how do people make it day-to-day, and how are differently located people affected? What does it mean that income inequalities have increased so dramatically over the past thirty years? For example, according to Serge Halimi (2013) the Walton family, owners of the Walmart corporation, "had a fortune 61,992 times greater than the median U.S. income" during the 1980s. Today their wealth is 1,157,827 times greater, or as much as the total income of America's 48,800,000 poorest families (Halimi 2013). Does this growth in wealth trickle down as neoliberal theorists promise, or does it depend on the low wages and precarious employment policies of their company? In other words, how are the conditions, means, and work of social reproduction for adults and children affected by political and economic change, and how are gender, race, and class implicated in these changes?

These questions challenge dominant discourses that assume improvements in capital accumulation are a necessary step toward achieving improvements to living conditions, and that dump all people into a single genderless, raceless, classless category. They also help to reframe nonfeminist economic and political discourses that call for alternatives to capital accumulation by showing how a limited focus on the wage relationship misses the actual complexities of class relations and suggests that gender and race relations are contingent—rather than essential—to capitalist class relations. The answers to these questions, together with others emerging from a social reproduction perspective, reveal inequities and possibilities, allowing us to work toward liberatory change.

However, this ferment of scholarship and activism has led to a wide variety of definitions, conceptions, and applications of social reproduction, with significant slippages, overlaps, and analytical messiness. For example, social reproduction is sometimes operationalized primarily as a descriptive category, to describe a specific set of activities (Laslett and Brenner 1989; Broomhill and Sharp 2007). Other scholars use it as an analytical concept with explanatory power (Luxton and Corman 2001; Duffy 2010). Some authors slide between these usages, demonstrating, for example, the relationship between child care and capitalism, but then deploying a more descriptive conception to discuss policy regimes (Mahon 2005).

Such conceptual differences produce different critiques and stimulate a variety of strategic approaches. One dominant conceptual strand critiques and also draws upon the ubiquitous liberalism of contemporary politics to take on the important work of demonstrating how neoliberal political economies negatively affect the conditions of everyday life (Bakker and Gill 2003; Bezanson 2006b). This strand shows a tendency to deploy a concept of social reproduction that slips between two definitions: the reproduction of the population and the reproduction of labor power. This slippage obscures and ignores issues of class, while the tendency to focus on "population" without examining race, racialization, racism, ethnicity, nationality, and other social hierarchies misses other key relations of inequality. Whether intentional, pragmatic, or otherwise, the alternative, more equitable vision these concepts suggest is social democracy—a kinder, gentler capitalism.

Another dominant conceptual strand places class relations centrally by critiquing and drawing on Marxist theories, where social reproduction is described in reference to "the laboring population." In this strand, several developments have created conceptual fuzziness, related to the concept of "domestic labor," honed through this strand's scholarship and activism (such as various "wages for housework" campaigns [James 2012]). Domestic labor refers to the *unpaid* household work involved in ensuring the capacity of workers to continue to work for wages, thus demonstrating that this work is key to the production of labor power for capital accumulation. The strategic vision emanating from this strand looks to end capitalism. Yet conceptual and political clarity has been compromised by slippages in terminology, such as when "domestic labor" is used to describe the oppressive conditions of domestic employees; the work of maids, nannies, and others; or the domestic work of women and men in managerial classes (Giles and Arat-Koç 1994). While dealing with important issues, this usage abandons the analytical possibilities latent in the original conception, leaving only a descriptor of paid/unpaid work involved in reproducing "populations" and failing to analyze the interconnections of gender, race, and class.

Further conceptual murkiness is created when the terms "domestic labor" and "social reproduction" are used interchangeably. This slippage ignores the fact that social reproduction is not always kin- or affective-relationship-based, and it is sometimes accomplished by those who work for wages, not only through private household arrangements but also through markets and states (O'Connor, Orloff, and Shaver 1999). Variations in how social reproductive work is accomplished are significant to understanding the relation between capital developments and class formation. The knowledge developed through workers' struggles and union politics offers important understandings of paid reproductive labor, as some analyses illustrate (Armstrong and Jansen 2000; Braedley 2009; Baines 2011; Armstrong and Laxer 2012).

In addition to these issues and despite frequent assertions that the intersections of gender, race, and class are core topics of study, very few scholars actually succeed in dealing adequately with all three. Gender and class are well analyzed, as are gender and race. Nonfeminist analyses of race and class are well developed (Gilroy 1982; Balibar and Wallerstein 1991). The challenge remaining is to fully theorize and operationalize the three in relation to each other and to show how they operate in processes of social reproduction. In this collection and others, this work is being undertaken. There remains much to be done.

Another challenge is that by its very nature, capitalism is always changing. Some feminists have taken up the globalization of capital seriously, proposing new frames for thinking about social reproduction in the context of this shift, such as Katz's "countertopographic" approach (Katz 2001). But recent developments in finance capital have yet to be deeply considered. Marx observed that profit resulted from the accumulation of surplus value, which was the difference between the value of goods and services produced and the wage. Feminists showed that the wage is the cost of social reproduction, which is historically contingent (Picchio 1992). However, the primary sources of profit fluctuate between finance capital and production. The effects of "casino capitalism" (Sinn 2010) on social reproduction, especially at the level of households and daily life, have yet to be analyzed. For example, how is social reproduction affected when companies' intrinsic value is not based solely upon their past or present economic performances or their net worth, but also upon the competitive strategizing of fund managers (Harvey 2005; Madrick 2011)? The fallout from the economic crisis of 2008 has affected working-class people around the globe, as governments respond with policies that often download the costs of propping up capital onto their bodies and lives (Brenner 2011; Stuckler and Basu 2013). The horror of these policies, such as the gross increase in male suicides across Europe, widespread youth unemployment, homelessness, and significant declines in health status in many countries, is well documented (De Vogli, Marmot, and Stuckler 2013; Elson 2013; Stuckler and Basu 2013). These tragedies lend urgency to the need to theorize the relationship between these economic relations of capital and social reproduction during this neoliberal, globalizing period, including all its unevenness (Harvey 2006; Roberts 2013).

The relations of social reproduction have been the ground from which much activism, feminist or otherwise, has sprung since the earliest days of capitalism— from campaigns for birth control, environmental protection, and fair wages to overthrowing colonial governments and capitalist economics. These struggles invert the assumption of capitalist economics that capital accumulation will eventually lead to human well-being. Instead, their activists argue that human well-being is necessary to a sustainable economic base. The Idle No More campaign, stimulated by indigenous women in Canada, spread across North America in 2012–13, mobilizing an understanding of social reproduction gleaned through the perspectives and experiences of indigenous peoples.[1] This conception links the conditions for social reproduction of indigenous peoples to environmental, economic, political, social, and spiritual factors, made possible partly by their traditional holistic cultural views and the organization of communal life and property, especially on their land. It is also informed by indigenous experiences that reveal the central role of capital accumulation in inflicting and perpetuating horrific conditions of life resulting from a centuries-old assimilation/extermination campaign. In our view, this contradiction embedded in indigenous conditions of social reproduction has led to an activist burgeoning, but certainly not for the first time (Williams 2012).

These kinds of scholarship and activism alert us to new approaches and new opportunities to evaluate, rethink, and reimagine social reproduction in order to contribute to bold, emancipatory futures.

NOTE

1. See *Idle No More,* "The Movement," September 12, 2014, http://www.idlenomore .ca/vision.

REFERENCES

Arat-Koç, Sedef. "Importing Housewives: Non-Citizen Domestic Workers and the Crisis of the Domestic Sphere in Canada." In *Through the Kitchen Window: The Politics of Home and Family,* 2nd ed., edited by Meg Luxton, Harriet Gail Rosenberg, and Sedef Arat-Koç, 81–103. Toronto: Garamond, 1990.

Armstrong, Pat, and Irene Jansen. *Assessing the Impact of Restructuring and Work Reorganization in Long Term Care Worker's Health Issues.* Ottawa: National Network on Environments and Women's Health, 2000.

Armstrong, Pat, and Olga Kits. "One Hundred Years of Caregiving." In *Caring for/Caring about: Women, Home Care, and Unpaid Caregiving,* edited by Karen R.Grant, Carol Amaratunga, Pat Armstrong, Madeline Boscoe, Ann Pederson, and Kay Willson, 45–73. Toronto: Garamond, 2004.

Armstrong, Pat, and Kate Laxer. "Precarious Work, Privatization, and the Health Care Industry: The Case of Ancillary Workers." In *Precarious Employment: Understanding Labour Market Insecurity in Canada,* edited by Leah F. Vosko, 115–140. Montreal: McGill-Queens University Press, 2006.

———. "Demanding Labour: The Aging Health Care Labour Force." 2012 RC19 Annual Conference, Oslo, Norway, 2012.

Baines, Donna. "Staying with People Who Slap Us Around: Gender, Juggling Responsibilities and Violence in Paid (and Unpaid) Care Work." *Gender, Work & Organization* 13, no. 2 (2006): 129–151.

———. "'If We Don't Get Back to Where We Were Before': Working in the Restructured Non-Profit Social Services." *British Journal of Social Work* 40, no. 3 (2011): 928.

Bakker, Isabella. *Unpaid Work and Macroeconomics: New Discussions, New Tools for Action.* Ottawa: Status of Women Canada, 1998.

———. "Who Built the Pyramids? Engendering the New International Economic and Financial Architecture." *femina politica* 11, no. 1 (2002): 13–25.

Bakker, Isabella, and Stephen Gill. *Power, Production, and Social Reproduction: Human In/security in the Global Political Economy*, Basingstoke, U.K.: Palgrave Macmillan, 2003.

Bakker, Isabella, and Rachel Silvey. *Beyond States and Markets: The Challenges of Social Reproduction*. New York: Routledge, 2008.

Balibar, Etienne, and Immanuel M. Wallerstein. *Race, Nation, Class: Ambiguous Identities*. London: Verso, 1991.

Bezanson, Kate. "Gender and the Limits of Social Capital." *Canadian Review of Sociology/Revue canadienne de sociologie* 43, no. 4 (2006a): 427–443.

———. *Gender, the State, and Social Reproduction: Household Insecurity in Neo-Liberal Times*. Toronto: University of Toronto Press, 2006b.

Bezanson, Kate, and Meg Luxton, eds. *Social Reproduction: Feminist Political Economy Challenges Neo-Liberalism*. Montreal: McGill-Queens University Press, 2006.

Bowles, Samuel, and Herbert Gintis. *Schooling in Capitalist America: Educational Reform and the Contradictions of Economic Life*. New York: Basic, 1976.

Braedley, Susan. "Someone to Watch Over You: Gender, Class and Social Reproduction." In *Social Reproduction: Feminist Political Economy Takes on Neoliberalism*, edited by Kate Bezanson and Meg Luxton, 215–230. Montreal/Kingston: McGill-Queens University Press, 2006.

———. "A Ladder Up: Ontario Firefighters' Wages in Neoliberal Times." *Just Labour* 14 (Autumn 2009): 129–149.

———. "Accidental Health Care: Masculinity and Neoliberalism at Work." In *Neoliberalism and Everyday Life*, edited by Susan Braedley and Meg Luxton, 136–162. Montreal and Kingston: McGill-Queens University Press, 2010.

———. "The Masculinization Effect: Neoliberalism, the Medical Paradigm and Ontario's Health Care Policy." *Canadian Women's Studies* 29, no. 3 (2012): 71–83.

Braedley, S., and M. Luxton, eds. *Neoliberalism and Everyday Life*. Kingston and Montreal: McGill-Queens University Press, 2010.

Brenner, Johanna. "Caught in the Whirlwind: Working-Class Families Face the Economic Crisis." *Socialist Register 2011: The Crisis This Time* (2011): 64–82.

Broomhill, Raymond, and Rhonda Sharp. "The Problem of Social Reproduction under Neoliberalism." In *Remapping Gender in the New Global Order*, edited by Marjorie Griffen-Cohen and Janine Brodie, 85–108. New York: Routledge, 2007.

Cameron, Barbara. "Social Reproduction and Canadian Federalism." In *Social Reproduction: Feminist Political Economy Takes on Neoliberalism*, edited by Kate Bezanson and Meg Luxton, 45–74. Montreal: McGill-Queens University Press, 2006.

Connell, Raewyn W. *Gender*. Cambridge, U.K.: Polity, 2002.

Coontz, Stephanie, and Peta Henderson. *Women's Work, Men's Property: The Origins of Gender and Class*. London: Verso, 1986.

De Vogli, Roberto, Michael Marmot, and David Stuckler. "Strong Evidence That the Economic Crisis Caused a Rise in Suicides in Europe: The Need for Social Protection." *Journal of Epidemiology and Community Health* 67, no. 4 (2013): 298.

Doyal, Lesley. "Women and Domestic Labour: Setting a Research Agenda." In *Health and Work: Critical Issues*, edited by Norma Daykin and Lesley Doyal. London: Macmillan, 1999.

Duffy, Mignon. "Reproducing Labor Inequalities: Challenges for Feminists Conceptualizing Care at the Intersections of Gender, Race and Class." *Gender and Society* 19, no. 1 (2005): 66–82.

———. *Making Care Count: A Century of Gender, Race, and Paid Care Work.* New Brunswick, N.J.: Rutgers University Press, 2010.

Elson, Diane. "Austerity Policies Increase Unemployment and Inequality—but Don't Reduce Budget Deficits and Government Borrowing." *Journal of Australian Political Economy* 71 (2013): 130.

Folbre, Nancy. "Measuring Care: Gender, Empowerment, and the Care Economy." *Journal of Human Development* 7, no. 2 (2006): 183–199.

Folbre, Nancy, and Julie A. Nelson. "For Love or Money—or Both?" *Journal of Economic Perspectives* 14, no. 4 (2000): 123–140.

Gardiner, Jean. *Gender, Care and Economics.* London: Macmillan, 1997.

Giles, Wenona, and Sedef Arat-Koç, eds. *Maid in the Market: Women's Paid Domestic Labour.* Halifax: Fernwood, 1994.

Gilroy, Paul. "The Empire Strikes Back: Race and Racism in 70s Britain." London: Hutchinson, in association with the Centre for Contemporary Cultural Studies, 1982.

Halimi, Serge. "The Tyranny of the One Percent." *Le Monde Diplomatique* (English version), May 2013. mondediplo.com/2013/05/01tryanny. Accessed January 17, 2015.

Harvey, David. *A Brief History of Neoliberalism.* Oxford: Oxford University Press, 2005.

———. *Spaces of Global Capital: Towards a Theory of Uneven Geographic Development.* London: Verso, 2006.

James, Selma. *Sex Race and Class: The Perspective of Winning: A Selection of Writings 1952–2011.* Oakland, Calif.: PM Press, 2012.

Katz, Cindi. "Vagabond Capitalism and the Necessity of Social Reproduction." *Antipode* 33, no. 4 (2001): 709–728.

Laslett, Barbara, and Johanna Brenner. "Gender and social reproduction: Historical perspectives." *Annual Review of Sociology* (1989): 381–404.

Luxton, Meg. *More than a labour of love: Three generations of women's work in the home,* Toronto: Womens Press, 1980.

———. "Two hands for the clock: Changing patterns in the gendered division of labour." *Studies in Political Economy* 12 (1983): 27–44.

———. "The UN, women, and household labour: Measuring and valuing unpaid work." *Women's Studies International Forum* 20, no. 3 (1997):431–439.

———. "Friends, Neighbours and Community: A Case of the Role of Informal Caregiving in Social Reproduction." In *Social Reproduction: Feminist Political Economy Challenges Neo-liberalism,* edited by Kate Bezanson and Meg Luxton, 263–292. Kingston/Montreal: McGill Queen's University Press: 2006.

———. "Doing Neoliberalism: Perverse Individualism in Personal Life." In *Neoliberalism and Everyday Life,* edited by Susan Braedley and Meg Luxton, 163–183. Montreal / Kingston: McGill Queens University Press: 2010.

Luxton, Meg and June Shirley Corman. *Getting by in hard times: gendered labour at home and on the job,* Toronto: University of Toronto Press, 2001.

Luxton, Meg, Harriet Gail Rosenberg, and Sedef Arat-Koç,. *Through the kitchen window: The politics of home and family.* Toronto: Garamond Press, 1990.

MacDonald, Martha and M. Patricia Connelly. "Women's Work: Domestic and Wage Labourers in a Nova Scotia Community." *Studies in Political Economy* 10, Winter (1983): 45–72.

Madrick, Jeff. *Age of Greed: The Triumph of Finance and the Decline of America, 1970 to the Present.* Toronto,New York: Vintage, 2011.

Mahon, Rianne. (2005). "Rescaling social reproduction: childcare in Toronto/Canada and Stockholm/Sweden." *International Journal of Urban and Regional Research* 29(2): 341–357.

———. "Babies and Bosses: Gendering the OECD's Social Policy Discourse." In *The OECD and Transnational Governance*, edited by Rianne Mahon and Stephen McBride, 260–275. Vancouver: University of British Columbia Press, 2008.

Mahon, Rianne, Anneli Anttonen, Christina Bergqvist, Deborah Brennan, and Barbara Hobson. "Convergent care regimes? Childcare arrangements in Australia, Canada, Finland and Sweden." *Journal of European Social Policy* 22, no. 4 (2012): 419–431.

Naylor, R. T. *Crass Struggle: Greed, Glitz, and Gluttony in a Wanna-Have World.* Montreal/Kingston: McGill-Queens University Press, 2011.

O'Connor, Julia S., Ann Shola Orloff, and Sheila Shaver. *States, markets, families: Gender, liberalism and social policy in Australia, Canada, Great Britain and the United States.* Cambridge: Cambridge University Press, 1999.

Picchio, Antonella. *Social reproduction: the political economy of the labour market.* Cambridge: Cambridge University Press, 1992.

Roberts, Adrienne. "Financing Social Reproduction: The Gendered Relations of Debt and Mortgage Finance in Twenty-first-century America." *New Political Economy* 18, no. 1 (2013): 21–42.

Seccombe, Wally. *A Millennium of Family Change: Feudalism to Capitalism in Northwestern Europe.* London: Verso, 1992.

———. *Weathering the Storm: The History of Working Class Families.* London: Verso, 1993.

Sinn, Hans-Werner. *Casino capitalism: How the financial crisis came about and what needs to be done now.* Oxford: Oxford University Press, 2010.

Stuckler, David, and Sanjay Basu. *The Body Economic: Why Austerity Kills-Recessions, Budget Battles, and The Politics of Life and Death.* New York: Basic Books, 2013.

Waring, Marilyn. *Counting for Nothing: What Men Value and What Women Are Worth.* Toronto: University of Toronto Press, 1999.

Williams, Carol. *Indigenous Women and Work: From Labor to Activism.* Champaign: University of Illinois Press, 2012.

ACKNOWLEDGMENTS

We would like to thank Nik Heynen, Cindi Katz, Sallie Marston, and Katharyne Mitchell for early encouragement; and Alex Loftus for his enthusiasm for the volume and thoughtful insights. At the University of Georgia Press we would like to thank our editor, Mick Gusinde-Duffy, and Nik Heynen, Deborah Cowen, and Melissa Wright of the Geographies of Justice and Social Transformation Series for helping to guide this book to fruition. We also received helpful and constructive comments from two anonymous reviewers, which made the book a stronger and more coherent volume.

Kendra wants to acknowledge the invaluable conversations with colleagues and friends that shaped the ideas in the introduction: Judy Fudge, Kate Derickson, and Abby Neely deserve special thanks for providing a listening ear over the years; and Rosie Cox for helping clarify (or start to) her thinking on social reproduction and care. Katie would like to acknowledge the Wayne Morse Center for Law and Politics at the University of Oregon, which provided generous support in the form of a fellowship and intellectual camaraderie; and to extend warm thanks to Sallie Marston, for being a mentor, friend, and coauthor; to Brian Marks, for his brilliant thoughts on social reproduction and nature; and to Julie Graham, whose light we still miss.

The editors also gratefully acknowledge the financial support of the SFU University Publications Fund in preparing the book manuscript for publication.

Precarious Worlds

New Frontiers in Life's Work

KENDRA STRAUSS AND KATIE MEEHAN

This volume explores new frontiers in "life's work" (Mitchell, Marston, and Katz 2004), with a focus on how and why it is becoming increasingly precarious for many in our contemporary moment. Precariousness and precarity are multivalent concepts grounded in different intellectual and political genealogies (McDowell and Christopherson 2009). In feminist political economy, the concept of precarious work describes the feminization of labor markets (what Vosko calls, in the subtitle of her 2000 book, "the gendered rise of a precarious employment relationship"); and in political philosophy, Judith Butler (2004) has developed a social ontology of precarity to articulate a more generalized concept of mutual dependency as a condition of human life. The extension of the idea of precariousness *in* work (Vosko 2010) to precarity as an ontological condition *of workers* has been taken up by theorists like Guy Standing (2011), who contentiously describes the precariat as a class. In geography, research on migrants and asylum seekers has drawn on both intellectual traditions to explore labor market experiences *and* "work-life" conditions (Dyer, McDowell, and Batnitzky 2011; Waite, Valentine, and Lewis 2014). In other words, more synthetic approaches are starting to explore the relationships between precarious work and precarious life.

Our goal in this volume is also exploratory and synthetic: to bring into conversation different approaches to conceptualizing and resisting inequality and exploitation, and to consider whether new alliances of theory and justice might be forged through a feminist materialist politics grounded in the concept of social reproduction (SRP). Social reproduction, we argue, provides a framework for examining the interaction of paid labor and unpaid work in the reproduction of bodies, households, communities, societies, and environments and the ways in which these activities are organized to support—or undermine—human flourishing. In other words, it potentially facilitates the exploration of both precarious work and precarious life as mutually constitutive conditions of subordination and oppression, while recognizing—as Butler does—that all bodies, all social and ideological formations, are reproduced through human labor and are therefore precarious to a degree. The concept of social reproduction, however, grounded in the recognition of the structural exercise of economic and social power, is also a lens for focusing on the unequal distribution of conditions of flourishing that render some bodies, some workforces, and some communities far more precarious than others. As economic restructuring has intensified demands for time, labor, and value extraction "at work," we recognize that recent crises—economic, political, and environmental—have also reconfigured the conditions and possibilities for *life's* work. Consider, for example, these three vignettes.[1]

> A child sits with her mother in a clinic waiting room in the town of Anand in the Indian state of Gujarat. She leans her head against the dome of her mother's belly and feels the baby inside kick against her cheek. Her mother has told her that this baby will not live with them but will grow up in a city called London, which is far away and very cold, with a different family. The child hopes the baby will have warm clothes. She thinks about the new apartment they will move into after her family gets money from the baby's new parents and is excited; where they live now the rain drips through the roof during the monsoon.[2]

> In a Starbucks in Seattle, Washington, a man shows his husband an Associated Press story about the elevated levels of caffeine, cinnamon, and artificial vanilla that University of Washington scientists have detected some 640 feet below the surface of Puget Sound. While they joke about fish with a taste for lattes, the man idly wonders if he should ask Betty, their Filipino nanny, not to buy local salmon for their two-year-old son.[3]

> In a small house on a steep hillside in Mexico City, a woman fills her washing machine with clean water. Her husband used to wire her money from the United States every month, but since he lost his construction job she now takes in neighbors' laundry to make ends meet. She already purchases bottled water for drinking and cooking (at prices one thousand times the municipal rate), so during the rainy season, rather than pay for municipal water, she collects rooftop rain and recycles sudsy greywater to use for her laundry business. Even though her house is connected to the municipal network, the woman enjoys managing her own water. "I feel more independent because I can turn off the tap," she explains. "It has changed our relationship with city government."[4]

If social reproduction is fundamentally about how we live (Mitchell, Marston, and Katz 2004), then such stories suggest that lived worlds are increasingly on edge: our livelihoods and the inequalities they engender are being engineered in new ways. From global warming to the most recent financial meltdown, crises have dramatically reshaped conditions of economic production and social reproduction, in turn destabilizing—and sometimes fracturing—the relations that we have historically understood as grounds for political change.[5] Governments enact drastic cuts to social spending and welfare services in the name of deficit reduction; states "get tough" on immigration but not financial profiteering; hurricanes and other natural disasters scour livelihoods and landscapes; and unregulated and informal employment balloons as old certainties expire with the standard employment relationship.

While it is true that public support for social reproduction—what Esping-Anderson (1990) conceptualized as welfare regimes facilitating decommodification (freedom from dependence on markets)—has been historically and geographically uneven (see chapters by Parker and Smith and Winders in this volume), significant institutional shifts have occurred in both the global North and South in the last several decades. As Isabella Bakker and Stephen Gill (2003) suggest, the contradictions between the extended reach of capital and its protection by the state, and progressive forms of social reproduction, have intensified. The costs of global economic restructuring are increasingly "downloaded" onto daily life in ways that are deeply gendered, classed, racialized, and militarized (Feldman, Geisler, and Menon 2011). Long after the workday expires and the shop floor is shuttered, these crises hemorrhage into the spaces of life's work. Yet as Marston, Mitchell, and Katz argue in the conclusion to this volume, much political economy remains production oriented and capital centric, continuing to ignore and downplay unpaid work, care labor, and the myriad "unproductive" activities and practices that contribute to the continuation of societies worldwide. This produces a ghettoization of social reproduction, which is considered (if considered at all) the purview of feminist theorists; but many approaches to conceptualizing the interrelationship of "the economy," "society," and "capitalism" still fail to take into account the relationship between paid labor and unpaid work, or to understand value in ways that don't rely on monetization and traditional definitions of productive activity.

Social reproduction—conceptualized by Karl Marx and Frederick Engels as the labor necessary to ensure that workers arrive the next day at the factory gate—has long been used by feminists as a critical lens onto the entwined spheres of paid labor and the unpaid work of daily life. This relationship has been understood as inherently dialectical, and critical and radical feminist epistemologies of social reproduction sought to theorize production and reproduction under capitalism in this way (Cameron 2006, 46). But one critique of some conceptual and analytical mobilizations of SRP is that production and social reproduction have nevertheless been represented as a binary, with wage labor as the central signifier and unpaid work as its domestic, gendered, unvalued "other" (Gibson-Graham 1996).

At the same time, socialist feminist critiques of Marx (especially the early second wave analyses of domestic labor, such as the important writings of Margaret Benson) treated the experiences of white working- and middle-class women homemakers as typical. This ignored the ways in which the male breadwinner model was grounded in racialized and heteronormative social and economic structures that excluded many people, including in what Nandita Sharma (2006) calls "the minority world." Taken together, these critiques highlight key challenges to social reproduction mounted by feminists toward the end of the second wave.

For geographers, these critiques suggest serious implications for spatial and place-based understandings of the world and the politics they engender. In their breakthrough collection *Life's Work: Geographies of Social Reproduction*, Katharyne Mitchell, Sallie Marston, and Cindi Katz attempted to push back against binary thinking while retaining a core engagement with SRP's foundations in critical and radical feminist political economy. They argued that imagining social reproduction as a separate "sphere" from production is particularly problematic in contemporary capitalism. They pointed to the "growing obfuscation of the boundaries between 'work' and 'non-work' . . . this widespread and profound shift in both the material spaces and cognitive understandings of life's work" (2004, 3) and illustrated how, given the extreme polarization of labor markets in many places, these processes are highly uneven (see Smith and Winders, this volume). Notably, they also drew on Katz's characterization of the "messy, fleshy" aspects of everyday life, and on the "multiple inter-lined forces within which the body of the laborer is constituted and hegemonic norms develop" (2004, 13).

Their focus thus spotlighted the role of *bodies, spaces,* and *material practices* in social reproduction. Our goal with this volume is to explore, in a way that reflects the pluralistic and outward-looking approaches of the best of human geography scholarship and praxis, the productive possibilities of social reproduction as a theoretical lens and analytical framework for what Geraldine Pratt (2004, 3) called "a vigorous, materialist transnational feminism"—one centrally concerned with cultivating geographies of justice. For example, we examine how feminist critiques of political economy (e.g., J. K. Gibson-Graham 1996 and The Community Economies collective) and new materialist ontologies (e.g., Coole and Frost 2010) might be brought into conversation with critical and radical approaches to the production/reproduction dialectic.

In so doing, we seek to understand sites of social reproduction without pre-imagining categories of social difference, which include the full range of material practices, forms, objects, and beings—human and otherwise. This project is the outgrowth of our interests in different approaches to conceptualizing life's work grounded in Marxist feminist political economy (Strauss 2013; Fudge and Strauss 2014) and political ecology and new materialist philosophies (Bennet 2010; Coole and Frost 2010; Shaw and Meehan 2013). The book therefore reflects our own attempts to discover and navigate conceptual and theoretical terrain for exploring shared preoccupations with exploitation, oppression, injustice, and hope in life's work. It is intended to be *provocative*—of debate, critique, and flights of imagination—and *generative*—of new epistemological and political engagements. Our work is compelled not by a desire for intellectual harmony or unity (this volume represents a range of disciplines, positions, and perspectives) but by the possibilities for progressive alliances and politics that such conversations open up.

Although several years in the making, this project speaks to a reinvigorated interest in social reproduction that recognizes its historical challenges while advocating strongly for its relevance in tackling contemporary issues. Nancy Fraser (2014, 55–56) argued recently for the continued relevance of capitalism as a central category of analysis in diagnosing our most pressing "heterogeneous ills—financial, economic, ecological, political, social," but she also pointed to the ways in which many "veterans" of capitalist critique are hampered by the failure "to incorporate the insights of feminism, postcolonialism and ecological thought systematically into their understandings of capitalism." Her suggestions build on Marx but acknowledge the lacunae in Marx's thought: failures to reckon systematically with gender, ecology, and political power. While theorists of social reproduction have made huge strides in conceptualizing the interrelationship of the construction of social and economic categories of difference, aspects of ecology and political power remain less integrated within SRP frameworks.

Feminist geography offers a disciplinary context in which such a project of integration can be debated and, potentially, taken forward. Contemporary studies of social reproduction are highly interdisciplinary, coming from sociology (Bezanson and Luxton 2006; Feldman, Geisler, and Menon 2011), international political economy (Bakker and Gill 2003; Bakker and Silvey 2008), political theory (Weeks 2011), and feminist economics (Folbre 1994, 2001), yet we find that the fundamentals of SRP have remained somewhat immune to other tendrils of feminist, political, and environmental thought. Feminist geographers, for example, have confronted and challenged dilemmas in life's work via the community economy approach (Gibson-Graham 1996, 2006), care studies (Pratt 1999; Cox 2007), and critical geographies of precarity (Ettlinger 2007; Waite 2009). It is for this reason, and in direct response to the above challenges, we mobilize a politics of an expansive feminist materialism. We see resonances in our approach with Fraser's (2013, chap. 10) attempt to revisit Polanyi's double movement in order to bridge the recognition/redistribution divide that has come to characterize differences between feminism(s) grounded in critical engagements with historical materialism, and poststructuralist feminisms concerned with very different theorizations of materiality.

A Genealogy of Social Reproduction

As a concept, social reproduction has closely tracked the history of the *idea* of capitalism. The development of the language of SRP is grounded in concepts that predate, and exist in tension with, what Gibson-Graham (1996) calls "capitalo-centric" models of human society: that is, models that give primacy to capitalist market relations. As Silvia Federici (2004) argued in her seminal book *Caliban and the Witch*, however, capitalism itself also evolved out of moments of dispossession and oppression (including of women's bodies and labor power) with specific gendered and racialized characteristics. The erasure of these moments from narratives of capitalist development and the elision of unpaid work from theories of value occurred alongside the creation of the "disciplines" of economics, political science, geography, and more described below.

Bakker and Silvey (2008) trace the concept of SRP to Enlightenment notions about the biological metabolism of human society. Capitalist societies were understood, within the nascent disciplines of economics and sociology, as having natural reproductive cycles that were fundamental to their continuation over time, across space, and in place—reflecting ecological theories of (nonhuman) community development. Enlightenment models were grounded in ancient Greek understandings of the social as the realm of free associations and the economic—typified by household relations between, for example, husband and wife or master and slave—as the realm of necessity, whose reproduction was assured by seemingly natural rhythms.

John Locke's concept of the social contract posited household relations as the domain of individual choice and free contract (that is, moved them into the realm of the social). This happened at the same time that the discipline of political economy emerged, with a central focus on the reproductive cycles of society: the study of social reproduction. Thus, as industrial capitalism took hold, the development of European universities produced a division of labor in which sociology specialized in the study of social relations and economics handled economic relations (Caffentzis 2002).

Disciplines such as economics and political economy sought to understand the creation of economic value, which under capitalism became associated with the labor theory of value in general and wage labor in particular. As Antonella Picchio (1992) has described, social reproduction was in fact a foundation for the classical political economy of David Ricardo, Adam Smith, and Thomas Malthus. Marx drew on Ricardo's conceptualization of the labor theory of value to produce a theory of the labor *process*. He also articulated a concept of social reproduction in *Capital* (Marx 1976) through his development of notions of simple reproduction and the reproduction of social capital. Simple reproduction describes the general conditions under which the amount of capital remains constant because part of the profit (itself generated by the surplus derived from the labor process), beyond what is needed to maintain the capital stock, is spent on consumption in order to maintain the current rate of production.

> A society can no more cease to produce than it can cease to consume. When viewed, therefore, as a connected whole, and as flowing on with incessant renewal, every social process of production is, at the same time, a process of reproduction. . . . The conditions of production are also those of reproduction. No society can go on producing, in other words, no society can reproduce, unless it constantly reconverts a part of its products into *means of production, or elements of fresh products.* (Marx 1906, VII.XXIII.1, emphasis added)

For Marx, the interrelationship between production and reproduction is clearly evident. Engels (2004) goes further, suggesting that in a materialist conception of history the determining factors are, in the final instance, the production and reproduction of immediate life and the conditions under which these occur. In his emphasis on immediate life, labor power was the link between the reproduction of the *means* and *relations* of production. Engel's insights located gendered processes, and particularly unpaid work done by women, at the center of theories about production. But as Meg Luxton (2006, 35) pointed out, "sex blindness and race blindness means that political economy, particularly Marxism, has inadequately theorized one of its own key insights about the production of labor power and its market." In other words, Marx granted equal weight to production and reproduction (for which consumption is necessary) but conceived and analyzed reproduction within relatively narrow bounds.

The study of economics was thus purged of any and all "social" relations; the centrality of social reproduction to political economy was bifurcated into spheres of "economy" and "society"; and the material or environmental aspects of life's work were shunted to the domain of "ecology." Marx and Engels's theorization of social reproduction has been pivotal to subsequent developments of SRP, but SRP theorists have often taken critical aim at the limits of the Marx/Engels approach and the productivist bias in Marxian political economy (Weeks 2011).

Perhaps most crucial, but least explored, are the ways in which Marx's notion of species-being is linked to production of nature and human life. Generally these processes are analyzed and understood in relation to the commodification of labor under capitalism: that is, the way in which workers become alienated from the means of production and subsistence, or the ways in which nonhuman labor (e.g., trees, water, air, land) is abstracted, commodified, and exploited. Indeed, Marx uses species-being to distinguish humans—who labor freely and universally— from nonhumans, who produce for basic or familial survival (Loftus 2012).

Marx clearly gave centrality to the processes by which people produce, allocate, and consume the products of human labor in ways that shape their social relations and organization (Luxton 2006). While criticisms of species-being are valid, Alex Loftus (2012, 34) suggests "there is a far more nuanced sense of the potential for a creative and symbiotic relationship between human and nonhuman to be achieved through sensuous engagement in the present and for the future." Such insights imply that social reproduction must be understood as *more* than the simple reproduction of laboring populations (Katz 2001).

It was this insight that animated a renewed interest in social reproduction during the 1970s. Socialist and Marxist feminists used the concept to spotlight the contribution of women's unpaid work to "the economy." Dalla Costa and James (1972) challenged the understanding of wage labor as productive labor and nonwage labor—especially household and care work—as unproductive; this point in turn dislocated value as something generated only in and through the production process. Within feminist political economy scholars sought to understand the historical, materialist, and dialectical processes through which gender and class oppressions are produced, and they theorized the relation between SRP and capitalist accumulation through interactions at the levels of production, distribution, circulation, institutions, and politics (Bakker and Silvey 2008). Such efforts resulted in a plurality of theoretical and political approaches, in particular the domestic labor debate and "Wages for Housework" movement (see, for example, Dalla Costa and James 1972; James 1975; see Weeks 2011 for an overview) and the theorization of the sex-gender system and gender order (Rubin 1975; Lerner 1986). As Luxton (2006, 33) has pointed out, domestic labor studies advanced historical materialism by integrating the production of life into theories of modes of production. According to Mitchell, Marston, and Katz (2004, 2), this relates to the larger project of linking structures and social relations:

> From Marx through Althusser to Leacock and Dalla Costa, the theoretical imperative has been to elucidate the correspondences and contradictions among structures and between them and particular social relations, to understand the form, logic and practices through which capitalism as a socioeconomic system is able to sustain its dynamic via the capacity to reproduce itself on an expanded scale.

In relation to feminist epistemology, then, social reproduction represents a framework for theorizing and analyzing correspondences and contradictions between structures, social relations, and practices. It is through these structures (such as state institutions of social welfare), social relations (such as class and gender), and practices (such as heterosexual marriage) that both means and relations of production, and those activities and institutions associated with the domain of social life, are reproduced in uneven ways over time and in space

(Massey 1984). Feminist political economists insist that capitalism is a *socio-economic* system, and that wage work/production and nonwage work/social reproduction are fundamentally co-constitutive (Folbre 2001, 2004).

Intellectual and political work in the 1970s and 1980s thus led to a generalized definition of social reproduction as involving "a range of activities, behaviors, responsibilities, and relationships that ensure the daily and generational social, emotional, moral, and physical reproduction of people" (Bezanson 2006, 175). Laslett and Brenner (1989, 382) similarly described it as "the activities and attitudes, behaviors and emotions, responsibilities and relationships directly involved in the maintenance of life on a daily basis, and intergenerationally." Seeking more clarity, Bakker and Gill (2003, 4) identified the main processes relevant to SRP as: biological reproduction, the reproduction of labor power, and social processes connected to caring and socialization.

Yet this movement toward a generalized definition and framework for understanding social reproduction did not always take adequate account of the role of the state. From the 1990s feminists began to theorize social reproduction in relation to the changes brought about by neoliberalism. Whereas earlier work by feminists located social reproduction within a framework of state-led development, for Bakker and Gill (2003) and Bakker and Silvey (2008) recent changes needed to be understood in relation to new, reorganized relations of governance that were shifting responsibilities for SRP in the context of intensified globalization. Their approach echoed claims that the state is not disappearing under neoliberalism but instead being dramatically restructured (Mitchell, Marston, and Katz 2004); the increasing commodification of women's labor and commoditization of care work are dimensions of these changes (McDowell et al. 2006, quoting Ehrenreich 1984).[6]

In the discipline of geography SRP had relatively little purchase, despite the radical turn since the late 1970s. Mitchell, Marston, and Katz's (2004) edited collection brought together work by feminist geographers on the spatial dimensions of social reproduction. They and their contributors demonstrated that approaches to SRP have tended to relate specifically to the social relations between capitalists and laborers at the point of production. This insight implies two assumptions: first, that workers are *waged* (which neglects forms of labor not contracted or paid for in monetary exchange); and second, that workers are necessarily constituted as free wage laborers.

Mitchell, Marston, and Katz (2004) object to these assumptions on three grounds. First, they argue that the class relation is not formed solely through the coercion into paid work; noncapitalist relations and activities exist and are reproduced even within primarily capitalist social formations (see also Gibson-Graham 1996). Moreover, as engagements with their work have shown, even when commodification takes place it is often not in the way envisaged by political economists, whose theories rely on the stylized facts of frictionless markets and a process of free contract (Strauss 2012, 2013). Second, while recent work has continued to advance our understanding of articulations among capitalism, patriarchy, and racism, there often remains a separation between theory and actually existing *spaces* of material reproduction. And third, migration challenges the assumption that the alienation of labor from its owner occurs in the same place (or at least within the same nation-state or territory) as the site of its reproduction (an argument that also has a longer history in industrial sociology—see Burawoy 1976).

These objections (and Luxton's [2006] assessment of dual systems theory) resonate, although in different ways, with J. K. Gibson-Graham's critique of political economy. In *The End of Capitalism (as We Knew It)* she explored socialist feminist conceptualizations of social reproduction as a small part of her engagement with anti-essentialism and Althusser's reworking and extending of the dialectic as he found it in Marx. Dual systems theory and the gendered, capitalocentric conceptualization of production, Gibson-Graham argued, reinscribed the binary of the social and the economic without rescuing (women's) unpaid labor from its subordinate status. Similarly, the "Wages for Housework" movement was critiqued for seeking to commodify social reproduction rather than resisting equivalence with wage labor (compare Weeks 2011).

Thus, while social reproduction was never a hegemonic epistemology within the diverse milieus of second wave feminism, its association with Marxian approaches and the more generalized shift from "redistribution" to "recognition" (Fraser 1997) meant that *other* approaches to life's work have gained traction over SRP. In particular, concepts of care and caring work (Smith 2005; Lawson 2007; Dowler et al. 2009; Datta et al. 2010), emotional labor and body work (McDowell 2004; Dyer et al. 2008; England and Dyck 2011), and precarity and precarious work have emerged in certain disciplinary, theoretical, and political contexts. While we do not have the space to delve into these diverse literatures and debates in detail, we suggest that their efflorescence represents challenges to the notion of social reproduction that need to be taken seriously: What *doesn't* social reproduction account for that these approaches seek to explore? Can other feminist epistemologies be brought into dialogue with approaches associated with political economy, in productive ways?

In particular, there are orders of materialist processes and encounters that have not been "metabolized" by the body of theory generally associated with social reproduction. Two challenges stand out: issues of embodiment and identity, and social difference, emerging from over two decades of poststructuralist thought; and the resurgence of materiality in social theory, including the urgent challenges regarding environmental, geopolitical, and economic change that the "materialist question" invokes. While these two areas are not exhaustive of the conceptual and categorical challenges to SRP, here we tap them specifically for their potential to deeply enrich SRP approaches and engage their strengths toward a materialist feminism rooted in a radically open notion of justice.

New Horizons of Social Reproduction

In the introduction to *Life's Work*, Mitchell, Marston, and Katz set out three aims in relation to their project of exploring "how people produce value in all domains of their lives" (2004, 1). These aims—to explore the separation of production and reproduction, to critically relate the problematic of this separation to the contemporary period of capitalist transformation, and to investigate the role of the state in these processes—grounded their exploration very much in the tradition of feminist political economy and socialist feminism. Yet as their chapter unfolds, it is clear that they are also seeking to address lacunae in these approaches. In particular, they mobilize Ferdinand Braudel's long view of the history of capitalism to explore paracapitalist activities and dense social networks of obligations and ties wherein forms of coercion and exploitation may involve processes "other than or in excess of those associated with the separation of the individual from the means of production" (quoted in Mitchell, Marston, and Katz 2004, 8).

They also explicitly, pace Foucault, insist on the analysis of forms and processes of hegemony and the body: "We need to examine the multiple inter-lined forces within which the body of the laborer is constituted and hegemonic norms develop" (Mitchell, Marston, and Katz 2004, 13). The chapters in this book (see especially Fredericks, Marks, Parker, and Smith and Winders) seek to further the project of addressing these lacunae, building also on Katz's (2001) assertion that the lens of social reproduction allows us to focus not only on the making, maintenance, and exploitation of the labor force but also on the productions and destructions of nature.

BODIES, IDENTITY, AND DIFFERENCE

To this end, embodiment and identity represent the first of our two challenges. As the first vignette of the introduction suggests, bodies are enrolled in processes of value creation and accumulation in fast-changing and highly uneven ways (see also Gidwani and Reddy 2011 on urbanism and waste). Work by Linda McDowell, for example, described how bodily performances relate to the social construction of categories of difference like gender in the realm of paid labor (McDowell and Court 1994). Recent scholarship on food and race (Slocum and Saldhana 2013) has made explicit the links between embodiment, racialization, and the production and consumption of food. Both of these literatures clearly relate to the conceptual categories, activities, and processes of interest to theorists of social reproduction, and both draw on theories and theorists associated with poststructuralism. Scholarship on food also touches on the fraught politics of consumption, often underexplored in social reproduction approaches.

Work that seeks to directly link social reproduction, labor, and the body is, however, surprisingly rare: the research of Smith and Winders (2008), which has explored processes of flexibilization, Latino migration, and changing demands on the body (and the spaces different bodies inhabit, or are restricted from, at different times), is a notable exception. What Bakker and Gill (2003) have called, following Saskia Sassen, the "feminization of survival" refers to the systematic links between debt servicing and new strategies of survival, which in the context of structural adjustment policies, for example, means the downloading of the costs of crisis not only onto the sphere of social reproduction but also onto women's, men's, and children's bodies in particular ways. Recent work in feminist political economy (Bedford and Rai 2010) has also sought to explore how to conceptualize and analyze the bodily effects of different kinds of labor on reproductive capacities: Rai, Hoskyn, and Thomas's (2013) development of the concept of depletion is a promising example.

Processes of identity formation are also related but not reducible to the processes by which bodies are gendered, racialized, and labeled as productive or unproductive. As Mitchell, Marston, and Katz (2004, 3) have pointed out, the growing obfuscation between "work" and "nonwork" is related to the interpellation of subjects: "rendering . . . permanently mobilized bodies in new kinds of technologies of power." This mode of conceptualization is clearly important for understanding class as a *process*, but so too are the ways in which individuals and groups are increasingly *unable* to commodify their labor (the massive increase in youth unemployment in much of the EU in the wake of the 2008 financial crisis is a pertinent example). Identity must thus be understood as relating to, but never reducible to, individual subjectivities and is enmeshed with processes of value creation in which the state, capital, and labor are all enrolled. For example, Gidwani and Reddy (2011) showed how some groups, individuals, and bodies in contemporary Indian cities become constituted as waste through "eviscerating urbanism" (on the gendered politics of garbage collection in Senegal, see Fredericks, this volume). Conversely, work within the community economies tradition gestures to the ways in which identities are equally shaped by noncapitalist activities and forms of social meaning (Morrow and Dombroski, this volume).

THE MATERIALITY QUESTION

Social reproduction, as Cindi Katz (2008) pointed out, is vibrantly lived and stubbornly material. In recent years, geography and cognate disciplines have witnessed the resurgence of the "material" and even the "real" in approaches that draw attention to the embodied, grounded, and material aspects of political and social life (Robbins and Marks 2010; Shaw and Meehan 2013). These approaches differ from the historical geographical materialism that has been influential in geography since the late 1970s, epitomized by the work of inter alia David Harvey and Neil Smith. While the framing and usage of materiality varies across the discipline—indeed, the term may reveal diverse and even incompatible onto-logical commitments—recent work in relation to commodities, corporeality, and hybridity offers fresh perspectives on political economy (Bakker and Bridge 2006). Importantly, the focus on materiality is directed at "not only [making] the non-humans 'matter,' but to rethink the ontological status of the 'social'" (Robbins and Marks 2010, 177)—including, we suggest, the "social" aspects of social reproduction.

The field of feminist political ecology (FPE), for example, reflects such an evolution. Since the 1990s, FPE differed from "mainstream" political ecology by its explicit attention to gender and power relations (Rocheleau, Thomas-Slayter, and Wangari 1996; Rocheleau 2008). Early studies revealed how environmen-tal knowledge, institutions, and management practices were deeply gendered (Schroeder 1999; Sundberg 2004); women were important if unacknowledged (or marginalized) environmental managers in cities and the countryside (Hovorka 2006); and assumptions about "community" and the "local" were often wrongly homogenizing (Rocheleau, Thomas-Slayter, and Wangari 1996). While FPE and political ecology share an emphasis on empirical data, political-economic orien-tation, and scalar-based explanations, feminist insights emphasized the gendered nature of material life.

Yet in recent years FPE has brought sharper focus to the nature of materiality *itself*. Not surprisingly, much of this work springs from feminist thinking on the body. The body is a volatile, messy, mysterious thing, resisting dualistic explana-tions and enduring long after the fierce deconstruction of gendered categories and discourse (Grosz 1994). Indeed, the body matters not only as a "visceral protagonist" that shapes knowledge and political encounters (Coole and Frost 2010; see also Haraway 1991 and Sundberg 2005) but also as the material *site* in which value, geopolitics, and meaning is produced and contested (Sundberg and Kaserman 2007; Sundberg 2011; see also Clark, this volume).

New materialist philosophies have recently urged thinking past the specifically human body, toward a radical reappraisal of subject objectivity and material reality (Coole and Frost 2010). Matter, they argue, is no mere template for predictable or predetermined causal forces, but it possesses the agentic capacity to transform and rearrange new subjects, objects, relations, conditions, and events (Whatmore 2002; Bennett 2010; Coole and Frost 2010; Shaw and Meehan 2013). As Coole and Frost (2010, 7) point out, the intellectual development of capitalist theory—as well as social reproduction—inherited Cartesian models of materiality, in which matter was unambiguous, unassailable, just "there."

Many of our ideas about materiality in fact remain indebted to Descartes, who defined matter in the seventeenth century as corporeal substance, constituted of length, breadth, and thickness, and also as extended, uniform, and inert. This provided the basis for modern ideas of nature as quantifiable and measurable and hence for Euclidean geometry and Newtonian physics. According to this model, material objects are identifiably discrete; they move only upon an encounter with an external force or agent, and they do so according to a linear logic of cause and effect.

The problem with such thinking, argue Coole and Frost (2010, 25), is the ways that inert materiality fails to explain the complexities of environmental change or meet the challenges spawned by technoscience and global capitalism in its diverse, localized effects on everyday lives. Indeed, it is precisely the seemingly insignificant daily activities of social reproduction—what to eat, what to drink, where to live, how to get to work—that operate synergistically to produce effects that devastate the global environment. For Coole and Frost (2010, 29), "renewed attention to structures of political economy complements new materialist sensitivities to the resilience of matter in the face of its reconstruction, the agency of nonsubjective structures, the importance of bodily experience, and the myriad interrelated material systems needed to sustain citizens before they can vote or deliberate."

For social reproduction, the key insights here are threefold. First, women are not the only bodies that perform social reproduction: this point is repeatedly made in broad strokes but rarely operationalized in actual research on social reproduction (see Gorman-Murray, this volume). Second, and more crucial, human bodies are not the only producers of life's work (see Marks, this volume). The material world consists of all types of laboring bodies and objects—alternately referred to as webs (Rocheleau 2008), hybridities (Whatmore 2002), or assemblages (Robbins and Marks 2010)—all of which work to transform the world in significant ways. In many ways, this second point underscores the conceptual distance found between studies on social reproduction and the environment—a gap that has seemed wider as Marxist political economy and political ecology have come together to challenge the traditional divides among environmental and anticapitalist politics (Loftus 2012; Huber 2013). Finally, and perhaps on a more inspiring note in terms of radical politics, new materialisms challenge us to consider not only how global change is unevenly "downloaded" onto the sphere of social reproduction but also how material bodies, objects, and practices collectively "upload" new dynamics and changes to the global realm. To borrow an insight from Coole and Frost (2010, 4): "what is at stake here is nothing less than a challenge to some of the most basic assumptions that have underpinned the modern world, including its normative sense of the human and its beliefs about human agency, but also regarding its material practices such as the ways we labor on, exploit, and interact with nature."

Conclusion

Our intention in this volume is not to provide definitive answers to these challenges or to supply a normative road map for SRP approaches and feminist engagements. Instead, our aim is to advocate for social reproduction's continued and increasing salience by bringing different approaches to SRP into conversation in a way that highlights productive tensions and opens up new routes for exploration. As geographers, we have also sought to demonstrate the salience of space, place, and scale to the transformations in structures and relations of social reproduction—from the rescaling of obligations for social welfare in Canada to the immobilizing effects of state-level immigration law on the lives of undocumented migrants in the United States and the relationship between public space and care work in housing estates in Xining, China. While the choice of case studies in a volume of this type is shaped by many factors, we have striven to include work that illustrates *both* diversities and particularities, *and also* commonalities, among contemporary relations of social reproduction in different regions and settings. These include not only the intensification of precariousness in life's work but also forms of resourcefulness (Mackinnon and Derickson 2013) and agency.

The book is organized into four parts that reflect these key themes. In part 1, "State Transformations," Kate Bezanson demonstrates how the current Conservative government in Canada is seeking to reconcile neoliberal promarket and conservative patriarchal ideologies through an open federalist framework that removes central responsibility for national social welfare guarantees. Jessie H. Clark highlights the ways in which the Turkish national and Kurdish local state enroll the spaces and practices of social reproduction in geopolitical processes of nation-building and the fortification of ethnic identities in Eastern Turkey. In both chapters, the rescaling of state interventions in the reproduction of households and communities signals evolving technologies of governance and sites of struggle.

In part 2, "Re-placing Care," Andrew Gorman-Murray uses the story of one man's attempts at negotiating life's work in Australia to reflect on how gendered expectations of care and waged labor create irreconcilable tensions for men as well as for women. Oona Morrow and Kelly Dombroski, on the other hand, draw on the work of J. K. Gibson-Graham to mobilize examples of diverse relations of care in the very different urban contexts of the United States and China. Their chapter suggests that actually existing noncapitalist or more-than-capitalist dimensions of everyday life represent points of departure for a journey to a postcapitalist politics of social reproduction. The different foci of these chapters—on the constraints and opportunities offered by gendered relations of care—point to significant tensions within larger debates about social reproduction and care.

Part 3, "Bodies and Barriers," illustrates the different ways in which bodies and embodied experiences of production and social reproduction in the United States vary along intersecting and interlocking axes of class, race, ethnicity, and status (whether a citizen or noncitizen). Barbara Ellen Smith and Jamie Winders critically and empirically challenge the spatial and social disintegration of the separate spheres of home and work, arguing that for undocumented migrants in some American states life's work is becoming literally a spatial paradox. Brenda Parker reflects on the ways in which the challenges of life's work for poor African American women in neoliberal Milwaukee are "amplified" by the history of, on one hand, state abandonment, and on the other, disciplinary interference and punitive strategies of control of the racialized working poor and their children.

In the final section, "Working Materialities," Rosalind Fredericks illustrates the active role of dirt and norms of cleanliness in the gendered politics of municipal waste restructuring in Senegal. Brian Marks, comparing the fortunes of small-scale shrimp producers in the United States and Vietnam, discusses the importance of more-than-human agency to what we might commonly understand as the political economy of the shrimp industry in both places. Both chapters illustrate the challenge to political and economic frameworks for understanding changing relations of production, social reproduction, and consumption and for theorizing how different materialities interact and co-construct each other in ways that have political implications and potentialities.

The volume concludes with a provocative set of reflections from Sallie A. Marston, Katharyne Mitchell, and Cindi Katz on the evolution of approaches to social reproduction (and related, if differently named, ontological questions involving the politics of labor, care, and everyday life) since the publication of *Life's Work* over a decade ago. They pull no punches. In their essay they challenge the continued masculinist bias in (but certainly not limited to) human geography that continues to ignore or devalue that which is not defined, in dominant epistemologies, as production. It is precisely this continued rendering *in*visible of what Marston calls "the quotidian work of enabling and maintaining life—both human and non-human" that also renders invisible and normalized racialized and class oppressions, the exploitation of workers, and the abrogation and denial of collective responsibility for the care of the young, the sick, those unable to engage in paid work, and the material world that supports us.

While our ambitions for this volume are conceptual, they are also intended (and hoped) to be catalytic: in our lives and activism, in the various sites and struggles of our research partners, and on the shopfloor of academia. Social reproduction remains as vital now as it was to arguments over wages for housework or struggles for the rights of exploited migrant domestic workers in previous decades—if not more so. Socioenvironmental transformations and depredations, new and intensifying ways of exploiting and commodifying bodies as well as their labor, and relentless logics of uneven development demand our continued commitment to its intellectual and political development—especially because "nonproductive" work, and low-paid feminized labor, continue to be ignored in many analyses, including from the Left. Social reproduction is worth debating and arguing over and for because of the ways in which it makes us see what those in power would have remain unseen. Such visibility is worth struggling for, and over, now more than ever.

NOTES

1. *Life's Work: Geographies of Social Reproduction* begins with "three vignettes of contemporary life" to illustrate the relationship between the production of value "at work" and the social reproduction of labor-power along with the conditions that enable its deployment. The opening of our collection deliberately mirrors their strategy, with three vignettes that reflect moments of embodiment and identity, human/nonhuman materialities, and community economies.

2. This vignette is based on a story by Jason Burke, "India's Surrogate Mothers Face New Rules to Restrict 'Pot of Gold,'" *Guardian*, July 30, 2010, http://www.guardian.co.uk/world/2010/jul/30/india-surrogate-mothers-law.

3. See the final paragraphs of Peter Wollheim, "A Fish Problem This Big," *Boise Weekly*, January 17, 2007, http://www.boiseweekly.com/boise/a-fish-problem-this-big/Content?oid=930703.

4. Based on field research by Meehan (Interview, Mexico City, July 2012).

5. Debates about the status and salience of the concept of class are an example.

6. Commodification refers to the process by which something, especially labor, is made into a commodity (e.g., a good or thing produced for sale); commoditization is the process by which something becomes treated as a commodity (e.g., in legal or governance frameworks). Therefore care labor might be increasingly commodified in the sense of

being performed for a wage under conditions of employment; it then may be thought of as something that *should be* performed as wage labor (and thus be subject to expectations about cost reduction and efficiency).

REFERENCES

Bakker, Isabella, and Stephen Gill, eds. *Power, Production, and Social Reproduction: Human In/security in the Global Political Economy.* London: Palgrave Macmillan, 2003.

Bakker, Isabella, and Rachel Silvey, eds. *Beyond State and Markets: The Challenges of Social Reproduction.* New York: Routledge, 2008.

Bakker, Karen, and Gavin Bridge. "Material Worlds? Resource Geographies and the 'Matter of Nature.'" *Progress in Human Geography* 30, no. 1 (2006): 5–27.

Bedford, Kate, and Shirin Rai. "Feminists Theorise International Political Economy: The State of the Field." *Signs* 36, no. 1 (2010): 1–18.

Bennett, Jane. *Vibrant Matter: A Political Ecology of Things.* Durham: Duke University Press, 2010.

Bezanson, Kate. "The Neo-Liberal State and Social Reproduction: Gender and Household Insecurity in the Late 1990s." In *Social Reproduction: Feminist Political Economy Challenges Neo-Liberalism*, edited by Kate Bezanson and Meg Luxton, 173–214. Montreal: McGill-Queen's University Press, 2006.

Bezanson, Kate, and Meg Luxton, eds. *Social Reproduction: Feminist Political Economy Challenges Neo-Liberalism.* Montreal: McGill-Queen's University Press, 2006.

Burawoy, Michael. "Functions and Reproduction of Migrant Labor—Comparative Material from Southern Africa and United-States." *American Journal of Sociology* 81, no. 5 (1976): 1050–1087.

Butler, Judith. *Precarious Life: The Powers of Mourning and Violence.* London: Verso, 2004.

———. "Performativity, Precarity, and Sexual Politics." *Revista de Antropología Iberoamericana* 4, no. 3 (2009): i–xiii.

Caffentzis, George. "On the Notion of a Crisis of Social Reproduction: A Theoretical Review." *Commoner* 5 (2002): 1–22.

Cameron, Barbara. "Social Reproduction and Canadian Federalism." In *Social Reproduction: Feminist Political Economy Challenges Neo-Liberalism*, edited by Kate Bezanson and Meg Luxton, 45–74. Toronto: McGill-Queens University Press, 2006.

Coole, Diana, and Samantha Frost. "Introducing the New Materialisms." In *New Materialisms: Ontology, Agency, and Politics*, edited by Diana Coole and Samantha Frost, 1–42. Durham and London: Duke University Press, 2010.

Cox, Rosie. "The Au Pair Body—Sex Object, Sister or Student?" *European Journal of Women's Studies* 14, no. 3 (2007): 281–296.

Dalla Costa, Mariarose, and Selma James. *The Power of Women and the Subversion of the Community.* Bristol, U.K.: Falling Wall Press, 1972.

Datta, Kavita, Cathy Mcilwaine, Yara Evans, Joanna Herbert, Jon May, and Jane Wills. "A Migrant Ethic of Care? Negotiating Care and Caring among Migrant Workers in London's Low-Pay Economy." *Feminist Review* 94 (2010): 93–116.

De Sario, Beppe. "Precari su Marte: An Experiment in Activism against Precarity." *Feminist Review* 87 (2007): 21–39.

Dowler, Elizabeth, Moya Kneafsey, Rosie Cox, and Lewis Holloway. "'Doing Food Differently': Reconnecting Biological and Social Relationships through Care for Food." *Sociological Review* 57, no. 2 (2009): 200–221.

Dyer, Sarah, Linda McDowell, and Adina Batnitzky. "Emotional Labour/Body Work: The Caring Labours of Migrants in the U.K.'s National Health Service." *Geoforum* 39, no. 6 (2008): 2030–2038.

———. "Migrant Work, Precarious Work-Life Balance: What the Experiences of Migrant Workers in the Service Sector in Greater London Tell Us about the Adult Worker Model." *Gender Place and Culture* 18, no. 5 (2011): 685–700.

Ehrenreich, Barbara. "Life without Father: Reconsidering Socialist-Feminist Theory." *Socialist Review* 73 (1984): 48–57.

Engels, Frederick. *The Origin of the Family, Private Property and the State.* Chippendale, NSW: Resistance, 2004.

England, Kim, and Isabel Dyck. "Managing the Body Work of Home Care." *Sociology of Health and Illness* 33, no. 2 (2011): 206–219.

Esping-Anderson, Gøsta. *The Three Worlds of Welfare Capitalism.* Cambridge: Polity, 1990.

Ettlinger, Nancy. "Precarity Unbound." *Alternatives: Global, Local, Political* 32, no. 3 (2007): 319–340.

Federici, Silvia. *Caliban and the Witch: Women, the Body and Primitive Accumulation.* New York: Autonomedia, 2004.

Feldman, Shelley, Charles Geisler, and Gayatri A. Menon. "Introduction: A New Politics of Containment." In *Accumulating Insecurity: Violence and Dispossession in the Making of Everyday Life*, edited by Shelley Feldman, Charles Geisler, and Gayatri A. Menon, 1–23. Athens: University of Georgia Press, 2011.

Folbre, Nancy. *The Invisible Heart: Economics and Family Values.* New York: New Press, 2001.

———. *Family Time: The Social Organization of Care.* New York: Routledge, 2004.

Fraser, Nancy. *Justus Interruptus: Critical Reflections on the Post-Socialist Condition.* New York: Routledge, 1997.

———. *Fortunes of Feminism: From State-Managed Capitalism to Neoliberal Crisis.* London: Verso, 2013.

———. "Behind Marx's Hidden Abode." *New Left Review* 86, March–April (2014): 55–72.

Fudge, Judy, and Rosemary Owens. "Precarious Work, Women and the New Economy: The Challenge to Legal Norms." In *Precarious Work, Women and the New Economy: The Challenge to Legal Norms*, edited by Judy Fudge and Rosemary Owens, 3–28. Oxford and Portland, Ore.: Onati International Institute for the Sociology of Law, 2006.

Gibson-Graham, J. K. *The End of Capitalism (as We Knew It): A Feminist Critique of Political Economy.* Minneapolis: University of Minnesota Press, 1996.

———. *A Postcapitalist Politics.* Minneapolis: University of Minnesota Press, 2006.

Gidwani, Vinay, and Rajyashree N. Reddy. "The Afterlives of 'Waste': Notes from India for a Minor History of Capitalist Surplus." *Antipode* 43, no. 5 (2011): 1625–1658.

Grosz, Elizabeth A. *Volatile Bodies: Toward a Corporeal Feminism*. Bloomington: Indiana University Press, 1994.

Haraway, Donna. *Simians, Cyborgs, and Women: The Reinvention of Nature*. New York: Routledge, 1991.

Hovorka, Alice J. "The No.1 Ladies' Poultry Farm: A Feminist Political Ecology of Urban Agriculture in Botswana." *Gender, Place and Culture* 13, no. 3 (2006): 207–225.

Huber, Matt T. *Lifeblood: Oil, Freedom, and the Forces of Capital*. Minneapolis: University of Minnesota Press, 2013.

James, Selma. *Sex, Race and Class*. London: Falling Wall Press, 1975.

Katz, Cindi. "Vagabond Capitalism and the Necessity of Social Reproduction." *Antipode* 33, no. 4 (2001): 709–728.

———. *Growing Up Global: Economic Restructuring and Children's Everyday Lives*. Minneapolis: University of Minnesota, 2004.

———. "Bad Elements: Katrina and the Scoured Landscape of Social Reproduction." *Gender, Place and Culture* 15, no. 1 (2008): 15–29.

Laslett, Barbara, and Johanna Brenner. "Gender and Social Reproduction: Historical Perspectives." *Annual Review of Sociology* 15 (1989): 381–404.

Lawson, Victoria. "Geographies of Care and Responsibility." *Annals of the Association of American Geographers* 97, no. 1 (2007): 1–11.

Lerner, Gerda. *The Creation of Patriarchy*. New York: Oxford University Press, 1986.

Loftus, Alex. *Everyday Environmentalism: Creating an Urban Political Ecology*. Minneapolis: University of Minnesota Press, 2012.

Luxton, Meg. "Feminist Political Economy in Canada and the Politics of Social Reproduction." In *Social Reproduction: Feminist Political Economy Challenges Neo-Liberalism*, edited by Kate Bezanson and Meg Luxton, 11–44. Montreal: McGill-Queen's University Press, 2006.

MacKinnon, Danny, and Kate Derickson. "From Resilience to Resourcefulness: A Critique of Resilience Policy and Activism." *Progress in Human Geography* 37, no. 2 (2013): 253–270.

Marston, Sallie A. "The Social Construction of Scale." *Progress in Human Geography* 24, no. 2 (2000): 219–242.

Marx, Karl. *Capital—Volume 1*. Harmondsworth: Penguin, 1976.

———. *Capital: A Critique of Political Economy, Vol. 1: The Process of Capitalist Production*, edited by Frederick Engels and Ernest Untermann and translated by Samuel Moore and Edward Aveling. Library of Economics and Liberty, 1906. Accessed August 13, 2013, http://www.econlib.org/library/YPDBooks/Marx/mrxCpA23.html.

Massey, Doreen. *Spatial Divisions of Labour: Social Structures and the Geography of Production*. London: Macmillan, 1984.

McDowell, Linda. "Work, Workfare, Work/Life Balance and an Ethic of Care." *Progress in Human Geography* 28, no. 2 (2004): 145–163.

McDowell, Linda, and Susan Christopherson. "Transforming Work: New Forms of Employment and Their Regulation." *Cambridge Journal of Regions, Economy and Society* 2, no. 3 (2009): 333–342.

McDowell, Linda, and Gill Court. "Performing Work: Bodily Representations in Merchant Banks." *Environment and Planning D: Society and Space* 12, no. 6 (1994): 727–750.

McDowell, Linda, Kevin Ward, Colette Fagan, Diane Perrons, and Kath Ray. "Connecting Time and Space: The Significance of Transformations in Women's Work in the City." *International Journal of Urban and Regional Research* 30, no. 1 (2006): 141–158.

Mitchell, Katharyne, Sallie A. Marston, and Cindi Katz. "Life's Work: An Introduction, Review and Critique." In *Life's Work: Geographies of Social Reproduction*, edited by Katharyne Mitchell, Sallie A. Marston, and Cindi Katz, 59–69. Malden, Mass.: Blackwell, 2004.

Picchio, Antonella. *Social Reproduction: The Political Economy of the Labour Market.* Cambridge: Cambridge University Press, 1992.

Pratt, Geraldine. "From Registered Nurse to Registered Nanny: Discursive Geographics of Filipina Domestic Workers in Vancouver, B.C." *Economic Geography* 75, no. 3 (1999): 215–236.

Rai, Shirin, Catherine Hoskyns, and Diana Thomas. "Depletion." *International Feminist Journal of Politics* http://dx.doi.org/10.1080/14616742.2013.789641, 2013.

Robbins, Paul, and Brian Marks. "Assemblage Geographies." In *The SAGE Handbook of Social Geographies*, edited by Susan J. Smith et al., 176–195. London: SAGE, 2010.

Rocheleau, Dianne E. "Maps, Numbers, Text, and Context: Mixing Methods in Feminist Political Ecology." *Professional Geographer* 47, no. 4 (1995): 458–467.

———. "Political Ecology in the Key of Policy: From Chains of Explanation to Webs of Relation." *Geoforum* 39, no. 2 (2008): 716–727.

Rocheleau, Dianne E., Barbara Thomas-Slayter, and Esther Wangari. *Feminist Political Ecology: Global Issues and Local Experiences.* London and New York: Routledge, 1996.

Rubin, Gayle. "The Traffic in Women: Notes on the 'Political Economy' of Sex." In *Towards an Anthropology of Women*, edited by Rayna Reiter, 157–209. New York: Monthly Review Press, 1975.

Schroeder, Richard A. *Shady Practices: Agroforestry and Gender Politics in the Gambia.* Berkeley: University of California Press, 1999.

Sharma, Nandita. *Home Economics: Nationalism and the Making of "Migrant Workers" in Canada.* Toronto: University of Toronto Press, 2006.

Shaw, Ian G. R., and Katharine Meehan. "Force-Full: Power, Politics, and Object-Oriented Philosophy." *Area* 45, no. 2 (2013): 216–222.

Slocum, Rachel, and Arun Saldhana, eds. *Geographies of Race and Food.* Farnham: Ashgate, 2013.

Smith, Barbara Ellen, and Jamie Winders. "'We're Here to Stay': Economic Restructuring, Latino Migration, and Place-Making in the U.S. South." *Transactions of the Institute of British Geographers* 33, no. 1 (2008): 60–72.

Smith, Susan J. "States, Markets and an Ethic of Care." *Political Geography* 24, no. 1 (2005): 1–20.

Standing, Guy. *The Precariat: The Dangerous New Class.* London: Bloomsbury Academic, 2011.

Strauss, Kendra. "Coerced, Forced and Unfree Labour: Geographies of Exploitation in Contemporary Labour Markets." *Geography Compass* 6, no. 3 (2012): 137–148.

———. "Unfree Again: Social Reproduction, Flexible Labour Markets and the Resurgence of Gang Labour in the U.K." *Antipode* 45, no. 1 (2013): 180–197.

Strauss, Kendra, and Judy Fudge. "Introduction." In *Temporary Work, Agencies and Unfree Labour: Insecurity in the New World of Work*, edited by Judy Fudge and Kendra Strauss, 1–25. New York: Routledge, 2014.

Sundberg, Juanita. "Identities-in-the-Making: Conservation, Gender, and Race in the Maya Biosphere Reserve, Guatemala." *Gender, Place and Culture* 11, no. 1 (2004): 44–66.

———. "Looking for the Critical Geographer, or Why Bodies and Geographies Matter to the Emergence of Critical Geographies of Latin America." *Geoforum* 36, no. 1 (2005): 17–28.

———. "Diabolic Caminos in the Desert and Cat Fights on the Río: A Post-Humanist Political Ecology of Boundary Enforcement in the United States–Mexico Borderlands." *Annals of the Association of American Geographers* 101, no. 2 (2011): 318–336.

Sundberg, Juanita, and Bonnie Kaserman. "Cactus Carvings and Desert Defecations: Embodying Representations of Border Crossings in Protected Areas on the Mexico-U.S. Border." *Environment and Planning D: Society and Space* 25, no. 4 (2007): 727–744.

Vosko, Leah F. *Temporary Work: The Gendered Rise of a Precarious Employment Relationship*. Toronto: University of Toronto Press, 2000.

———. *Managing at the Margins: Gender, Citizenship, and the International Regulation of Precarious Employment*. Oxford: Oxford University Press, 2010.

Waite, Louise. "A Place and Space for a Critical Geography of Precarity?" *Geography Compass* 3, no. 1 (2009): 412–433.

Waite, Louise, Gill Valentine, and Hannah Lewis. "Multiply Vulnerable Populations: Mobilising a Politics of Compassion from the 'Capacity to Hurt.'" *Social & Cultural Geography* 15, no. 3 (2014): 313–331.

Weeks, Kathi. *The Problem with Work: Feminism, Marxism, Antiwork Politics, and Postwork Imaginaries*. Durham, N.C.: Duke University Press, 2011.

Whatmore, Sarah. *Hybrid Geographies: Natures, Cultures, Spaces*. London: SAGE, 2002.

Wright, Melissa W. *Disposable Women and Other Myths of Global Capitalism*. New York: Routledge, 2006.

PART ONE

State Transformations

CHAPTER 1

Return of the Nightwatchman State?

Federalism, Social Reproduction, and
Social Policy in Conservative Canada

KATE BEZANSON

On the tail of the global financial crisis of 2008, Canadians reelected Stephen Harper's Conservatives to parliamentary office with a majority in the spring of 2011, in effect continuing Conservative rule since 2006. Although the economic crisis struck Canada with comparatively less force than it did the United States or some European Union nations, it worsened and multiplied existing poverty and disadvantage and cleared the terrain for a series of changes in federal scope and spending. In the Canadian case, and especially in a climate of economic uncertainty, the Conservative government's project of open federalism laid the foundation for a realignment in the distribution of the work of social reproduction. This recent economic crisis, and the return of the Conservatives despite their anti-redistribution policies, underscores the need to focus attention on social reproduction and production at a broad level and on the ways in which economic changes are mediated by states, families, and individuals more specifically. Put simply, we must direct attention to how the physical, social, and psychological work of caring for people is done or not done, by whom (women, men, states, markets, charities), under what conditions (forced/coerced, voluntary, subsidized), and with what effect (more or less time seeking wages/income; more or less time provisioning; gendered, class-based, or racialized stratification) in order to understand the implications of open federalism for Canadian society.

The principle of classical federalism promoted by the Conservative government builds on existing neoliberal tendencies (see Mahon 2008) but adds a neoconservative twist by emphasizing family life and traditional values even as such policies erode the conditions for familial reproduction and life's work. While Canada is a highly decentralized federation, the Conservatives are deepening this decentralization via an emphasis on criminal justice, commerce, the military, and trade at the federal level while further divesting federal responsibility and standards for a host of "soft" issues, such as the environment, labor, and income support to provincial and municipal governments that frequently lack the requisite resources. In an effort to explore what appear to be deeply gendered, racialized, and class-based consequences to an emerging nightwatchman federal state, the lens of social reproduction is applied here to pull apart the dynamics and ideological basis of this new federalism.

This chapter seeks to draw out the alliance between neoliberalism and neoconservatism and begin to understand its material consequences for families and households. Thus, the chapter sketches the kind of state that may be emerging by asking three key questions: (1) What might be the implications of Prime Minister Harper's federalism and governance in relation to social reproduction? (2) How do socially conservative approaches to gender and family life animate Conservative social policy? and (3) Do social policy changes, proposals, and omissions suggest a broader reconfiguration of the existing gender order?

The chapter begins with a brief discussion of Canadian legal tradition, structure, and form. The chapter then examines Conservative Party views of "open federalism" and maps the contours and consequences of the neoconservative and neoliberal approach. Finally, the chapter explores the material impacts of Harper government policies, such as childcare, maternity leaves, and families' income splitting, arguing that such policies resurrect male-breadwinner family norms even as they prioritize families with high incomes, while subjecting those who are socially and economically vulnerable to an escalated disciplinary neoliberalism (see Gill and Roberts 2011). The gendered tasks and processes of social reproduction, including transforming welfare incomes into the necessities of life and internalizing/normalizing social stigma, are decentralized to provinces and to families as the state is transformed from a safety net into a "nightwatchman" (Rice and Prince 2013), with the result of making the lives of the most vulnerable even more precarious.

Federalism and Social Reproduction in Canada

FEDERALISM, NEOLIBERALISM, AND NEOCONSERVATISM IN CANADA

Canada in the 2011 federal election was a different place than it was in 2006. In the 2006 election, the Canadian economy was booming and boasted significant budget surpluses. The federal Liberal Party, in power for thirteen years, had negotiated agreements with the provinces for the creation of a *national* system of early learning and childcare. The central topics in the federal leaders' debate were equality issues: childcare, reproductive rights, and the Canadian charter of rights. The expansion of segments of Canada's welfare state infrastructure was curtailed when the Conservative Party won a minority in that election. Issues of equality were also transformed through a series of funding decisions (Dobbin 2010). By the 2008 election, the economy moved to the fore of public priorities as a global recession began to take hold; Canadians faced this recession with greater financial uncertainty because of significant tax cuts over the intervening two years. By the 2011 election, despite a $56 billion federal deficit, the key issue in the leaders' debate pertained to governance and accountability, especially in relation to the proroguing of Parliament (twice) and the unprecedented contempt of Parliament judgment against the Conservatives. Issues of equality were totally absent, and women were mentioned only during a discussion on gun control in reference to their being killed by guns. In the seven years since 2006, the foundations of federalism and governance have changed.

Canada is a complex federation whose history is shaped by a vast geography, proximity to the United States, and an ongoing negotiation over federal and provincial/territorial areas of jurisdiction, especially with reference to the French-speaking province of Quebec. Canada has a federal government that sits in Ottawa (Ontario) in central Canada and thirteen provincial and territorial governments. Canada is a constitutional monarchy with a Westminster-style parliamentary democracy. It has a bicameral national legislature, with an appointed Senate (upper house) and an elected House of Commons (lower house). Constitutional divisions of power and responsibility between the federal and provincial/territorial governments have evolved from being highly centralized in the hands of the federal government to being one of the most decentralized federations in the Organization for Economic Cooperation and Development (OECD) (Gray 2010).

Despite this decentralization, important programs remain federally administered and/or regulated, such as employment-based social insurance policies like Employment Insurance, the Canada Pension Plan, and workers' compensation. Transfers of federally collected tax dollars (some conditional on meeting certain national standards) are made to the provinces/territories for areas such as health care, education, and social assistance (welfare). Until recently, the federal government played a direct role in areas such as social housing and homelessness, childcare, and training. Although it funds hospital and physician services for citizens, Canada is a liberal welfare state in which responsibility for social reproduction "is largely conceived of as a choice, and thus the responsibility primarily of the family, and in the absence of the family, the market" (White 2012, 661). Who does what—federal or provincial, municipal or collective, market or individual—matters in terms of mobilizing and sharing resources, establishing and maintaining standards, and attending to issues of equality and voice. Federalism, in other words, matters.

The Conservative federal government under the leadership of Stephen Harper came to power with a vision for decentralizing key elements of the federal state, transforming its institutions (especially the judiciary), and enshrining property rights in the Canadian constitution (see Bezanson 2010). While it built upon the neoliberal (later social investment) approach of the long-governing Liberal

Party (Jenson 2009a), it drew its road map from a melding of social conservatism, western Canadian populism, and the ideas of neoliberal intellectuals such as Hayek and Friedman (Boily, Boisvert, and Kermoal 2005; Boily 2007; Bezanson 2010). "Open federalism" is a term employed by Prime Minister Harper (Harper 2004) to capture his vision for Canadian federalism (see Jeffrey 2011). It involves a strong adherence to the constitutional division of powers between federal and provincial/territorial governments (a variant on states' rights approaches in the United States). This vision views all matters of social reproduction as provincial and local, and it understands the federal role as strictly related to commerce, the military, and corrections (Kent 2008). It is consistent with the neoliberal approach to federalism, which centralizes most "market-enabling policy capabilities at the federal level" (Harmes 2006, 736) while decentralizing tax and regulatory powers in order to encourage competition among provinces/territories.

Open federalism, a centerpiece of the 2006 Conservative election, has, in practice, reduced fiscal room for existing and new social policy initiatives via increased spending on law and order issues, despite declining crime rates and austerity budgeting (see Prince 2012). This kind of paradigmatic restructuring (Orloff and Palier 2009) involves dropping support for a set of principles that have served as a basis for policy action (Rice and Prince 2013). Open federalism must be viewed, then, as part of a broader philosophical and ideological approach to transforming the role of the federal government in Canada. This approach is at once neoliberal and moral in orientation.

The Conservative Party vision is one in which the welfare state is reduced and/or abolished and a socially conservative morality is brought to bear in areas such as the courts, charter rights, crime, private property, family, the military, and immigration (Bezanson 2010; Arat-Koc 2012; Porter 2012). The moral orientation of the party has been obscured during its minority tenure (2006–11), as Prime Minister Harper (Harper 2003) argued that the only way to make the Conservatives into what he called the "natural governing party" was to emphasize economic ideas while downplaying moral ones. The explicit policy visage of incremental change has been successful in casting the leader of the party as a center-right fiscal conservative. The values conservatism that forms a large part of the conservative base and philosophical orientation, however, has made strong inroads in meaningful and hard-to-reverse ways, particularly around how the responsibility for social policy is shared between the federal and provincial/territorial governments, senate and judicial appointments, and, consequently, around family policy (MacDonald 2011).

The majority government, in its first session of Parliament, substantially laid the groundwork for further decentralization, a reduced social infrastructure, and an altered distribution of the work of social reproduction. The incremental

Conservative approach is changing the landscape of Canadian constitutionalism and federalism, and these changes now have a lasting legacy: the prime minister made more appointments to the senate than any other prime minister, and the upper chamber is now Conservative dominated. This guarantees the passage of key Conservative pieces of legislation, but it also blocks future attempts by other parties to alter current initiatives.

Some of the façade of moderation that accompanies the Harper government's incrementalism stems from its response, albeit much delayed, to the economic crisis that took hold in 2008. While the prime minister has appeared to compromise on key Conservative Party ideals, especially when he agreed to stimulus spending in the 2009 budget, extending to but not beyond the 2010 budget, the spending was overwhelmingly infrastructural. This spending boosted mostly male employment and has been termed a "macho stimulus plan" (Abelde 2008). Canadian banks were comparatively better regulated and less exposed to the subprime market than their OECD peers, yet banks received significant sums from both the Canadian (CDN$75 billion) and U.S. (US$111 billion) governments (Government of Canada 2008; Slater 2010; see also Bakker 2012). The automotive sector was also assisted, but the bulk of public attention was directed at spending on primarily "shovel-ready" projects. In fact, unlike the United States, where elected representatives debated bailout packages, no such parliamentary process occurred in Canada. Moreover, the Keynesian-style measures served as a highly visible source of political capital of federal government dollars invested into local constituency projects. The series of major tax cuts that preceded the economic crisis positioned the Conservatives so that the budget surplus was largely eliminated, and thus the need to respond to calls for expansions of social spending at the federal level could be avoided.

The neoliberal "disembedded federalism" (Harmes 2007) approach coexists with a deeply moral social project. The prevalence of such strong social conservatism is unusual in Canadian politics. Social conservatism is, however, a core facet of the Conservative Party: many of its Members of Parliament have strong ties to antichoice, pro-gun, and traditional family, religious, and lobbying organizations. In fact, in 2009, 75 percent of the Conservative Caucus were members of the secretive Pro-Life Parliamentary Caucus (Haussman and Rankin 2009). The name "Conservative" itself is misleading as it reflects a compromise reached in the merger between the former Progressive Conservative Party and the right-wing, religiously based Alliance Party in 2003. Responding to social conservative grievances, a series of changes in laws, courts, and equality issues have occurred, including: changing the way judicial appointments are made, in part in response to Conservative concerns about judicial interpretations of the charter's equality provisions; eliminating the national gun registry; cutting the federal agency Status of Women Canada and removing the word "equality" from its mandate; eliminating the Court Challenges Program and funding for the National Association of Women and the Law while appointing conservative jurists to federal courts and regulatory agencies (MacDonald 2010); proposing an international maternal and child health initiative that does not include reproductive rights; and *eliminating* the nascent national system of early learning and care. According to Porter (2012, 24), since 2006, "more than 30 women's organizations and research bodies have had their funding cut or been defunded," primarily when the government was posting a surplus. These cuts and changes followed at least a decade of neoliberal delegitimatization of advocacy groups as "special interests" (Jenson 2009b, 463).

Socially conservative values thus infuse the more neoliberal open federalism project, at once individualizing and familializing its effects. The economic crisis provided a pathway for the project of open federalism and the attendant dismantling of social entitlements, federal bureaucracy, and social services. These changes have far-reaching implications and appear to have begun a process of shifting the existing class and gender orders in Canada. We now turn to a specification of the relationship between social reproduction and Canadian federalism under the Harper government.

SOCIAL REPRODUCTION AND CANADIAN FEDERALISM

> My version of conservatism is summed up in three Fs: freedom, family and faith.
> —PRIME MINISTER STEPHEN HARPER, Speech to the Manning Institute for Democracy, March 2009

Unusual on the Canadian political menu, defense of "family values"—especially paired with religion—is a powerful political invocation: it serves discursively as a made-in-Canada approach to realigning the work of social reproduction, under the auspices of attending to Canadian women's very real need for greater balance between their paid work and their family lives. The Harper government's form of open federalism is buttressed by a rearticulation of the relationship between the state and the household that relies heavily on rhetoric of "the ordinary Joe" and his family. Family, however, is normatively construed. Put plainly, "Joe" lives with "Jane" and they have kids; even as they embrace a particular and often simplistic commonsense view of social and economic issues, Joe and Jane still must find ways to absorb the insecurities produced by neoliberal atomization and individualization. Framing political strategy around families is not unique to the Harper government, but their focus is on the traditional family. Conservative campaign slogans and proposals such as "standing up for families" and "family tax-cuts" naturalize the family as the site for collective identity. This version of family values embraces the idea that the welfare state has been instrumental in fostering family breakdown, leading to a host of social ills, including deterring innovation and ambition vis-à-vis the labor market (see Crowley 2010). Despite the appeal to Jane and Joe, as we shall see, the traditional family who benefits from Conservative family policies is one with a high income and a single (usually male) earner.

The way people put together the necessities of life—nourishment, shelter, security, socialization, affection, belonging, culture—varies historically and socially. All economic systems require that people be reproduced and their capabilities be formed and sustained to assist in group life. The feminist political economy concept of social reproduction offers an important lens for viewing the ways in which institutions such as states and families mediate the process of the accumulation of capital. As I have argued elsewhere (2006, 26–27), social reproduction refers to:

> the day to day work of maintaining and reproducing people and their labor power, including creating space for the building of their capacities such as learning, caretaking, and playing. . . . It involves negotiations over power and resources within households, usually between men and women . . . and is characterized by an unequal division of labor and a gender specific socialization process. It also includes provisioning beyond individual households, through volunteer work, intra-household care work, and local initiatives pertaining to shared social space or services. Social reproduction involves pooled risk services and programs, such as getting access to income via citizenship based entitlements such as those which have been provided through the welfare state. . . . In short, social reproduction encompasses the work that must be done in order to ensure that people at least survive and ideally thrive and develop as well as to ensure that the economic system is perpetuated.

In capitalism, the work of social reproduction is separated from production, is made mostly invisible, and is assumed to be externally accomplished with little regard for those undertaking the tasks. The process of capital accumulation involves conflict and tension between production and social reproduction because profit maximization and standard-of-living maximization are rarely compatible (Bezanson 2006, 28). Because standards of living and degrees of profit extraction vary, the work of social reproduction cannot be understood as automatic: it is socially, historically, and culturally determined and likewise varies over time and in place (Picchio 1992). To shape, reshape, and stabilize the conflict, specific class and gender orders are required (Bakker and Gill 2003). These conflicts between social reproduction and production thus always require mediation;

the state often plays a central role as regulator while the family takes a role of alternator (Picchio 1992).

It is the state that most often, depending on its degree of regulation, intervenes to absorb or shift the high costs of social reproduction. The family, and usually women's labor within it, absorbs the tasks, and/or a space is created for markets or the third sector to take on the work. The state, then, plays a substantial role in establishing the conditions *under which* social reproduction takes place through its roles in regulating capital, labor markets, and financial obligations in families and in providing socialized services (Bezanson 2006, 27). In the current period of renewed neoliberalism and austerity, a specific vision of family life and, hence, a reframing of the gendered work of social reproduction is forwarded, while at the same time the model of neoliberal federalism promises to decentralize and restrict social services.

Barbara Cameron's (2006) important review of social reproduction and Canadian federalism considers the ways in which federal division of powers have historically informed the Canadian state's mediation of social reproduction. She argues, "the way the 1867 constitution institutionalized an accommodation between capital accumulation and social reproduction . . . worked as long as social reproduction was primarily the responsibility of private or local institutions" (Cameron 2006, 48). The extension of this original accommodation (related to a French-speaking national minority but also to new social forces with political claims) has most recently produced tendencies to employ intergovernmental arrangements to manage conflicts around social reproduction (ibid.). Cameron's review makes clear that the type of neoliberal state embraced by federal and provincial governments since at least the 1980s "introduces a new dynamic into intergovernmental relations as elite strategies of limiting the role of the state in social reproduction through provincialization dovetail with historic Quebec demands . . . over all matters of social reproduction" (ibid., 73).

The version of open federalism forwarded by the Harper government entrenches a centralizing role for the federal government in facilitating "exit options" for capital (Hayek 1963). Using the logic of a strict interpretation of federal and provincial jurisdictions in the constitution, this "market-enabling" federalism provincializes "market-inhibiting policy capabilities such as labor and environmental regulation and certain forms of tax collection and social spending" (Harmes 2007, 424). The hostility of the Conservative Party to the Canadian welfare state makes administrative reform under the guise of open federalism a means through which two aims can be achieved: first, a neoliberal economic approach can be enacted at the federal level; and second, the provinces can compete with one another and engage in a race to the bottom in terms of social services, labor standards, and environmental regulations.

The admixture of neoliberal economic views—especially in creating exit options for capital at the federal level while leaving the messy, fleshy matters of the social (Katz 2001) to lower levels of government and families, along with traditional views of family forms and a policy compass guided by a neoconservative morality—leaves women especially exposed to economic and social insecurity. The near-hegemonic lexicon of "choice," so prevalent in Canada's individualized, "self-help" society (see Beck-Gernshiem 2002), offers the illusion that individual decisions and approaches, rather than structural social relations and attendant institutional norms, will lead to desired equality outcomes. Put more simply, if we find ourselves poor or in ill health, we have but ourselves to blame, irrespective of the stubborn fact that gender and race/ethnicity are stalwart predictors of social stratification.

The postwar federal state was capable and willing to guarantee greater national uniformity in the quality and availability of social entitlements to Canadians, but federal first-tier social insurance income supports have been scaled back in terms of eligibility, replacement income rate, and length of coverage, while also made more "active" in terms of pushing people into what is an increasingly precarious labor market. In the recession of the late 2000s, half of the unemployed did not receive Employment Insurance benefits, and among those who did, many exhausted their benefits before finding employment (Pasma 2010). The problem of unemployment and the need for income replacement moved to the provinces, whose volume of social assistance (welfare) cases rose. For provinces, which have jurisdiction over areas such as education, health care, and social assistance, the retreat of the federal state's role in key areas of social provisioning and support promises to Balkanize welfare infrastructures. Indeed, as Andrew (2010, 87) notes, because provinces have social services, they "have women." Despite the appearance of greater control, most provinces have significant deficits and are unlikely to be able to maintain existing social spending. Some provinces, such as Ontario, have remained committed to social investments in early learning, maintaining funding for full-day four- and five-year-old kindergarten despite great pressure to halt the program (see Drummond 2012). Other social programs, however, are subject to increased means-testing and marketization. With reduced federal incomes resulting both from tax cuts and shortfalls related to the economic recession, coupled with a concerted effort to create a decentralized federalism in relation to most social infrastructure and social regulations, the terrain of negotiation over the work of social reproduction is shifting.

The austerity/restructuring path has been trodden before in Canada, as elsewhere, and produced an intensification of the work of social reproduction (Bakker 1994; Chant 2011; Elson 2011). The moving of work from the public sector, such as in the case of earlier releases for hospital patients, relies on the unpaid work of usually female family members who provide increasingly complex care for which they are neither trained nor compensated. Such work is also subject to increasing surveillance (see Braedley 2006), a hallmark of disciplinary neoliberalism (Gill 1995; Gill and Roberts 2011). Social reproduction, and within it the persistently unequal division of care work among men and women, racialized groups, and social classes, is assumed to be elastic (Elson 1995) and able to stretch and contract as needed to make up for shortfalls in market income, welfare, Employment Insurance, or all other inputs, especially socialized ones such as health care or education. Yet there are threshold effects to such constant reliance on the resilience of social support networks and families; degraded household infrastructures leave households and their members in crisis and threaten the very relationships meant to support them by overburdening them (Elson 1995).

Because of the adaptability of neoliberalism to crisis (Brenner, Peck, and Theodore 2010; Harvey 2010), the period of austerity after stimulus spending is bringing significant changes. As Yalnizyan (2013) recently argued, the rise in social inequality in Canada threatens the economic recovery of the nation. The persistent increase in reliance on the work of social reproduction, while consistently failing to meaningfully support and redistribute it, is unsustainable for most families. The crisis tendencies in social reproduction can be seen in a host of social processes, including: greater formal or informal labor market participation in spite of an absence of care provision, especially for children; reduced/delayed/forgone childbearing; intervention on the part of social services to remove so-called at-risk children from families; and, most severely, social dislocation and crime. In the current period of economic austerity and economic uncertainty, in which the majority of Canadian women with children are employed full-time and in which Canada does not have a replacement fertility rate, understanding how the daily and generational work activities of social reproduction are accomplished is pressing. Conservative approaches to families and gender, along with attendant Conservative policy tools, are resurrecting a male breadwinner norm while simultaneously retaining a central place for the market.

The project of open federalism is nested in a neoliberal political economy and overburdens the social in its pursuit of market liberalism. Proponents of neoliberalism, however, tend not to view gender or families in atavistic ways, and they are unconcerned about who attends to which labor market roles and at what rates of pay. Neoliberal proponents seek a climate of social stability for investment and are largely disinterested in how the work of social reproduction is accomplished, heeding it only when the effects of failures to invest in household and community sectors affect markets. The neoliberal project of the Harper Conservatives, however, competes with a social conservatism around family life and moral issues. In addition to moving toward a traditional nightwatchman

TABLE 1.1. Net Value of the UCCB, Families in Ontario, 2006

Earnings	One-Earner Couples	Two-Earner Couples	One-Parent Families
$0	$0–1,200	$0–1,200	$0–1,200
$10,000	$1,176	$1,176	$1,176
$30,000	$673	$460	$607
$50,000	$1,049	$827	$802
$100,000	$1,032	$778	$655

Source: Adapted from Battle, Torjman, and Mendelson 2006, 2.

version of federal governance, the Conservatives are using the tools at their disposal to hem how families put together the necessities of life, including which relationships are given financial support and who does the bulk of the work of caregiving.

A key argument to be taken forward is that the Conservative version of federalism brings with it a traditional vision of family life, and thus a neoliberal individualization emphasis competes with a strong familializing thrust in its approach to social policy. The family, and in particular women's roles within it, are important to open federalism. The lens of social reproduction reveals the shifting of responsibilities for the work of care in the public sector and market arenas, at various levels of government and not-for-profit organizations and, crucially, at the microlevel of gender relations and family care arrangements. The Conservatives are positioned to deepen their efforts at reworking the existing mediation between the state, the market, and the family around the work of social reproduction, with socially conservative ideas about family life competing with neoliberal adult worker norms.

Refamilializing and Individualizing? Gender and Social Policy

One of the first acts of the newly elected Conservative government in 2006 was to cancel the agreements between the federal government and the provinces for the creation of a national system of early learning and childcare. The Universal Child Care Benefit (UCCB) served as its replacement. It consists of a $100-per-month taxable payment to families for each child under six years old (see table 1.1). The money neither covers childcare nor allows for labor market exit. A 2006 analysis by the Caledon Institute of Social Policy demonstrates the refamilialization leanings of this policy (Battle, Torjman, and Mendelson 2006). The allowance favors *one-earner* couples over single parents and two-earner couples (Bezanson 2010). Single-earner families tend not to have significant childcare expenses; thus such a structure is consistent with Prime Minister Harper's conservative views on gender and family life, if not entirely consistent with an approach favoring smaller decentralized government.[1]

The government also convened an advisory committee on Canada's Child Care Spaces Initiative, which reported its findings in 2007. Among other recommendations, it sought to encourage private-sector employers to establish day care close to or at their facilities, and to increase the tax credits parents receive for payments they make for childcare. What is unique about this document is its recommendation to *decrease* demand for childcare via an extension of maternity and parental benefits and worksharing for those covered under the Canada Labour Code. The document discusses parental leave, which suggests that either parent could take the leave, but Conservative Party actions and views on gender, family, and equality suggest that the neutral language should be read with some caution. The report recommends extending Employment Insurance, Maternity, and Parental benefits incrementally up to two-and-a-half years. It also recommends increasing the income replacement rate. Such a policy direction mirrors classical conservative welfare state approaches that encourage female labor force exit, support a male breadwinner model, and provide little support for nonfamilial childcare or elder care.

The proposal to create income splitting is another area in which a traditional vision of family life is forwarded, and federal policy reach is employed to hem the distribution of the work of social reproduction. Launched as part of its "family tax cut" in the 2011 Conservative electoral campaign, the proposal would cost an estimated $2.5 billion and would favor high-income single-earner families (MacCharles 2011). The language of choice and flexibility for families is identical to the language used in proposing the UCCB in the 2006 election campaign (then called the Choice in Childcare Allowance). The proposal would allow spouses to divide their total taxable income, thus resulting in a higher-earning spouse being taxed at a lower marginal rate, potentially reducing household taxation. In practice, no individual in a couple with earnings under $41,000 would qualify. Economist David Macdonald notes that Canadians with children under eighteen with incomes between $50,000 and $100,000 would get 39 percent of the benefit, and the remaining 61 percent of the benefit would go to those families who make over $100,000 (see table 1.2) (Macdonald 2011). Legal scholar Kathleen Lahey views income splitting as "the Conservative government's last and best attempt to try and roll the clock back on childless marriage, unmarried cohabitation, lesbian and gay marriage and any form of non-traditional family" (Fagan 2011).

Income splitting is an expensive proposal that suggests a support and recognition of the work of social reproduction done in the home by ostensibly rewarding it via a change in taxation rate. Increased dependence on a male wage, however,

TABLE 1.2. Family Tax Cut Distribution

Family Income Range	No. of Families with Children under 18 yrs	Yearly Average Family Tax Cut Savings	Cost	% of Total Families with Children under 18 yrs	% of Total Benefit
Under $50,00	628,000	$20	$12 Mil	24%	0%
$50,000–$100,000	1,105,000	$962	$1,100 Mil	44%	39%
$100,000–$150,000	643,000	$1,393	$896 Mil	21%	33%
Over $150,000	399,000	$1,929	$770 Mil	11%	28%

Source: MacDonald 2011.

increases women's insecurity in the short term and over the life course. Moreover, it creates a context in which return to the labor market is potentially a financial liability to families because of tax breaks for single-earner households (Lahey in Mrozek 2011). As economist Frances Woolley (2011) notes, in cases where one partner specializes in the care and maintenance of households and their members, s/he both has greater time to attend to these labors (and a reduced need to hire others to attend to them) and has a reduced need for transport, clothing, and the like associated with labor market attachment; households with one earner, therefore, often have significantly reduced costs and greater time flexibility.

The tax system as it stands now recognizes this. Policies such as the "family tax cut" reprivatize the work of social reproduction by failing to invest in early learning and care while making labor-market exit or reliance on market provision of care the only options available to families. Moreover, single mothers, the poorest group in Canadian society, receive no support. Tax policy can be a vehicle for recognizing the costs of social reproduction, such as with deductibility for childcare costs, but the family tax cut and the UCCB policy shore up an atavistic and class-biased vision of familial life in a context in which a dual-earner model is normative. In the case of the family tax cut, an individualization approach is favored in the sense that the family and the market—not pooled social supports—are chosen as the mechanism for delivering income and caregiving, while familialization is encouraged so that wealthy families can entrench labor-market exit for women.

There are distinct gendered outcomes to policy tools and trends associated with individualization and familialization. Mandel (2009) considers configurations of gender inequality across welfare regime types; she suggests that liberal welfare states like Canada tend to adopt understandings of gender equality based on the idea of sameness (women's status as workers and not mothers), whereas conservative states such as Germany tend to rely on a difference approach (based on motherhood and not labor market attachment). Relating her characterization to individualization and familialization, it is evident that both have significant inegalitarian consequences. Policy initiatives nested in individualization tendencies include keeping lone mothers' claim for public support low and promoting their labor market attachment, and the granting of some rights to children (Daly 2011, 9). The more familializing policy approaches—such as longer maternity leaves, family income splitting, and the UCCB—often produce decreased female labor force participation, greater "dependence," and lower lifetime earnings. Moreover, women in Canada suffer from a "motherhood gap," incurring "larger wage penalties unrelated to their skills, education and experience" (TD Bank Financial Group 2010, 6) and related to the length of time away from paid work. Women also experience a stubbornly segmented labor market despite massive educational gains. Payments to families around care—such the UCCB—in lieu of *de*familialized supports for childcare can have the effect of intensifying work-life balance issues in families, given that the need for two earners has not disappeared.[2] Indeed, some have argued that it is women's labor market participation that buffered families most in the recent so-called he-cession or mancession (Hennessy and Yalnizyan 2009; Rampell 2009). Individualizing policy trajectories entrench the market as the source of income and social support, guaranteeing high levels of female poverty.

The secular, neoliberal element of the Harper government's approach is unconcerned about leaving family support to the market, while the religious/social conservative element is concerned with the effects of the adult worker model on "the family" and supports some state spending that aligns with breadwinner/caregiver models. Processes of refamilialization fit with neoliberal aspirations, as shifting the work of social reproduction onto individuals—usually women in households—is the cheapest way for this work to be accomplished. Yet as Daly (2011, 18) aptly notes, "ideology always counts when it comes to matters relating to gender and family," and it is not a stretch to come to the conclusion that the Harper Conservatives are "closer to organized anti-feminism than any regime in the country's history" (Bashevkin 2009, 121). The assumptions guiding family-related social policy are more than they seem and appear to reflect a socially conservative desire to resurrect a version of female-carer, one-earner (most likely) family forms, despite a retention of the central liberal welfare state ideal of markets as the source of social goods and services. The tension here fosters competing negative consequences: higher levels of female poverty, low levels of childcare, higher levels of female "dependence," and greater work-life balance pressures resulting from policies that aspire to a one-earner norm in an economy that requires dual-earner households.

Conclusion

Seven years of a Harper government has left a lasting imprint. The neoliberal policy orientations of open federalism have fostered a deepening of provincial-ization, in a context in which federal decommodification supports have eroded and spending room has been ceded to harsh corrections and crime approaches. Academic, elite, and interest group perspectives have been shut out of federal policy processes, and expert data from federal statistical agencies and federal scientists has been silenced or altered. Replaced by a kind of "epistemological populism" (Saurette and Gunster 2011), a commonsense neoliberal individual-ism has been forwarded, situated alongside traditional family values. The two forces—neoliberal individualism and neoconservative familialism—work in concert and, at times, against one another, depending on socioeconomic status and family form. For those households requiring two earners, the pressures on increasingly residualist liberal Canadian and provincial welfare states re-quire them to be unencumbered workers with limited state inputs or supports for social reproduction, with markets, the third sector, and families provid-ing for human needs. These families do not readily benefit from the family support proposals that frame federal initiatives and inform processes of tax transfers; those higher-income male breadwinner families are comparatively well served. Yet as the architecture of social citizenship is redrafted, individu-alization requires familialization because the work of social reproduction must continue to be accomplished, creating for some crisis conditions, for others ever-expanding work.

Points of entry matter for resistance strategies. Building on the work of schol-ars of multilevel governance, I agree with Sawer and Vickers (2011, 11–12), who assert that it may be worse to have policy power left to the political agendas of one level of government, leaving no recourse to other overlapping jurisdictions. Yet having to advocate to multiple levels of government is a structural hindrance to social movements, and it weakens their reach (see Rice and Prince 2013, 234). As the open federalism project proceeds, and as citizen attention focuses more on provincial struggles with debt and social spending restraint, attention to the erosion of a more uniform national social policy agenda is diverted. The hos-tility of the federal government to expert perspectives suggests that legal and constitutional challenges must be a basis for political action, while simultane-ously pursuing cross provincial solidarities. The astonishing number of women who are provincial/territorial premiers (from zero in 2008 to six in 2013) and, depending on political party, a general provincial/territorial commitment to elements of a social investment state, offers greater opportunity structures at the provincial level of governance.

The blend of social conservatism and neoliberalism has pushed at the borders of the existing gender order. The third term in office in a majority setting may nurture a gender order in which income splitting, along with a lack of childcare, income entitlements, and benefits, forces some women to either intensify an existing dual-earner female career model or reduce—even leave—paid work and become dependent on a (usually) male earner. This is all in a context in which the realities of the postrecession labor market are bleaker than the precarious work characteristic of the booming early twenty-first-century economy. We must refocus political economy attention on the dynamics of the tension between accumulation and social reproduction. The ways these tensions are mediated in Canada today is producing crisis tendencies, and these are exacerbated by the economic crisis and resulting budget deficit.

NOTES

1. In the 2010 federal budget, a change was introduced to rectify the situation in which a single-parent family paid more income tax on the UCCB than did a one-earner couple with the same income. Yet as Battle, Torjman, and Mendelson (2010, 7) note, single-parent families who claim their UCCB payments as part of the income of a dependent child pay no federal tax on their UCCB, while one-earner and two-earner couples continue to pay tax on the UCCB.

2. The individualization approach, characterized by an adult worker model and a social investment approach, is deeply problematic. The focus in this model is on childcare as part of a strategy to encourage women's labor market participation. It does not view early learning and care as a good in itself. Social investment approaches tend to foreground social capital and human capital arguments for investing in childcare, reflecting a utilitarian rather than developmental emphasis. A truly robust view of early learning and care unties it from the labor market practices of parents, and includes significant investments in the training and remuneration of childcare workers as well as broader societal changes in employment norms. A dual-earner/female-carer model is not sustainable, and a redistribution of care between men and women, the public and private, and within labor markets is required.

REFERENCES

Abelde, Randy. "The Macho Stimulus Plan." *Boston Globe*, November 28, 2008. Accessed March 1, 2013, //www.boston.com/news/nation/articles/2008/11/28/the_macho_stimulus_plan/.

Andrew, Caroline. "Federalism and Feminism: The Challenge for Women's Urban Safety." In *Federalism, Feminism and Multilevel Governance*, edited by Melissa Haussman, Marian Sawer, and Jill Vickers, 83–96. London: Ashgate, 2010.

Arat-Koc, Sedef. "Invisibilized, Individualized, and Culturalized: Paradoxical Invisibility and Hyper-Visibility of Gender in Policy Making and Policy Discourse in Neoliberal Canada." *Canadian Woman Studies* 29 (2012): 6–17.

Bakker, Isabella. *The Strategic Silence*. London: Palgrave MacMillan, 1994.

———. *The Unfinished Business of Women's Economic Empowerment: A Call for a New Economic Equity Commission*. Ottawa: Trudeau Papers, 2011.

Bakker, Isabella, and Stephen Gill. *Power, Production and Social Reproduction: Human In/security in the Global Political Economy*. New York: Palgrave Macmillan, 2003.

Bashevkin, Sylvia. *Women, Power, Politics: The Hidden Story of Canada's Unfinished Democracy*. New York: Oxford University Press, 2009.

Battle, Ken, Sherri Torjman, and Michael Mendelson. *More Than a Name Change: The Universal Child Care Benefit*. Ottawa: Caledon Institute of Social Policy, 2006.

———. *The Déjà Vu All Over Again Budget*. Ottawa: Caledon Institute of Social Policy, 2010.

Beck-Gernshiem, Elizabeth. *Reinventing the Family*. Cambridge, U.K.: Polity, 2002.

Bezanson, Kate. *Gender, the State and Social Reproduction*. Toronto: University of Toronto Press, 2006.

———. "Childcare Delivered through the Mailbox: Social Reproduction, Choice and Neoliberalism in a Theo-Conservative Canada." In *Neoliberalism and Everyday Life*, edited by Susan Braedley and Meg Luxton, 90–112. Montreal and Kingston: McGill-Queen's University Press, 2010.

Boily, Frédéric, Natalie Boisvert, and Natalie Kermoal. "Portrait intellectuel de l'ecole de Calgary. Definition et influence." *International Journal of Canadian Studies* 32 (2005): 175–203.

———. *Stephen Harper: De l'Ecole de Calgary au parti conservateur: les nouveaux visages du conservatisme canadien*. Levis, Quebec: Les Presses de L' Universite Laval, 2007.

Braedley, Susan. "Someone to Watch over You: Gender, Class and Social Reproduction." In *Social Reproduction: Feminist Political Economy Challenges Neoliberalism*, edited by Kate Bezanson and Meg Luxton, 215–230. Montreal and Kingston: McGill-Queen's University Press, 2006.

Brenner, Neil, Jamie Peck, and Nik Theodore. "After Neoliberalization?" *Globalizations* 7, no. 3 (2010): 327–345.

Cameron, Barbara. "Social Reproduction and Canadian Federalism." In *Social Reproduction: Feminist Political Economy Challenges Neoliberalism*, edited by Kate Bezanson and Meg Luxton, 45–74. Montreal and Kingston: McGill-Queen's University Press, 2006.

———. "Harper, Quebec and Federalism." In *The Harper Record*, edited by Teresa Healy, 419–434. Ottawa: Canadian Centre for Policy Alternatives, 2008.

Chant, Sylvia. *The International Handbook of Gender and Poverty: Concepts, Research, Policy*. London: Edward Elgar, 2011.

Crowley, Brian Lee. *Fearful Symmetry: The Fall and Rise of Canada's Founding Values*. Toronto: Key Porter, 2010.

Daly, Mary. "What Adult Worker Model? A Critical Look at Recent Social Policy Reform in Europe from a Gender and Family Perspective." *Social Politics* 18 (2011): 1–23.

Dobbin, Murray. "Harper Runs Roughshod over Women's Rights." *rabble.ca*, February 8, 2010. Accessed March 1, 2013, http://rabble.ca/columnists/2010/02/harper-runs -roughshod-over-womens-rights.

Drummond, Don. *Public Services for Ontarians: A Path to Sustainability and Excellence.* Toronto: Queen's Printer, 2012.

Elson, Diane. *Male Bias in the Development Process.* Manchester, U.K.: Manchester University Press, 1995.

———. *Gender and Poverty in the 21st Century.* Panel discussion at the LSE Gendering the Social Sciences public lecture series, March 11, 2011. Retrieved at http://www2.lse .ac.uk/genderInstitute/home.aspx.

Fagan, Noreen. "Singles, Gays, Women Punished by Income Splitting: Professor." *Xtra*, March 30, 2011. Accessed March 1, 2013, http://www.xtra.ca/public/National/Singles _gays_women_punished_by_income_splitting_professor-9946.aspx.

Gill, Stephen. "Globalization, Market Civilization, and Disciplinary Neoliberalism." *Millennium: Journal of International Studies* 24, no. 3 (1995): 399–423.

Gill, Stephen, and Adrienne Roberts. "Macroeconomic Governance, Gendered Inequality and Global Crises." In *Questioning Financial Governance from a Feminist Perspective*, edited by Brigitte Young, Isabella Bakker, and Diane Elson. London: Routledge, 2011.

Government of Canada. "Government of Canada Announces Additional Support for Canadian Credit Markets." Ottawa: Department of Finance Canada, 2008. Available at: www.fin.gc.ca/n08/08-090-eng.asp.

Gray, Gwendolyn. "Federalism, Feminism and Multilevel Governance: The Elusive Search for Theory?" In *Federalism, Feminism and Multilevel Governance*, edited by Melissa Haussman, Marian Sawer, and Jill Vickers, 19–35. London: Ashgate, 2010.

Harmes, Adam. "Neoliberalism and Multilevel Governance." *Review of International Political Economy* 13 (2006): 725–749.

———. "The Political Economy of Open Federalism." *Canadian Journal of Political Science* 40 (2007): 417–437.

Harper, Stephen. "Rediscovering the Right Agenda." Speech to the Civitas meeting, Toronto, Ontario, 2003. Accessed March 1, 2013, http: www.ccicinc.org.

———. "My Plan for 'Open Federalism.'" *National Post*, October 24, 2004.

———. "Does Conservatism Still Matter?" Speech to the Manning Institute of Democracy, March 12, 2009.

———. *The New Canada Plan.* Ottawa: Reform Party of Canada, N.D..

Harvey, David. *The Enigma of Capital and the Crises and Capitalism.* London: Oxford University Press, 2010.

Haussman, Melissa, and Pauline Rankin. "Framing the Harper Government: 'Gender-Neutral' Electoral Appeals While Being Gender-Negative in Caucus." In *How Ottawa Spends: Economic Upheaval and Political Dysfunction*, edited by Allan M. Maslove, 241–262. Montreal and Kingston: McGill-Queen's University Press, 2009.

Hayek, Friedrich von. *The Constitution of Liberty.* London: Routledge, 1963.

Hennessy, Trisha, and Armine Yalnizyan. *Canada's "He-cession": Men Bearing the Brunt of Rising Unemployment.* Ottawa: Centre for Policy Alternatives, 2009.

Jeffrey, Brooke. "Stephen Harper's Open Federalism and the Quebec Conundrum: Politicized Incompetence or Something More?" Paper presented at the Canadian Political Science Association Meetings, Concordia University, Montreal, Quebec, June 1–3, 2010.

———. "Prime Minister Harper's Open Federalism: Promoting a Neoliberal Agenda?" In *The Case for Centralized Federalism*, edited by Gordon Di Giacomo and Maryantonett Flumian, 73–107. Ottawa: University of Ottawa Press, 2011.

Jenson, Jane. "Writing Gender Out: The Continuing Effects of the Social Investment Perspective." In *Women and Public Policy in Canada: Neo-Liberalism and After?* edited by Alexandra Dobrowolsky, 25–47. Don Mills, Ontario: Oxford University Press, 2009a.

———. "Lost in Translation: The Social Investment Perspective and Gender Equality." *Social Politics* 16, no. 4 (2009b): 446–483.

Katz, Cindi. "Vagabond Capitalism and the Necessity of Social Reproduction." *Antipode* 33, no. 4 (2001): 709–728.

Kent, Tom. "The Federal Spending Power Is Now Chiefly for People, not Provinces." *Queen's Law Journal* 34, no. 1 (2008): 413–426.

MacCharles, Tonda. "Who Will Benefit from the Tories' Proposed Family Tax Cut?" *Toronto Star*, March 28, 2011.

Macdonald, David. *Robin Hood in Reverse: The Real Numbers behind Income Splitting.* Ottawa: Canadian Centre for Policy Alternatives, 2011.

Macdonald, Laura, and Lisa Mills. "Gender, Democracy and Federalism in Mexico: Implications for Reproductive Rights and Social Policy." In *Federalism, Feminism and Multilevel Governance*, edited by Melissa Haussman, Marian Sawer, and Jill Vickers, 197–198. London: Ashgate, 2010.

Mahon, Rianne. "Varieties of Liberalism: Canadian Social Policy from the 'Golden Age' to the Present." *Social Policy and Administration* 42, no. 4 (2008): 342–361.

Mandel, Hadas. "Configurations of Gender Inequality: The Consequences of Ideology and Public Policy." *British Journal of Sociology* 60, no. 4 (2009): 693–719.

McDonald, Marci. *The Armageddon Factor: The Rise of Christian Nationalism in Canada.* Toronto: Random House, 2010.

Mrozek, Andrea. "New Feminist Demand—Higher Taxes." *National Post*, April 7, 2011. Accessed March 1, 2013, http://fullcomment.nationalpost.com/2011/04/07/andrea-mrozek-new-feminist-demand-higher-taxes/.

Orloff, Ann. "Gendering the Comparative Analysis of Welfare States: An Unfinished Agenda." *Sociological Theory* 27, no. 3 (2009): 317–343.

Orloff, Ann, and Bruno Palier. "The Power of Gender Perspectives: Feminist Influence on Policy Paradigms, Social Science, and Social Politics." *Social Politics* 16, no. 4 (2009): 405–412.

Pasma, Chandra. *Bearing the Brunt: How the 2008–2009 Recession Created Poverty for Canadian Families.* Ottawa: Citizens for Public Justice, 2010.

Picchio, Antonella. *Social Reproduction: The Political Economy of the Labour Market.* Cambridge: Cambridge University Press, 1992.

Porter, Ann. "Neo-Conservatism, Neo-Liberalism and Canadian Social Policy." *Canadian Woman Studies*, 29, no. 3 (2012): 19–31.

Prince, Michael. "The Hobbesian Prime Minister and the Night Watchman State: Social Policy under the Harper Conservatives." In *How Ottawa Spends, 2012–2013*, edited by G. Bruce Doern and Christopher Stoney. Montreal and Kingston: McGill-Queen's University Press, 2012.

Rampell, Catherine. "The Mancession." *New York Times*. August 10, 2010.

Rice, James J., and Michael J. Prince. *Changing Politics of Canadian Social Policy*. 2nd ed. Toronto: University of Toronto Press, 2013.

Saurette, Paul, and Shane Gunster. "Ears Wide Shut: Epistemological Populism, Argutainment and Canadian Conservative Talk Radio." *Canadian Journal of Political Science* 44, no. 1 (2011): 195–218.

Slater, Joanna. "Big Five Tapped Fed for Funds." *Globe and Mail*, December 2, 2010.

TD Bank Financial Group. *Career Interrupted: The Economic Impact of Motherhood*. Toronto: Toronto Dominion Bank Financial Group, 2010.

White, Linda. "Must We All Be Paradigmatic? Social Investment Policies and Liberal Welfare States." *Canadian Journal of Political Science* 45, no. 3 (2012): 657–683.

Whyte, John D. "Federalism Dreams." *Queen's Law Journal* 34, no. 1 (2008): 1–28.

Woolley, Frances. "How to Win Women's Votes: Start a Mommy War." *Globe and Mail*, March 28, 2011.

Yalnizyan, Armine. "Income Splitting Won't Help Families in Need." *Globe and Mail*, March 28, 2011a.

———. "A Problem for Everyone." *National Post*, September 21, 2011b.

———. "Five Years of Economic Recovery Have Been Far From Equal." *Globe and Mail*, September 19, 2013.

CHAPTER 2

Just One Drop

Geopolitics and the Social Reproduction of Security in Southeast Turkey

JESSIE H. CLARK

> Being a mother is hard, but your children are your most valued things in the world. For our city, for our *memleket* [country or homeland] it is important to raise good people.[1] *Bir damla olsun* [let it be just one drop]. (Meltem Hoca, instructor)

Meltem Hoca, a volunteer instructor, explains the importance of good parenting to a class of fifteen young Kurdish mothers. They have gathered in the neighborhood laundry as part of a government-sponsored Mother's Education course. On this particular day, they are discussing the merits of proper hygiene—such as potential health dangers in sharing the same bath towel and water cup or not teaching your children how to properly brush their teeth. Hygiene is one of many topics—ranging from the seemingly mundane (brushing teeth, using birth control) to the serious (finding work, domestic violence)—that are taught to address family care and management during the three-month course.[2]

Located on the outskirts of an urban area in southeast Turkey, this particular neighborhood is one of many migrant communities to fall under government-led efforts toward socioeconomic and gendered development. Neighborhood "education centers" and "laundries" for women, located primarily within migrant communities in and around urban areas of southeast Turkey, have acted as the sole points of contact between migrant families and local and national governments since the formal end of the Turkish-Kurdish conflict in 2001. After fifteen years of civil struggle (*mucadele*) between the Turkish military and Kurdish separatist groups and forced displacement in the 1980s and 1990s, the migrant neighborhoods that house these spaces are visible reminders of the stain of war: unemployment, limited infrastructure, and domestic tensions. The centers also are a visible symbol of the new thrust of state power, concerned less with extensive mechanisms of violence and cultural oppression and more with intensive mechanisms of social, economic, and cultural production.

Perhaps it is the seemingly innocuous nature of these women's programs that allows gender to easily escape the geopolitical gaze. After all, what could possibly be political about brushing teeth and sharing a towel? But in much of the developing world in the last decade, and in conflict regions in particular, gendered development has become the primary mechanism through which humanitarian organizations, regional security groups, and the military articulate the tasks of liberal government, ranging from voting to minute tasks of caring for the body. In the post–Cold War period, particularly since 2000, the United Nations (UN), for example, initiated a number of declarations and resolutions linking gender, development, and security (for example, see UN *SCOR* 2000). United States military interventions have also been accompanied by distinct gendered components, such as the Marine Corps' Female Engagement Program, a program officially turned over to the Afghan Security Forces in 2012 (Watson 2011).

At the heart of these initiatives is a security imperative that takes social reproduction as its main target and method. If war is ultimately about government, as Foucault (2003) suggests, the increasing occupation of liberal development mechanisms with the management of community, family, and body constitute one part of what Gregory (2011) terms "the everywhere war." Shaped by ideas about ethnicity, national identity, citizenship, health, and work, sites such as the home, school, and neighborhood are where boundaries are drawn, territory staked, and social and cultural practices demarcated along lines of political belonging and exclusion. In government-led development efforts in southeast Turkey, they are the spaces where good Turkish *and* Kurdish citizens are produced. Thus far, these efforts have been focused primarily on women, as signified by an immense growth in women-targeted facilities and centers offering programs such as literacy classes, family planning, health seminars, and citizenship education. Through these projects, women—historically marginalized from geopolitical discourse and narratives of conflict—and domestic work have emerged as important targets in debates about what it means to be a Turkish citizen and an ethnic Kurd and, ultimately, in the ongoing struggle between these two political identities.

This chapter argues that social reproduction and geopolitics are "intimately"— both figuratively and literally—tied together. Drawing on work in feminist geopolitics and research conducted in Diyarbakır, Turkey, on government-sponsored gendered development programs, I suggest that spaces of social reproduction— in this case, the home, school, and laundry—are central to geopolitical struggles over territory, nation, and statehood. It is this relationship between social reproduction and geopolitics that undergirds the gendered character of the "everywhere war" and the fusion of traditional military interventions with development and humanitarian-oriented programs. I draw on anecdotes from field research conducted in 2009 and 2010 to describe the role of social reproduction in efforts to politically secure and nationalize the region and the resulting "territorialization" of neighborhood spaces as the national and local governments, aligned along different ethnic affiliations, compete for access and control over development activities.

Geopolitics and Social Reproduction

At a theoretical level, bringing geopolitics to the spaces of social reproduction—the home, the laundry, the classroom—follows in the steps of the work of feminist political geographers who have cast an eye on the everyday realm of political negotiation. Feminist geographers interrogate the materiality of geopolitical policy, war, and peacemaking to explore what happens at the ends of policy where dominant political narratives are upheld and, most importantly, challenged. For example, Dowler and Sharpe (2001, 171) argue:

> In order to start to think in terms of a feminist (or post-colonial feminist) geopolitics, it is necessary to think more clearly of the grounding of geopolitical discourse in practice (and in place)—to link international representations to the geographies of everyday life; to understand the ways in which the nation and the international are *reproduced* in the mundane practices we take for granted.

While Katz (2001) describes "life's work" as the "messy-fleshy" bits of capitalism, feminist political geographers employ similar terms to think about the operation of state power expressed in spaces where political belonging and exclusion are practiced day to day (Dowler and Sharp 2001, 2004; Hyndman 2001, 2004; Wastl-Walter and Staeheli 2004; Secor 2007; Dixon and Marston 2011). In the "geographies of everyday life"—the decision to not have a baby, the ritual of brushing teeth, or the whisper of Kurdish—the most intricate effects of power are felt. In Turkey, they are choices that immediately mark an outside and an inside in tangible ways. Speaking, dressing, gesturing, and even the most private decisions about raising children are activities that position individuals within a very distinct relationship to the state. In the words of Dowler and Sharpe (2001, 171), they "produce" the "national" and "international."

At the heart of feminist political work is attention to the body, as a scale and site of inquiry, but also in its materiality: as biology, as numbers, and as a site of physical trauma and care (Fluri 2011; Smith 2012). The corporeal experience of conflict and development tells a story about state formation and geopolitical struggle that is messy, but also complex and illuminating of political strategy concealed in formal narratives. As the central focus of socioeconomic development efforts by the Turkish state, women's bodies are becoming quite literally a part of what Dowler and Sharp (2001, 169) term "making the international." In this way, the body (and ideas about the body) is engaged in producing and struggling against ideas of political belonging as Turkish citizens. The body is defined through education programs as an object of liberal knowledge, foundational to ideas of health, care, citizenship, and family. Foucault (2000, 137) describes this relationship in "The Birth of Social Medicine," in which "the control of society over individuals is not conducted only through consciousness or ideology, but also in the body and with the body. For capitalist society biopolitics is what is most important, the biological, the somatic, the corporeal." Indirectly, Foucault was describing the importance of social reproduction—and the emerging economy of the body—to the tasks of government. This focus implicated all kinds of seemingly "nonpolitical" spaces—the household, the clinic, the school—as important sites of capitalism. Thus, from the outset, mundane practices, like brushing teeth, were part of a careful political project to maintain a productive population as well as a certain level of order.

The links between social reproduction and geopolitics take many forms. The 1990s turmoil in Bosnia and much of the Balkans revealed in great extent the place of the "personal"—school and household spaces and sexual violence—in political conflict (Toal and Dahlman 2011). The difference is that these are accounts of violence and sovereign power to *destroy* life. In the post–Cold War period, military intervention has taken on a decidedly biopolitical element in its focus to *produce* life (Dillon and Reid 2001; Dillon 2007; Duffield 2007; De Larrinaga and Doucet 2008). Spaces of social reproduction have become a critical, yet largely unquestioned, target of war in the last two decades at the development-security nexus, as noted by scholars in both political geography and international relations (Ackerly, Stern, and True 2006; Hyndman 2009; Hettne 2010; Orjuela 2010; Reid-Henry 2011; Lemanski 2012). For Duffield (2007, 4), concerns over social, cultural, and economic existence by security apparatuses constitute the "liberal problematic of security." This is the "everywhere war" (Gregory 2011). For Duffield (2007), it is also the "unending war," war to make legible and bring under governance the ungovernable. Nowhere is the unending war more apparent than in contemporary practical geopolitical theories that have helped shape Western military intervention in the last decade. In Thomas Barnett's (2003) "The Pentagon's New Map," for example, security is understood as an effect of economic and technological integration. As a military strategist during the Bush administration, Barnett's voice was one among many that saw globalization as the most effective force against political instability in the twenty-first century. The calls for development and humanitarian aid that accompanied conflict in Iraq and Afghanistan were and continue to be largely shaped by this body of practical geopolitical work. These theories place liberal idealism, free markets, and global economic integration alongside a development imperative at the core of contemporary geopolitical challenges. This "neoliberal geopolitics" (Roberts, Secor, and Sparke 2003) represents a marked deviation from prior geopolitical strategy, as the enemy is no longer to be contained or destroyed, but rather integrated and produced. The spaces of social reproduction are where autonomous, productive "neoliberal subjects" are formed (Mitchell, Marston, and Katz 2003).

The "everywhere war" and the "unending war" describe a politics that is as intensive as it is extensive, entirely obsessed with the day to day, the details, the minutiae of banal life. Surveillance cameras, cyberspace, and drones are technologies by which life is monitored externally in its details. Gendered development efforts extend these interventions into the home in order to govern the most intimate decisions of livelihood. The territorialization of political power under neoliberalism emerges alongside a reterritorialization of social and political life with the state comfortably still in control. To this end, the body and spaces of social reproduction have never been more important in thinking about the modern practices of war and geopolitics and their simultaneous work toward capitalist expansion and peacemaking, two processes that cannot be distinguished from one another. How people take care of themselves and each other are not just economic issues; they are also choices that draw political boundaries, as suggested by the case of gendered development in southeast Turkey.

Gendered Development and the Kurdish Question

The *Kurt Sorunu* (Kurdish Question or Kurdish problem) first appeared as a term in the Turkish press in 1988. It has since become formalized in policy, media, and popular terminology as a catchall phrase to describe the varied conceptual tools and methods by which different interest groups have problematized the presence of Turkey's largest minority group, the Kurds. Throughout much of the life of the Republic, the Turkish state has dealt with the Kurdish Question through policies of nonrecognition and forced ethnic assimilation. When the Kurdistan Workers Party (PKK) brought the Kurdish struggle for rights to the table with a paramilitary operation against the state in the 1980s and 1990s, the state responded with a network of linked and nonlinked intelligence agencies, police, military, and clandestine ultra-Turkish nationalist groups (the "deep state") to essentially place the region on lockdown. Millions of southeast residents were forcibly displaced from their villages, and approximately 40,000 Turks and Kurds were killed. With the capture of PKK leader Abdullah Ocalan in 1999, a cease-fire in 2001, and the election into national office of a new administration, the Justice and Development

Party (AKP), policy toward the region has changed dramatically. The Turkish state's approach to the Kurdish Question has changed over time, reflecting the different shades of ethnopolitical struggle.

During the 1980s and 1990s, southeast Kurdish residents experienced the state through repressive strategies of power: forced displacement, killings, kidnappings, rape, torture—methods that sought to destroy life. In the last decade military involvement in the region, while still continuing, has lessened. In its place, the Turkish state has invested in regional development programs—such as the Southeastern Anatolia Project, or GAP in Turkish—that *produce* life, rendering the biopolitical production of life a political necessity to the Turkish state *and* to its Kurdish counterpart. "The government hopes that economic development resulting from GAP will help it to minimize the number of political adherents to extremist Kurdish nationalist groups" (White 2000, 111). While opinions differ over the causes and solutions of the Kurdish Question, one thing remains consistent. There is a widespread view, across ethnicities and political alliances, that socioeconomic development is central to forging productive connections between people and governments (Bilgin and Yükseker 2005). Even further, many recognize that the Kurdish problem cannot be solved through military intervention alone. At the crux of this argument is an evolving notion of security as inherently linked to the social and economic welfare of a people. In southeast Turkey, gendered development programs reflect a fundamental shift in the way security is defined and security policy deployed. It is a definition shot through with tension—sometimes enacted through physical violence and sometimes through cultural violence—always through a specific claim as to what life should look like.

In the 1990s, politically active Kurds began to mobilize within formal pro-Kurdish parties to take up Kurdish cultural rights as a political platform. It is a bit ironic that this new institutional base for a pro-Kurdish political agenda was actually fostered by and within the oppressive conditions of the Turkish political system of the time that saw the imprisonment and death of numerous Kurdish activists (Watts 2006). To this end, the local pro-Kurdish facet of government had been heavily involved in seeing to it that development not be the sole work of the Turkish state. Women's centers and laundries are divided in sponsorship, with some funded by the Turkish national government, some by the local pro-Kurdish municipality (governed at this time by the Peace and Development Party, BDP), and others supported through nongovernmental organizations, largely affiliated with the pro-Kurdish government.[3]

As both the Turkish and pro-Kurdish governments have adopted similar development strategies to incorporate women within the body politic, gendered development has become a battleground for two competing national programs.

In this way, the spaces of social reproduction—where people live, eat, clean, and learn—are ground zero for ethnopolitical struggles along Turkish/pro-Kurdish lines. Day-to-day life for many women is increasingly infused with struggles that, at a policy level, rest between two parties—the AKP and the BDP; and at an ideological level, between two different political subject positions, one Turkish, one distinctly Kurdish. As the next section demonstrates, what women do in their home, how they raise their children, and how they provide for their families matters to government and geopolitical struggle in the southeast region.

The Geopolitics of Laundry and Education

The Mothers Education program is one of several classes taught in women's and family education centers in the migrant neighborhoods of Diyarbakır. In addition to physical education programs for children, women's health, and political seminars, the government offers a regular Turkish literacy and citizenship education class. In discussing the goals of the education units, Adem Hoca, a manager at one center, declares, "In addition to learning letters, we have to give social education—another kind of education—about how to *live life*." While the "face" and cause of women has taken on a decidedly public role, the actual work of development focuses on what are traditionally considered private spaces and practices: the household and household work. This gaze on the "personal" reflects the fuzzy line between the economic and the social that characterizes these neoliberal interventions. But it does so within a distinctly Muslim context. Gendered development in conservative Muslim neighborhoods, such as those where this research was conducted, recognizes the deep gendered boundaries between private and public life with an eye to changing these divides (Harris and Atalan 2002). In these conservative Muslim communities there exist simultaneously strict rules of honor for a woman's mobility alongside a general fear among some of leaving the neighborhood for the city. The work of development is first and foremost concerned with transecting these boundaries.

With the laundry program, launched in 2001, the local Kurdish municipality began a rather novel program to bring women out of the house. They built "laundries" in the centers of some of the poorest migrant neighborhoods and offered free use of washing machines and detergent. Also housed in these laundries are classrooms and day-care rooms. While attending to laundry, women can attend literacy or family planning/mother's education classes. Coming to "do laundry" was often just an excuse to attend class—one that was acceptable to husbands and fathers who did not approve of women leaving the house for non-domestic-related activities. Thus, this space of social reproduction—the laundry—and practice of social reproduction—actually *doing* laundry—are essential to the operation of development work. In hosting these activities in spaces and activities of social reproduction, the work of the state and pro-Kurdish government offices could and did happen. Housework brings women outside the home, and simultaneously it allows the home to be accessed by the outside world.

The development curriculum is focused heavily on the home. Core lessons involve issues pertaining to the number of children women should birth, understanding a woman's right to marriage/divorce, proper hygiene, the value of education and formal work, equal division of labor in the home between men and women, and so on. The home is recognized as a space that produces a set of relationships—relationships that are to be dramatically altered as programs like this develop. And this is an important point about the connection between social reproduction and geopolitics. Changing economic processes—the incorporation of new populations into the labor force and a formal education system—rely on a shift in household dynamics. In traditional Muslim communities where family and community act as the referent unit of political and personal organization (over the individual), such changes have immediate impacts on the relationships between members of the household.

As Meltem Hoca notes in the opening quote, decisions about the body, the home, and the family are *Bir damla olsun*, or "just one drop." Anecdotes like these are soft reminders that the relationship between state and subject is forged most intimately in the relationships between members of that nation—in the way that mothers raise their children, engage in work within and outside the home, or converse with their husbands. It is a fitting two-part metaphor for the kind of power Foucault first theorized in *A History of Sexuality*. Biopolitics, as such, is simultaneously concerned with the individual and the population, the drop and the bucket—both productive of one another.

In one Mother's Education course, at a Turkish-sponsored women's education center, Meltem Hoca says:

> We need to communicate with our young children. These are crucial times, and you need to be aware of the world. We can control our house—this is the one thing we can control. So, take control. Before we can strengthen others, we need to strengthen ourselves. We need to protect our bodies and the bodies of our children.

Meltem Hoca's words demonstrate clearly that brushing teeth and using a towel have a purpose beyond just "controlling the house" and "protecting our bodies"; they are the micropractices that extend the responsibility of care beyond the scope of the home to the city, region, country, and wider political community. At the same time that women have responsibility toward their children, they simultaneously have a responsibility to ensure the production of a "good society."

The theme of self-awareness is central to lessons on parenting and hygiene, as if the goal of education is to illuminate what already exists: a free-thinking, rational, liberal subject. These lessons attest to the process of knowledge production that is tantamount to processes of social reproduction. The production of knowledge about the self, home, and work is a central part of the work of social reproduction (Mitchell, Marston, and Katz 2003).

What makes these educational moments geopolitical is the way that they nationalize the home, body, and practices of care. This is best highlighted when they are contextualized, some more carefully than others, against the surrounding political tensions.

One day in an advanced literacy course, we read about Kemal Ataturk, founder of Turkey, and the events of World War II. One woman asks why there was a war. Our instructor, Betü Hoca, answers: "It is always for the same reasons, for land and resources." Someone mentions the Iraq War, and the discussion moves to the U.S. need for oil. Betü Hoca says, "Yes, there are wars everywhere. Not in Turkey . . . but we struggle with wars of a different kind . . . terror, crime, poverty. This is why we learn, so we can make ourselves better." Indeed "terror" was a theme that came up regularly in connection to development efforts, both in the grand halls of parliament and in conversations with development practitioners.

On March 9, 2010, Prime Minister Tayyip Erdoğan commemorated International Women's Day with these words:

> On the occasion of International Women's Day, I ask once again from all the women and mothers of our country to set their hearts on the end of this pain. I am also appealing to the mothers who lend support to the separatist terrorist organization: Please put yourselves in the shoes of mothers who lost their sons in the fight against terrorism. Please prevent your sons from going to the mountains as terrorists. Let's unite as the 72.5 million citizens of this country. It is firstly the women and mothers who will remove the seeds of discord sown among us. (*Today's Zaman*, March 8, 2010)

In one instance, Adem Hoca describes the work he is doing with children and parenting at his AKP-sponsored center to make the neighborhood, city, and nation safer. He says, "The stone-throwing children . . . 80 percent come from the municipality [BDP] neighborhoods. In our neighborhood, however, we are reaching a lot of people—for example, normally these children would be in the streets—crime, drugs—but they are here [at the center] learning folklore alongside their mothers."[4] "Stone-throwing children" (*taş atan çocuklar*) is a term used to describe children participating in political protests, who often throw stones at police and soldiers. Like the image of stone-throwing children in Palestine, the symbol of the stone has meaning for the Kurdish struggle. Adem

Hoca's description of the kind of work his center is doing to alleviate "terror" is a testament to the recognized relationship between national and international security, on the one hand, and neighborhood and home security, on the other, underpinning policy at the security-development nexus. The focus of education on parenting, health, and literacy is about raising better children and better citizens, who are productive and not destructive of state interests. The home is the eminent battleground for the Turkish-Kurdish struggle.

His words also reveal how localized the geopolitical struggle between Turks and Kurds actually is, playing out neighborhood to neighborhood, education center to education center. This is where the physical space of social reproduction and not simply the ideological and symbolic changes play a role. Migrant neighborhoods have become a new terrain for territorial control as they come under the interests of differently situated development efforts.

The Territorialization of Neighborhood Space

While stories of the importance of "private" spaces to public politics are not new and have been explored in impressive detail in feminist geopolitics literature to date, the case of southeast Turkey and the testaments of development affiliates show that these spaces are not just important, they are *physical targets* of the current geopolitical struggles between Turkish and pro-Kurdish factions.

The contrasting political ideologies undergirding gendered development practice in this region are reflected in the geography of political support across the urban landscape. The location of centers and laundries and their political support has a major impact on the kinds of education and governmental services that families access. Turkish state-led gendered development efforts have been met head to head with similar efforts by the local pro-Kurdish government. Current political struggles between the Turkish and Kurdish parties—the AK Party and the BD Party—over political legitimacy and nationhood both rely on gendered development programs to produce new political subjects. The uneven distribution of development activities across different political affiliations demonstrates the fine scale at which the formal struggles between the Turkish and pro-Kurdish political apparatuses are unfolding literally door-to-door and neighborhood-to-neighborhood.

Currently, household visits are a major component of both Turkish and pro-Kurdish development goals. Nearly every Tuesday evening I would accompany a center manager on his weekly visits to meet and talk with neighborhood families. These visits constitute a careful survey of the social makeup of the neighborhood. With questionnaires in hand, we would ask mothers and fathers about basic demographics (number, age, and sex of children; health concerns; documents owned; financial resources). For those conducting these visits, they are a way to begin the tedious and sometimes daunting task of building relationships between disaffected Kurds and the government through helping to secure documents, acquire access to social service programs, and assess medical concerns.

More broadly, they are the mechanisms by which a people become legible to the work of government or a society is made governable (Foucault 1991). On one Tuesday evening, I accompany Mehmet Hoca on his round of family visits. At some point we come to a street and he beckons me to turn around. "No," he says, "that is not our place." My research partner and I stare at him quizzically as he explains that there is an unspoken boundary where the work of the local wing of the Turkish government and the pro-Kurdish municipality divides. Indeed, neighborhoods that were "controlled," so to speak, by pro-Kurdish centers were often marked with pro-Kurdish graffiti, and individuals were much more likely to discuss openly their Kurdish political leanings. On the other hand, neighborhoods operated by Turkish government centers were politically "clean" save for the Turkish flags that would adorn the windows of the center or greet visitors outside on Turkish holidays.

The nature of the curriculum offered also differs between Turkish and pro-Kurdish affiliated spaces. As a pro-Kurdish municipality initiative, for example, the laundries to some extent bring a more sensitive eye to the kinds of cultural issues migrant Kurdish families face in these new urban environments. For one, seminars openly address the recent political violence and ethnopolitical character of the conflict. Kurdish rights—to speak Kurdish, to listen to Kurdish music, to criticize the Turkish government—are a motivation that is at the heart of much of the work of the pro-Kurdish municipality. In some neighborhood centers, Kurdish literacy classes are now being offered. This stands in stark contrast to the Turkish-sponsored centers where references to Kurdishness and government critique are quickly hushed, in spite of the fact that most of the individuals employed at these centers are Kurdish.

Adile Hoca and Leyla Hoca, both literacy instructors and both BDP supporters, termed the literacy program *devletçi*, *cumhuriyetçi*, or *Atatürkçi* (statist, republican, and Atatürk-an'—in other words, nationalist) due to the fact that education is strictly in Turkish and contextualized in lessons on Turkish history and government. When Adile Hoca and I discuss the primary goals of the literacy programs, she gives me a knowing look and firmly says, "For these classes, everyone who does not know *Turkish* must know *Turkish* [emphasis on "Turkish"]. . . . Do you understand?"

I understood. For certain individuals with pro-Kurdish leanings, the Turkish literacy and citizenship education programs are direct efforts to nationalize the Kurdish populations in order to produce good Turkish citizens. There are large numbers of Kurds who are suspect of the motives of Turkish-sponsored development efforts, fearing that they are simply new strategies for perpetuating the tiresome politics of cultural oppression and Turkish nationalism.

On the other side, those working for the national wing of the local government (the Turkish apparatus) point to the overt politicization of women's programs in Kurdish-controlled centers. One center manager, Mehmet Hoca, says:

> We were here first in the late 1990s, but then later places like the pro-Kurdish governmental and nongovernmental organizations opened. These are places that have a political bent—an ideology, you know. They use feminist terminology and they act more political.

Mehmet Hoca is alluding to the overt feminist character of the pro-Kurdish programs. In fact, it has become ubiquitous to see flags and clothing colored in green, red, yellow (the colors of the Kurdish flag), *and* purple (the color of the international feminist movement) in pro-Kurdish celebrations of any kind, such as at Nevros (the Kurdish celebration of the new year and the coming of spring) or at protests contesting the anniversary of PKK leader Abdullah Ocalan's incarceration. And International Women's Day is celebrated every year as an ode to the Kurdish struggle, bringing women out into the streets in thousands dressed in green, red, yellow, and purple. A feminist component has long been part of the Marxist-inspired PKK struggle, so it is not surprising that women remain a central face of the Kurdish struggle today, as Mehmet Hoca describes. The concern of those working in the Turkish-run centers is that the overt cultural agenda of municipality-sponsored programs will continue to enable ethnopolitical tensions in the city.

One can hypothesize on the tangible motivations of these programs for the parties—new votes (both the AKP and BDP deliver household wares to poor families during election time), new labor, and economic growth. For the individuals that work in these programs, the motivations are personal and sincere in a desire to make life better for poor migrant families. At a policy and curriculum level, women are tasked with giving their respective political communities a modern and legitimate face to the national and international community—perhaps that face is Turkish, perhaps it is Kurdish. This is a task that begins in the practices of homemaking, education, and "doing laundry."

Conclusion

The southeast Turkish region is in the process of reimagining its political identity, both externally and internally, after years of violence. This transformation is marked by an unfolding system of governance around gender and development.

In this regard, life's work is centrally embedded in the complex struggle for political power that has long shaped the region. Flagged in the landscape, references to "women's" and "women's education," "women's rights," and "women's work" occupy public billboards and banners, newspapers, and local TV programs. Attention to issues of motherhood, gender, and citizenship position Kurds in a different kind of relationship to the state: one that serves to produce and reproduce, and not just threaten and undermine, the nation (whether that be the Kurdish or the Turkish nation). Thus, Kurds are cast as laborers, mothers, fathers, and voters (against or in tandem with the most common racial pejoratives long directed at the Kurdish populations—*terorist* [terrorists], *cocuk katilleri* [child killer], *hain* [traitor]). Women migrant Kurds are the new liberal subjects of the state: family members given the task of socially reproducing the moral codes of national belonging, laboring bodies producing the material conditions of society, and political beings exercising a set of rights and freedoms.

To date, the Kurdish Question has largely been understood through very public images of protests, violence, warfare, and formal party politics. In reality, the most important "question(s)" are being answered in the not so obvious spaces of the home, laundry, and classroom. It is present, negotiated, and answered in the nuances of everyday life—ultimately, in the means, mechanisms, and values by which life is produced. These stories highlight the very real and important relationship between geopolitics and social reproduction as they visibly unite in policy at the security-development nexus. Considering the kinds of gender-related work ongoing in other predominantly Muslim conflict zones, such as Afghanistan and Iraq, these stories tell us about the linkages between gender, conflict, geopolitics, and social reproduction that are still largely underexplored, in spite of the turn in international and national policy.

I end this chapter with two important points to add to the above argument for taking more seriously the relationship between social reproduction and geopolitics. First, the decision to engage or disengage in gendered development is not overdetermined by a top-down politics, as described by the narratives of women in southeast Turkey who consciously and carefully maneuver within a complex web of expectations on citizenship, motherhood, homemaking, and work. While I highlight the ways that spaces of social reproduction (laundries, households, education centers) are targeted by development efforts, these spaces are also where political narratives are challenged. To that end, there is an "excess" of life's work that is not captured by a development curriculum. As the home becomes more politicized as an object of national security concern in southeast Turkey vis-à-vis development, and as more individuals are invited to participate in different kinds of political communities and subjectivities, the national and local governments will inevitably have to challenge and modify their strategies.

They will have to find new ways to incorporate and name or rename populations and, ultimately, to accommodate difference. In the process, sensitive issues (like cultural rights) will be negotiated and perhaps integrated within new definitions of security and vulnerability.

Second, such intense focus on the spaces of social reproduction brings an obvious worry about the biopoliticization of warfare. Ultimately, it is not really life but a certain kind of life that is to be made secure or *produced* secure. When Adem Hoca says "live life," it is not the "living" of life that is in question, it is how life is to be lived and what that kind of life means for the concerns of the larger political body. Life will go on, but whose life counts politically is always in question. According to Dillon (2007, 4), "securitization raises important concerns over the dangers of a too ready willingness by the state and professional groups to invoke the exceptionalism of security in relation to a widening range of life and society processes." In these migrant neighborhoods in southeast Turkey, women are positioned at the junction between different narratives about community, nation, and security. These are difficult positions to negotiate, and tensions could and do lead to increased violence in the home, where the behavioral and ideological changes associated with "modernization" and "development" meet their biggest challenge in the historically and culturally defined fabric of family life. The complex and differential ways that the state protects its citizens renders some lives livable and others exceptional (and sometimes these are marked on the same body in physical ways).

In the end, towels and toothbrushes are objects laden with political meaning. They are about modernization; they are about nationalization; they are about political stabilization and securitization. They are about geopolitics. In their use, how they are used, and what they represent, they are essential to the work of the nation and to the work of opposing nations. The case of gendered development in southeast Turkey is a story that exceeds its geographical borders. It is *somewhere* (Sparke 2007), but it is also *everywhere* (Gregory 2011); it mirrors pressing issues ongoing in other conflict and postconflict regions where the development arm of political power is pronounced and growing.

NOTES

1. The term *memleket* is used to describe a country (delimited by a bounded space) or the general region or area of someone's native homeland.

2. The "Mother's Education" class was one course among many in which I participated as both an observer and, at times, a student. Other classes included: literacy, hair styling, childcare, and craft making. I conducted sixty-seven semistructured and structured interviews with female students, instructors, and managers, along with participant

observation, in seven centers in five neighborhoods over the course of eleven months in 2009–2010 and 2006.

3. "Pro-Kurdish" refers to a political platform focused on the organized struggle for Kurdish cultural and linguistic rights in Turkey. The pro-Kurdish political movement, today institutionalized in the BD Party, is not representative of the Kurdish population as a whole. Rather, ethnic Kurds straddle a number of different parties. The AKP, for example, has fared well as a national Turkish party in the southeast, receiving 32–68 percent of the vote within southeast provinces in the June 2011 general elections. The AKP received 32 percent of the vote in Diyarbakır province, which was about average for the provinces in the deep southeast (excluding the Iraqi border provinces of Sirnak and Hakkari, which only gave the AKP 16 percent and 21 percent of the vote, respectively). Just north in Elazig, the AKP received 67 percent of the vote. The pro-Kurdish BDP increased its votes from the 2007 elections in a number of provinces, however. See: http://www.google.com.tr/intl/tr/landing/elections/2011/. In June 2014, the Peace and Development Party (BDP) dissolved and reformed under the People's Democratic Party (HDP). For the purposes of this chapter, I will continue to refer to the pro-Kurdish political party by its previous name, BDP.

4. Like the image of stone-throwing children in Palestine, the image and the act has similarly taken on symbolic meaning for the Kurdish struggle. After the passage of the Anti-Terror Bill in 2005, hundreds of children were tried as adults and imprisoned for such acts, considered "crimes against the state." The bill was overturned in 2010, but there are still children who remain behind bars.

REFERENCES

Ackerly, Brooke A., Maria Stern, and Jacqui True. "Feminist Methodologies for International Relations." In *Feminist Methodologies for International Relations*, edited by Brooke A. Ackerly, Maria Stern, and Jacqui True, 1–15. Cambridge: Cambridge University Press, 2006.

Barnett, Thomas. "The Pentagon's New Map." *Esquire*, March 1, 2003, 174–179, 227–228.

Bilgin, Ayata, and Deniz Yükseker. "A Belated Awakening: National and International Responses to the Internal Displacement of Kurds in Turkey." *New Perspectives on Turkey* 32 (2005): 5–42.

De Larrinaga, Miguel, and Marc Doucet. "Sovereign Power and the Biopolitics of Human Security." *Security Dialogue* 39, no. 5 (2008): 517.

Dillon, Michael. "Governing through Contingency: The Security of Biopolitical Governance." *Political Geography* 26, no. 1 (2007): 41–47.

Dillon, Michael, and Julian Reid. "Global Liberal Governance: Biopolitics, Security and War." *Millenium* 30, no. 1 (2001): 41–66.

———. *The Liberal Way of War: Killing to Make Life Live*. New York: Routledge, 2009.

Dixon, Deborah, and Sallie A. Marston. "Feminist Engagements with Geopolitics." *Gender, Place and Culture* 18, no. 4 (2011): 445–453.

Dowler, Lorraine, and Joanne Sharpe. "A Feminist Geopolitics?" *Space and Polity* 5, no. 3 (2001): 165–176.

Duffield, Mark. *Development, Security and Unending War: Governing the World of Peoples.* Cambridge, U.K.: Polity, 2007.

——. "The Liberal Way of Development and the Development-Security Impasse: Exploring the Global Life-Chance Divide." *Security Dialogue* 41, no. 53 (2010): 53–76.

"Erdogan Asks Women to Help End Pain of Terrorism." *Today's Zaman*, March 8, 2010.

Fluri, Jennifer. "Bodies, Bombs, and Barricades: Gendered Geographies of (In)Security." *Transactions of the Institute of British Geographers* 36, no. 3 (2011): 280–296.

Foucault, Michel. *The History of Sexuality.* Vol. 1. New York: Vintage, 1978.

——. "Governmentality." In *The Foucault Effect: Studies in Governmentality*, edited by Graham Burchell, Colin Gordon, and Peter Miller, 87–118. Chicago: University of Chicago Press, 1991.

——. "The Birth of Social Medicine." In *Michael Foucault, Essential Works III: Power*, 134–156. New York: New Press, 2000.

——. *Society Must Be Defended: Lectures at the Collége de France, 1975–76.* New York: Picador, 2003.

Gregory, Derek. "The Everywhere War." *Geographical Journal* 177, no. 3 (2011): 238–250.

Harris, Leila, and Nurcan Atalan. "Developing Women's Spaces: Evaluation of the Importance of Sex-Segregated Spaces for Gender and Development Goals in Southeastern Turkey." *Kadin/Woman 2000* 3, no. 2 (2002/2004): 17–46.

Hettne, Bjorn. "Development and Security: Origins and Future." *Security Dialogue* 41, no. 1 (2010): 31–52.

Hyndman, Jennifer. "Towards a Feminist Geopolitics." *Canadian Geographer* 45, no. 2 (2001): 210–222.

——. "Mind the Gap: Bridging Feminist and Political Geography through Geopolitics." *Political Geography* 23, no. 3 (2004): 307–322.

——. "Acts of Aid: Neoliberalism in a War Zone." *Antipode* 41, no. 5 (2009): 867–889.

Jamestown Foundation. "'No Miracles in the War on Terror': Turkish Chief of Staff Comments on Conflict with the PKK." *Terrorism Monitor* 7, no. 13 (October 1, 2009): 1–2.

Katz, Cindy. "Vagabond Capitalism and the Necessity of Social Reproduction." *Antipode* 33. no. 4 (2001): 709–728.

Lemanski, Claire. "Everyday Human (In)Security: Rescaling for the Southern City." *Security Dialogue* 43, no. 1 (2012): 61–78.

McDowall, David A. *A Modern History of the Kurds.* New York: St. Martin's Press, 2000.

Mitchell, Katharyne, Sallie A. Marston, and Cindi Katz. "Introduction: Life's Work: An Introduction, Review and Critique." *Antipode* 35, no. 3 (2003): 415–442.

Orjuela, Camilla. "The Bullet in the Living Room: Linking Security and Development in a Colombo Neighbourhood." *Security Dialogue* 41, no. 1 (2010): 99–120.

Reid-Henry, Simon. "Spaces of Security and Development: An Alternative Mapping of the Security-Development Nexus." *Security Dialogue* 42, no. 1 (2011): 97–104.

Roberts, Susan, Anna Secor, and Matthew Sparke. "Neoliberal Geopolitics." *Antipode* 35, no. 5 (2003): 886–897.

Secor, Anna. "Toward a Feminist Counter-Geopolitics: Gender, Space and Islamist Politics in Istanbul." *Space & Polity* 5, no. 3 (2001): 191–211.

———. "Between Longing and Despair: State, Space, and Subjectivity in Turkey." *Environment and Planning D: Society and Space* 25, no. 1 (2007): 33 –52.

Smith, Sara H. "Intimate Geopolitics: Religion, Marriage, and Reproductive Bodies in Leh, Ladakh." *Annals of the Association of American Geographers* 102, no. 6 (2012): 1511–1528.

Sparke, Matthew. "Everywhere but Always Somewhere: Critical Geographies of the Global South." *Global South* 1, nos. 1–2 (2007): 117–126.

Staeheli, Lynn, and Eleanor Kofman. "Mapping Women, Making Politics: Toward Feminist Political Geographies." In *Mapping Women, Making Politics: Feminist Perspectives on Political Geography*, edited by Lynn Staeheli, Eleanor Kofman, and Linda Peake. New York: Routledge, 2004.

Toal, Gerard, and Carl Dahlman. *Bosnia Remade*. Oxford: Oxford University Press, 2011.

UN *SCOR*. 2000. 55th Sess., 4213th mtg. at 1, U.N. Doc. S/RES/1325.

Waite, Louise. "A Place and Space for a Critical Geography of Precarity?" *Geography Compass* 3, no. 1 (2001): 412–433.

Wastl-Walter, Doris, and Lynn Staeheli. "Territory and Boundaries." In *Mapping Women, Making Politics: Feminist Perspectives on Political Geography*, edited by Lynn Staeheli, Eleanor Kofman, and Linda Peake. New York: Routledge, 2004.

Watson, Julia L. "Female Engagement Teams: The Case for More Civil Affairs Marines." *Marine Corp Gazette*, 95 no. 7 (2011): http://www.mca-marines.org/gazette/article/female-engagement-teams-case-more-female-civil-affairs-marines.

Watts, Nicole. "Activists in Office: Pro-Kurdish Contentious Politics in Turkey." *Ethnopolitics* 5, no. 2 (2006): 125–144.

White, Paul. *Primitive Rebels or Revolutionary Modernizers?: The Kurdish National Movement in Turkey*. London: Zed, 2000.

PART TWO

Re-placing Care

CHAPTER 3

Men at Life's Work

Structural Transformation, Inertial Heteronormativity, and Crisis

ANDREW GORMAN-MURRAY

crisis (noun):
1. A decisive or vitally important stage in the course of anything; a turning point; a critical time or occasion.
2. A condition of instability or danger, as in social, economic, political, or international affairs, leading to a decisive change.
3. A dramatic emotional or circumstantial upheaval in a person's life. (collated from *The Macquarie Dictionary* 2009, *The Collins Dictionary* 2009, *The Random House Dictionary* 2011)

Colluding Crises

Peter, a married father in his forties, is a "househusband": he is a primary homemaker, part-time worker, and supplementary breadwinner. In performing nontraditional gender roles, which invert the heteronuclear breadwinner/homemaker convention, Peter reconfigures hegemonic models of heteromasculinity. But simultaneously, he faces significant challenges in doing his life's work, manifest across domains of both home and work. These challenges have been amplified during the recent Global Financial Crisis. For Peter and similar men, crises collude at the juncture of economic pressures and nonconventional gender practices. Househusbands are caught in a friction of progress and inertia where old and new expectations about the gendering of paid employment, domestic labor, and care work collide. This confrontation unfolds across and interlinks the sites of production/reproduction and work/home. I contend that focusing on the life's work of househusbands extends insights into masculinity, structural crises, and productive/reproductive stresses. Feminist thinkers have long argued that men's engagement in the full spectrum of life's work could be a substantial aid for achieving gender equity and reordering relations of social reproduction. This chapter thus advances scholarship by considering men who attempt to *do* heteromasculinity *differently*, examining the possibilities and problems faced in relation to entangled socioeconomic and spatial structures.

In doing so, this chapter attends to life's work in crisis, underscoring the collusion of various imaginings of crisis. All of the definitions of "crisis" assembled above come into play in this discussion, inflecting each other. A crisis can be a change, turning point, or critical occasion. This can be a structural or personal experience, signifying instability in cultural, social, and economic processes, impelling change and adjustment, or creating an emotional upheaval in an individual's life. At times, these interpenetrate. Here I am interested in the layering of different crises: a personal crisis; an "ontoformative gender crisis," especially its characterization as a so-called (but contested) crisis of masculinity (Connell 2005); and the added influence of the ongoing crisis in global economic and financial processes. I am concerned with how these come together in Peter's life's work, in which crises of gender, masculinity, and work are interrelated, structurally and individually. Before exploring this case study, I begin with some contextual and conceptual definitions.

Life's Work, Crisis, and Househusbands

"Life's work," an extension and reworking of the concept of social reproduction, is one of the defining concepts for this collection and thus foundational for this chapter. As a conceptual frame, life's work contests the theoretical, practical, and analytical separation of production and social reproduction in contemporary society (Mitchell, Marston, and Katz 2004). The term "life's work" underscores the way in which material social practices *entangle* the relational spheres of paid and unpaid work, draw them together, and make them difficult to separate, because the material practices that comprise life's work are multidirectional and multilocated. Life's work intersects the activities and spaces of paid work with unpaid labor at home and elsewhere outside the workplace. It is "how we live *in space*—in and between schools, homes, neighbourhoods, workplaces, and institutions of civil society and the state, as mobile subjects both inside and outside the entwined projects of domesticity, schooling, and nation, among others" (Mitchell, Marston, and Katz 2003, 437). Life's work, then, is how we "keep it all together": the performative network linking the activities and spaces of paid and unpaid work.

Life's work involves collective social practices but is also intensely *personal* work with unfixed practices that vary among individuals, families, and households. The pressures of production and reproduction, of paid and unpaid labor, impinge upon and inflect life's work in different ways, and furthermore these practices are susceptible to additional demands and difficulties during episodes of cultural, social, and economic change or structural crisis—such as contemporary crises of gender relations or global financial processes. This raises notions of *change* and *crisis* as another key set of ideas for this chapter. As the definitions at the beginning of the chapter indicate, change and crisis are inextricably linked in and through discourses of transformation and upheaval. A turning point is often a crisis point, and this crisis can be both collective and individual. In this light, contemporary structural crises in production and reproduction vibrate through the web of life's work, shaking the tentative connections within and between different sites and threatening personal crisis—emotional and circumstantial upheaval—on top of structural change. The possibility of crisis is implicit in the idea of "keeping it together," where the intricate web of life's work threatens to unravel momentarily. The objective of this chapter is to consider the personal crisis in life's work that is entwined with structural transformations in production and reproduction, which extends across the interlinked domains of work and home.

Moreover, as suggested above, such structural change has simultaneous gendered dimensions alongside economic consequences, and this is a key part of my interpretation of structural-cum-personal crisis in this chapter. Feminist research in geography has identified the effects of structural transformations in culture, economy, and society, as well as resistance to these changes, on women in the West. Women's workforce participation has increased since the 1970s, yet lower rates of career advancement than men persist (Seager 2008), as does gender stereotyping in the workplace (McDowell 1995; Massey 1996). There have been changes in men's working lives, too, with shedding of blue-collar manufacturing jobs and increasing work hours for white-collar professionals (McDowell 2005; Mac an Ghaill and Haywood 2007). Meanwhile, in terms of social reproduction in the domestic sphere, the gendered division of household labor endures. Time use surveys show that men in heterosexual couples have increased their domestic contributions, but women still tend to the greater share of tasks like housework and parenting (Singleton and Maher 2004). The traditional twentieth-century ideology of separate spheres persists, imputing natural binary associations of masculinity/femininity on public/private and work/home, and idealizing the male breadwinner and female housewife. Irving (2008) contends that this spatial model of gender, work, and home has been "stirred" by social and economic change but "is still only just beginning to be shaken" (Robinson and Hockey 2011, 32).

But persistence of conventional gendered divisions of productive and reproductive work is not universal. In a small but growing number of couples, women and men are equalizing, or reversing, breadwinner/homemaker responsibilities (Chapman 2004). It is one such family that interests me, in which the husband is the primary homemaker. Given continued correlation of masculine identity with paid work, this is not unproblematic (Robinson and Hockey 2011). There has been attention to men's troubles in the sphere of production, and the emotional trauma of demeaning work or unemployment (McDowell 2003a, 2003b), but there is little consideration of men's sometimes difficult engagement with social reproduction and of their attempts to reconcile productive and reproductive labor. The literature on life's work has exposed women's strained experiences of "keeping it together" (Johnson 2000), but there has been less consideration of men's attempts to do so. Yet men, like women, are subject to the inertial heteronormativity that reifies gendered expectations about the spaces and activities of paid and unpaid labor. Change is "sticky"—there is movement and inertia at the same time, a friction of progress and tradition, working in tension with each other.

To advance such insights, I offer a case study of a househusband who is a part-time worker. He embodies a particular nonhegemonic masculine subjectivity that ranges across productive/reproductive activities and home/work spheres, providing insights into the shifting gendered and emotional terrain of life's work. The term "househusband" is attributed to Beer (1983), who studied husbands in nuclear families who took primary housework duties in the context of social change in the 1970s United States. Since these men, like housewives, assumed principal responsibility for cooking, cleaning, shopping, and childcare, Beer denoted this counternormative subjectivity "househusband." While househusbands seem to have become more common since the 1970s (Sullivan 2000; Selinger-Morris 2012)—albeit still rarer than housewives—there is little examination of how these men manage home/work boundaries. It seems that househusbands (and stay-at-home dads, etc.) are often maligned in popular discourse for "doing" femininity, eschewing masculinity, and avoiding the demands of higher-level professional roles (Selinger-Morris 2012), but the literature has stressed how these men can foment alternative dynamics of both gender norms and work/life balance (Petroski and Edley 2006). This is not without personal and interpersonal stress, however, and research has highlighted the difficulties and possibilities men (in general) face in negotiating home/work relations (Smith and Winchester 1998; Gorman-Murray 2011a; Robinson and Hockey 2011). This chapter adds to work on masculinities, home, work, and productive/reproductive tensions by examining the colluding crises—economic, social, and personal—in life's work.

These colluding crises have been complicated by the Global Financial Crisis, or GFC, which swept through the world economy over 2008–9, with ongoing aftershocks. It seems the GFC has had particular consequences for men, compounding employment uncertainties, with flow-on tensions across work and home (Gorman-Murray 2011a). In the United States, for example, 80 percent of the 5.7 million jobs lost between December 2007 and May 2009 were held by men, affecting both blue-collar and white-collar workers, and the male-to-female jobless rate was (then) the widest recorded by the Labor Department, at 8 percent for women but 10.5 percent for men. Sommers (2009) reported that some economists labeled the GFC a "man-cession," noting that a University of Michigan economist (Mark Perry) "characterizes the recession as a 'downturn' for women, but a 'catastrophe' for men."

Australia has seen similar gendered effects. While Australia escaped the worst in terms of "national" macroeconomics, with one quarter of negative growth (November–December 2008) and unemployment holding at *approximately* 5.2 percent (up from 3.9 percent in February 2008), internal outcomes have been geographically diverse: export mining sectors in Western Australia and Queensland have grown, while Sydney, New South Wales, and much of the southeast have stagnated, with finance, property, retail, and manufacturing sectors flat (Australian Broadcasting Corporation 2009a, 2009b; Australian Bureau of Statistics 2010). Overall, a larger proportion of men than women lost jobs, especially in managerial, financial, and manufacturing occupations (Richardson 2009).[1] This has exacerbated stress on household finances and tensions between gender norms, production/reproduction, and the demands of life's work.

Methodology

To provide some insight into the crises of life's work, I elicit a "spatial story" (de Certeau 1984) of masculine trouble in the interpenetrating spheres of home and work. I do so via a case study that voices Peter's experiences. I focus on a single case because the messiness of life's work and the complexity of individual circumstances are not easily generalized; simultaneously, this approach allows me to elicit the gendered, economic, and emotional dimensions of Peter's personal crisis, and their relationship to wider structural change and social inertia around gendered, masculine, and heterosexual norms (Cameron 2000). My mode of interpreting Peter's experience is motivated by Aitken's approach in *The Awkward Spaces of Fathering* (2009). Aitken was interested in men's emotional adjustments to social transformations, which are framed and felt spatially. Social changes recalibrate spaces and their constituent practices—like those of work and home—which in turn foments personal crisis. Following Chamberlain and Leydesdorff (2004), he suggests that these emotional adjustments are accessed via narrative. The emotional intensity of narrative points to the effects of wider structural change; emotionally charged stories are both personal and collective constructions. He thus offers a narrative experiment to represent and interpret participants' voices, foregrounding their stories.

My project, *Men on the Home Front*, was also interested in men's emotional responses to sociospatial transformation. The project examined changing relations between masculinity, domesticity, and urbanity in twenty-first-century inner Sydney, seeking to understand reconfigurations in men's domestic lives (Gorman-Murray 2011a, 2011b, 2012, 2013a, 2013b, 2013c). Initially, I proposed to gather men's spatial stories in the context of shifting gender, employment, lifestyle, and household patterns, but between writing the proposal and undertaking the research, the transformative effect of the GFC was added. The timing of the research thus entwined a global economic crisis with ongoing changes in gender relations and practices—what Connell (2005) called an "ontoformative gender crisis." This has been characterized as a crisis of masculinity, with men seen as inhibited in educational attainment, career development, and interpersonal relationships.

The crisis discourse has been critiqued along several lines, including: its "newness" (McDowell 2000), since change is continual in social and economic systems; which men are marginal in the labor market (typically *not* white middle-class professionals, who are still advantaged in terms of career and economic achievement) (McDowell 2003b); and whether men understand their lives as "in crisis," regardless of employment barriers, occupational sector, or household type (Singleton 2007). Yet, even if the crisis of masculinity is debatable and uneven, I agree with Robinson and Hockey (2011, 19) that there is, regardless, "a proliferation of challenges to traditional forms of masculine identity," which might provoke discomfort and difficulty for some men, but choice and possibility for others. Thus, despite contestability, the crisis narrative provides opportunities for some men to question their lives and roles, and explore "alternative" formations of "being a man" (Selinger-Morris 2012).

Within this layered crisis context, the fieldwork focused on inner Sydney. In 2009–10, fifty-two men participated in three stages of data collection: an initial interview about home/work; a one-week reflective diary; and a follow-up interview-cum-home-tour. Meth and McClymont (2009) show that qualitative mixed-method approaches are apt for researching masculinities, enabling access to the contingency and complexity of men's identities, practices, emotions, and reflections. Mixed methods enhance insight, triangulation, and credibility of findings by both facilitating multiple avenues of participation and deepening researcher-participant rapport. Professional middle-class partnered men were prominent in the sample, facilitating an ethnographic window into masculine home/work configurations in a specific sociospatial context: 42 (81 percent) were working, 10 retirees; 36 (86 percent of working men) were professionals, managers, or administrators, 6 laborers or retail assistants; 46 (88 percent) had European heritage, 6 (12 percent) Asian heritage; 32 (62 percent) lived with partners or family, 15 (29 percent) alone, 5 in group households. In this chapter, as noted, I provide one focused case study from this sample: the case of a man who is the primary homemaker for his family. I do this to provide detail of his negotiations of home/work and production/reproduction and to draw out the emotional tenor of his spatial story. Peter's experiences exemplify how personal upheavals are entwined in wider structural changes in culture, economy, and society (Meth 2009).

Personal Crisis and Structural Transformation

In this section I present a spatial story through three themes about Peter's personal, emotional, and circumstantial experiences of colluding crises—crises that foment at the juncture of economic pressures, nonconventional gender practices, and expectations of masculinity. The first theme introduces Peter's family and their divisions of labor. Its spatial focus is the nexus of home, work, and the GFC. The next themes concentrate on the spatial spheres of work and home but point to how they interpenetrate in and through the demands of life's work. This is followed, in the subsequent section, by an analytical discussion of how these crises transcend home/work boundaries in life's work.

HOME, WORK, FAMILY, AND THE GFC

Peter and I met between October and December 2009. He was (then) forty-two years old. He and Rebecca, his partner, own and occupy a two-bedroom semi-detached house in Sydney's inner west suburb. Their home is mortgaged, with a fixed interest rate—a debt exacerbated by the GFC, which induced lower interest rates, *except* for those on fixed rates. This is a preoccupation for Peter: "We fixed into a high rate of interest because we thought it was a low one at the time. Of course it's not now, and it costs a lot of money to get out of that sort of thing. I feel very frustrated because we are really heavily indebted to the bank and I'm not able to earn the money. We're pretty stretched. I'm trying to work out how we can improve that part of our lives" (Interview, October 13, 2009). They have a two-year-old daughter, Sarah, and were (then) expecting another baby, adding to existing financial anxieties: "Lately I've been freaking out internally about finances. I will need full-time work to ensure enough income while [Rebecca] is on half pay for maternity leave" (Diary, October 14, 2009).[2]

As the above quotes intimate, Peter's personal GFC angst is yoked, moreover, with labor practices and the negotiation of shifting gender practices. Peter and Rebecca embody a nonconventional gendered division of reproductive and productive work. Rebecca is the main breadwinner, a senior public servant and parliamentary adviser with "regular" full-time hours (Monday to Friday, 9–5) but a heavy workload that sometimes demands overtime. Peter is the primary homemaker, and he also works multiple part-time jobs in the entertainment sector—acting, scriptwriting, staging, lighting, and machinery operation—to provide both parenting time and supplementary family income: "That's all casual work and that fits in where I can with the rest of what's going on. I'm looking after [Sarah] three weekdays, Wednesday, Thursday, Friday. [She's] in day care Monday and Tuesday" (Interview, October 13, 2009).

Balancing the demands of productive and reproductive labor is always awkward, but as a man performing as the principal homemaker and auxiliary breadwinner, Peter faces some specific challenges in his life's work. These are spatially contingent and reflect lingering gendered correlations of paid work and unpaid domestic labor, such as the "need" to work full-time to support his family. They materialize in embodied narrative experiences of work, home, and the nexus between them. I now present some difficulties of his work and home experiences, including consideration of how the two spheres impinged on each other in Peter's efforts to do both the productive and reproductive labor of life's work.

WORK

There is a robust and enduring synonymy between masculine identity, paid work, career success, and breadwinning (Chapman 2004; McDowell 2005; Robinson and Hockey 2011). Full-time paid employment is seen as a masculine ideal in Western societies—not just a right but a responsibility for meeting the expectations of "gendered citizenship." This is especially so for men who are husbands and fathers—those who are breadwinning to "keep" a family. This structural coalescence of social, cultural, and economic norms is upheld in Australia in public discourse, political and policy rhetoric, and, significantly, organizational cultures and labor force structures (Connell 2005). For example, a 2011 feature article in the *Sydney Morning Herald* on difficulties and possibilities for men working part-time stated, "There is still an entrenched culture in Australia that real men don't work part-time [and there is] great reluctance to let men work part-time in jobs that have been constructed as full-time" (Kind 2011, 5).

Despite calls to rupture the imbrication of masculinity and paid work, change is sluggish (Seidler 2007; Irving 2008). This reluctance is borne in labor markets: Australian Bureau of Statistics figures show 16 percent of employed men work part-time compared with 45 percent of employed women (Kind 2011). Likewise, 2011 Census data indicate that men comprise 64 percent of the full-time labor force but only 32 percent of the part-time labor force, "percentage figures [that] are almost identical to 2006 [Census data]," confirming the inertia of norms about gender and work status ("Men Twice as Likely to Work Full-Time" 2012).

Peter is among this minority of men working part-time. In preparation for Sarah's arrival and a new family structure, Peter and Rebecca negotiated their workforce participation to maximize income, minimize financial risk, and provide parenting while meeting career aspirations. They decided that Rebecca, whose work was permanent and well remunerated with parental benefits, would be the main breadwinner; Peter's work was contract based and inconsistent but flexible, so he would work part-time and be the principal homemaker. Nevertheless, the resilience of cultural norms about masculinity and breadwinning induces anxiety in men who are homemakers and work part-time. In his diary Peter narrated a sense of failure—as a man, husband, father, and breadwinner—for lacking a well-paid career:

> I beat myself up for my lack of material and professional success as though I were leaving a time capsule for my children so they could find out why their dad turned out such a failure. This is a regular theme in my life and why my kids will never be allowed to pursue a career in the arts without becoming independently wealthy first. (Diary, October 14, 2009)
>
> The fact that I am a loser who avoided responsibility for most of his life has come to a bit of a head lately. I have squandered all of life's opportunities and now have nothing to show for my many years. I am only just barely employable and even when I'm employed I have difficulty earning reasonable money. I'm trying to live a life that I can't afford in claustrophobic conditions. My exhausted pregnant wife is forced to work full-time. Why didn't I study medicine? (Diary, October 16, 2009)

We discussed these emotional diary entries in our follow-up interview. It seems that social inertia around masculine norms of productive labor inflamed a multidimensional sense of failure for Peter as a homemaker and part-time worker. This personal crisis entwines gender and labor market expectations, a failing of self and family, and is felt in the present and projected into the future. Moreover, his anxiety is aggravated in the employment downturn during the GFC, in which part-time work opportunities are further limited.

Peter didn't make these statements to suggest that he wants to work full-time and/or fulfill personal ambitions or masculine expectations. He wrote in his last diary entry: "I actually enjoy most of my life, where I live and with whom I live. I can't help feeling like an underachiever though" (Diary, October 20, 2009). Rather, he wants part-time work that is more conducive to supporting his parenting and family work: "Planning for time hasn't been easy at all and that's why I'm still looking for that perfect job where I can work regular hours, that sort of permanent part-time job, but it means changing what I do completely" (Interview, October 13, 2009).

We discussed this further in both interviews. His current casual jobs involve "weekend and night work" and "change from week to week." The ideal situation would be a permanent part-time weekday job, and he proffered "school secretary." He is not hindered by feminine cultural associations with this work but finds breaking into such female-dominated labor markets difficult. He tried but said he found they seemed to be highly protected by "mothers' networks," which were not "willing" to include househusbands and stay-at-home dads in their labor pool. In a corollary to the reluctance of male-dominated workplaces to allow men to work part-time, it appears that part-time female-dominated workplaces might also be reluctant to admit men as part-time workers (McDowell, Rootham, and Hardgrove 2014). Such inertia in labor markets and workplaces aggravates crises in social reproduction.

HOME

While Peter enjoys his homemaking and parenting responsibilities, there are some difficulties he faces at home as well. Some of these parallel tensions that are faced by working mothers, such as the time pressure: "to get as much done for the family as I can before I go to work [between 6–7 a.m. on a Saturday, before leaving for work at 7 a.m.]. Then I feel less like a deserter." (Diary, October 17, 2009)

Peter's assertion that he "feels . . . like a deserter" corresponds to pressures that some working mothers might feel about the need (and the expectation) to be *present* in order to provide emotional labor for their spouse and children, even while their paid employment also contributes to the financial resources and material support equally necessary for the family's well-being (Losoncz and Bortolotto 2009; Losoncz 2011). Life's work means shifting between different forms of paid and unpaid labor to secure individual and familial happiness. But leaving home for work—leaving domestic responsibilities for those at the workplace—can induce guilt and anxiety for working parents (Baxter et al. 2007). Peter's case suggests that househusbands experience self-reproach and emotional strain similar to working mothers.

Other difficulties, however, are specific to Peter's awkward work pattern, and make it hard to plan personal free time for his own social reproduction through leisure, even at home: "The annoying thing because of my work pattern is I can't plan free time at home. I'm always leaving time open for work that might come up. I plan probably two weeks in advance, and then that's going to change at any given moment" (Interview, October 13, 2009). Impediments to planning for free time are produced by tensions within work and home and between the imperatives of production and reproduction (Cameron 2000). The flexible and casual nature of Peter's paid work options—which, as discussed above, have certain gendered limits—means he cannot feasibly plan ahead for large chunks of free time, while parenting and homemaking responsibilities limit spontaneous free time. This makes home, as much as work, a site of uncertain schedules and commitments.

Further difficulties for househusbands and stay-at-home fathers—or "hussifes," as Peter put it—are found in tensions about parenting practices and the ongoing assumption of mothers as "the benchmark for norms in fathering," which misses the nuanced differences and articulations between fathering and mothering practices (Aitken 2009, 25). Like social and cultural norms about men, work, and breadwinning, there are gendered norms of ideal parenting, where mothering is seen as primary and archetypical and fathering as auxiliary coparenting (Petroski and Edley 2006). This creates tensions and circumstantial crises for fathers who are primary parents (or at least the parent who is at home most). Persistent discourses about ideal parenting models—the "institution" of parenthood—infiltrate everyday parenting practices and inflect the relations between parents and their actions. This is despite calls for changing gender practices in and around the home, with more fatherly involvement in parenting (Gorman-Murray 2008; Johansson and Klinth 2008). Or, perhaps more accurately, this tension is part of the friction of ongoing change, and adherence to ideals can erupt in disagreements in everyday practice.

In this light, Peter related an incident in his diary about parenting tensions:

> 7:45 a.m.: Dressing my daughter often takes up to an hour. I'm happy to coax her slowly into clothes most mornings, though it is tedious. I'd like to take her to say goodbye to her mother at the station this morning so I try to push the issue of dressing along. There is a bit of resistance culminating in strong uncontrollable emotion. Naturally my partner intervenes to help, though I'd prefer she leave it to me to continue as she gets ready for work so she's not late, otherwise my purpose for being there seems diminished. My partner verbally corrects my parenting in front of our daughter. I don't see that this will help any of us in the search for control and harmony. (Diary, October 16, 2009)

In our follow-up interview, Peter said he was hurt because Rebecca assumed the "moral superiority" of mothering as the ideal model of parenting technique. This is particularly upsetting for Peter, since he is principal homemaker and primary caregiver, with this responsibility diminished by Rebecca's verbal correction in front of Sarah. This left him feeling out-of-place and failing at home as well as work (Aitken 2009), and he felt differences in parenting practice should have been discussed at another time. This example suggests some of the difficulties, related to gender norms, for men taking up the messy, indeterminate, material practices of social reproduction through parenting and homemaking.

Crises across Home/Work Boundaries

In this penultimate section, I draw Peter's crises at work and home back together—the inertia and difficulty around *doing* heteromasculinity *differently* in both the domestic sphere *and* at work—to further think about the challenges in life's work for men performing "alternative" masculinities (Smith and Winchester 1998). Here, I further analyze crises that connect across work and home. Work and home interpenetrate in life's work; so then do the crises in Peter's attempts to do both productive and reproductive labor, which are exacerbated in the social and economic pressures of the GFC.

The crises in life's work are underpinned by continuing notions of separate home/work spheres and the placement of normative heteromasculine identity in paid work in the public sphere. This informs men's perceptions of themselves and others' expectations of what men "do" in their day-to-day lives. On the one hand, in this discursive regime, doing masculinity is primarily identified with performing full-time work activities outside home (Robinson and Hockey 2011). On the other hand, the solidification of boundaries is itself enrolled in doing masculinity—the practice of compartmentalizing home and work, crossing the public/private boundary, and "leaving home" can be "central to masculine identification" (Whitehead 2002, 117). In the extreme version of this ideology of gendered home/work spheres and masculine identity, when men "return home" they do not (nor are they expected to) assist in doing life's work, but instead they benefit from the reproductive labor of others, typically wives or mothers (Cameron 2000). In this schema, home is not a site of work for men, neither productive nor reproductive labor, but a place of leisure and relaxation, seen as masculine domestic practice (to which Peter has limited access—see previous section, "Home") (Chapman 2004).

Interpreting Peter's life's work in this discursive regime, then, there are several crisis points for his gendered sense of self. One basic crisis is the compartmentalization and separation of home and work. This is untenable for Peter and his casual employment in the entertainment sector. He has little guarantee that he will be "leaving home" for work day-to-day, week-to-week; the hours, days, and location of work change, with no fixed time or space in which to cultivate a sense of masculinity through work activities; and preparatory *work* (e.g., scriptreading) occurs *at home*. Uncertainty conflicts with enduring expectations that full-time work underpins normative breadwinning masculine identity. Peter, arguably like most men, internalizes this discourse and feels personal failure for not meeting this gender-based responsibility for his family. Further, as established in prior research, men in nontraditional careers—such as the arts—may find their masculinity under scrutiny and experience "gender identity strain" (Alvesson

1998; Robinson and Hockey 2011). By extension, I suggest that men like Peter in part-time/casual employment and eschewing the masculine model of full-time work—designated "precarious work"—are perhaps more likely to feel their masculinity under scrutiny, from self and others. Precarious work is paid work with uncertainty in terms of continuity, income, conditions, and protections. Significantly, precarious work is often gendered as "female employment," associated with feminized labor markets (Fudge and Owens 2006). Peter's situation shows some men experience precarity, especially in "creative" occupations with noncontinuous employment, which is aggravated further by post-GFC funding cutbacks.

For men like Peter, who are househusbands and supplementary breadwinners, this gender identity strain seeps into the home and reproductive work. Doing domestic labor, parenting, and care work is fundamental for reworking gender dynamics and generating new caring and nurturing norms for heteromasculinity (Petroski and Edley 2006; Johansson and Klinth 2008). Peter agrees with men's significant involvement in domestic social reproduction and embodies this in his role of primary homemaker and stay-at-home dad. He does not feel such a role is emasculating, but crises emerge.

One, which transcends home/work, is balancing parenting responsibilities with seeking part-time "school hours" work. In those sectors—like schools themselves—such work is seen as suitable for mothers but not fathers, who should be in full-time breadwinning jobs (McDowell et al. 2014). Another tension concerns parenting norms: the "moral ideal" of mothering as primary parenting and concomitant marginalization of fathering as "helping" (Aitken 2009). For stay-at-home dads, for whom fathering is a daily embodied practice that defines their selves as men—as *fathers*—this social and cultural discourse always threatens to undermine their sense of responsibility and self-worth. This becomes real when it erupts in confrontation with wives and their mothering practices, as Peter attests. Househusbands then experience placelessness at home as well as work, and a failure to perform reproductive as well as productive labor and to meet the responsibilities of life's work.

Conclusion

This chapter has explored the collusion of multiple imaginings of crises in production and reproduction through a case study of one man's experiences. I have teased out the messy practices of life's work in a period of critical and simultaneous change in economic processes and gender practices. Through the lens of life's work, we can see these transformations not only as structural crises but also as inducing personal crises: social, cultural, and economic reconfigurations necessitate everyday renegotiation of gender practices and labor relations. Moreover, through this discussion I have sought to be sensitive to how these structural-cum-personal crises transcend the porous boundaries of home and paid work, and to show how the spaces and practices of reproductive and productive labor inflect and affect the other as Peter tries to "keep it together" doing life's work.

These boundary-crossing crises have implications for achieving a feminist political project grounded in a transformation of relations of social reproduction. Crises around changing economic structures can present opportunities for challenging the normative gender order of paid employment and home/work relations. However, other social and personal crises can disrupt the material effects of shifting gender subjectivities for individuals and families. Using Peter's case I elicited the difficulties experienced by some men performing nonconventional masculinities, who face challenges and crises in—and crucially, because of—their attempts to *do* life's work *differently*. Men who are primary homemakers, part-time workers, and auxiliary breadwinners may be the vanguard of new gender relations and practices (Selinger-Morris 2012), but as such they are equally caught in the friction of progress and inertia, where old and new expectations collide—a confrontation that unfolds across sites of both production and reproduction at and between work and home.

NOTES

1. There was significant "hidden" female unemployment from the GFC, referring to those choosing to leave the labor market and not counted in official statistics. Women comprise approximately 80 percent of Australia's hidden unemployed.

2. Federal law provides eighteen weeks paid parental (maternity/paternity) leave for one parent and two weeks for their partner, paid at the minimum wage (approximately A$606/week). Maternity leave is the favored option. Some enterprise agreements, including those for government employees like Rebecca, provide additional benefits and flexibility, such as longer leave at half-pay.

REFERENCES

Aitken, Stuart. *The Awkward Spaces of Fathering.* Aldershot: Ashgate, 2009.
Alvesson, Mats. "Gender Relations and Identity at Work: A Case Study of Masculinities and Femininities in an Advertising Agency." *Academy of Management Review* 24 (1998): 413–434.
Australian Broadcasting Corporation. "Unemployment Rate 1999–Present: Global Financial Crisis Special Coverage." *ABC News*, 2009a, http://www.abc.net.au/news/events/financialcrisis/charts/unemployment.htm.

———. "Finance Sector Hit by Latest Job Cuts: Global Financial Crisis Special Coverage." *ABC News*, January 22, 2009b. http://www.abc.net.au/news/stories/2009/01/22/2472446.htm?section=justin.

Australian Bureau of Statistics (ABS). "The Global Financial Crisis and Its Impact on Australia." *Year Book Australia 2009–2010*. Canberra: Commonwealth of Australia, 2010.

Baxter, Jenny, Matthew Gray, Michael Alexander, Lyndall Strazdins, and Michael Bittman. *Mothers and Fathers with Young Children: Paid Employment, Caring and Wellbeing*. Social Policy Research Paper No. 30. Canberra: Department of Families, Community Services and Indigenous Affairs, 2007.

Beer, William. *Househusbands: Men and Housework in American Families*. New York: Praeger, 1983.

Cameron, Jenny. "Domesticating Class: Femininity, Heterosexuality, and Household Politics." In *Class and Its Others*, edited by J. K. Gibson-Graham, Stephen Resnick, and Richard Wolff, 47–68. Minneapolis: University of Minnesota Press, 2000.

Chamberlain, Mary, and Selma Leydesdorff. "Transnational Families: Memories and Narratives." *Global Networks* 4, no. 3 (2004): 227–241.

Chapman, Tony. *Gender and Domestic Life: Changing Practices in Families and Households*. Basingstoke: Palgrave Macmillan, 2004.

Connell, Raewyn. *Masculinities*. 2nd ed. Crow's Nest, N.S.W.: Allen & Unwin, 2005.

de Certeau, Michel. *The Practice of Everyday Life*. Berkeley: University of California Press, 1984.

Fudge, Judy, and Rosemary Owens, eds. *Precarious Work, Women and the New Economy: The Challenge to Legal Norms*. Oxford: Hart, 2006.

Gorman-Murray, Andrew. "Masculinity and the Home: A Critical Review and Conceptual Framework." *Australian Geographer* 39, no. 3 (2008): 367–379.

———. "Economic Crises and Emotional Fallout: Work, Home and Men's Senses of Belonging in Post-GFC Sydney." *Emotion, Space and Society* 4, no. 4 (2011a): 211–220.

———. "'This Is Disco-Wonderland!' Gender, Sexuality and the Limits of Gay Domesticity on *The Block*." *Social and Cultural Geography* 12 (2011b): 435–453.

———. "Queer Politics at Home: Gay Men's Management of the Public/Private Boundary." *New Zealand Geographer* 68, no. 2 (2012): 111–120.

———. "Liminal Subjects, Marginal Spaces and Material Legacies: Older Gay Men, Home and Belonging." In *Queer Presences and Absences: Time, Future and History*, edited by Yvette Taylor and Michelle Addison, 93–117. Basingstoke: Palgrave Macmillan, 2013a.

———. "Urban Homebodies: Embodiment, Masculinity and Domesticity in Inner Sydney." *Geographical Research* 51, no. 2 (2013b): 137–144.

———. "Straight-Gay Friendships: Relational Masculinities and Equalities Landscapes in Sydney, Australia." *Geoforum 49 (2013c):* 214–223.

Irving, Zoe. "Gender and Work." In *Introducing Gender and Women's Studies*, edited by Diane Richardson and Victoria Robinson, 160–183. Basingstoke: Palgrave Macmillan, 2008.

Johansson, Thomas, and Roger Klinth. "Caring Fathers: The Ideology of Gender Equality and Masculine Positions." *Men and Masculinities* 11, no. 1 (2008): 42–62.

Johnson, Louise. *Placebound: Australian Feminist Geographies*. South Melbourne: Oxford University Press, 2000.

Kind, Kim. "Working Part Time Work." *Sydney Morning Herald, My Career*. August 20, 2011, 5.

Losoncz, Ibolya. "Persistent Work-Family Strain among Australian Mothers." *Family Matters* 85 (2011): 79–88.

Losoncz, Ibolya, and Natalie Bortolotto. "Work-Life Balance: The Experience of Australian Working Mothers." *Journal of Family Studies* 15, no. 2 (2009): 122–138.

Mac an Ghaill, Máirtín, and Chris Haywood. *Gender, Culture and Society: Contemporary Femininities and Masculinities*. Basingstoke: Palgrave Macmillan, 2007.

Massey, Doreen. "Masculinity, Dualisms and High Technology." In *BodySpace: Destabilizing Geographies of Gender and Sexuality*, edited by Nancy Duncan, 109–126. London: Routledge, 1996.

McDowell, Linda. "Body Work: Heterosexual Gender Performances in City Workplaces." In *Mapping Desire: Geographies of Sexualities*, edited by David Bell and Gill Valentine, 75–95. London: Routledge, 1995.

———. "The Trouble with Men? Young People, Gender Transformations and the Crisis of Masculinity." *International Journal of Urban and Regional Research* 24, no. 1 (2000): 201–209.

———. *Redundant Masculinities? Employment Change and White Working-Class Youth*. London: Blackwell, 2003a.

———. "Masculine Identities and Low-Paid Work: Young Men in Urban Labour Markets." *International Journal of Urban and Regional Research* 27, no. 4 (2003b): 828–848.

———. "The Men and the Boys: Bankers, Burger Makers and Barmen." In *Spaces of Masculinities*, edited by Bettina van Hoven and Kathrin Horschelmann, 19–30. London: Routledge, 2005.

McDowell, Linda, Esther Rootham, and Abby Hardgrove. "Representations, Respect and Resentment: Labour Market Change and Discourses of Masculine Disadvantage." In *Masculinities and Place*, edited by Andrew Gorman-Murray and Peter Hopkins, 387–400. Farnham: Ashgate, 2014.

"Men Twice as Likely to Work Full-Time: ABS." *Sydney Morning Herald National Times*, October 30, 2012, http://www.smh.com.au/opinion/political-news/men-twice-as-likely-to-work-fulltime-abs-20121030-28hpa.html.

Meth, Paula. "Marginalised Men's Emotions: Politics and Place." *Geoforum* 40, no. 5 (2009): 853–863.

Meth, Paula., and Katie McClymont. "Researching Men: The Politics and Possibilities of a Qualitative Mixed-Method Approach." *Social and Cultural Geography* 10, no. 8 (2009): 909–925.

Mitchell, Katharyne, Sallie A. Marston, and Cindi Katz. "Life's Work: An Introduction, Review and Critique." *Antipode* 35, no. 3 (2003): 415–442.

———, eds. *Life's Work: Geographies of Social Reproduction*. Malden: Blackwell, 2004.

Petroski, David, and Paige Edley. 2006. "Stay-at-Home Fathers: Masculinity, Family, Work, and Gender Stereotypes." *Electronic Journal of Communication* 16, nos. 3–4 (2006): http://www.cios.org/EJCPUBLIC/016/3/01634.HTML.

Richardson, David. *The Impact of the Recession on Women*. Canberra: Security4Women, 2009.

Robinson, Victoria, and Jenny Hockey. *Masculinities in Transition*. Basingstoke: Palgrave Macmillan, 2011.

Seager, Joni. *The Penguin Atlas of Women in the World*. 4th ed. New York: Penguin, 2008.

Seidler, Victor. "Masculinities, Bodies, and Emotional Life." *Men and Masculinities* 10, no. 1 (2007): 9–21.

Selinger-Morris, Samantha. "The Masculine Mystique." *Sydney Morning Herald, Life and Style*. August 19, 2012, http://www.smh.com.au/lifestyle/the-masculine-mystique -20120814-246ct.html.

Singleton, Andrew. "Boys in Crisis? Australian Adolescent Males beyond the Rhetoric." *Journal of Men's Studies* 15, no. 3 (2007): 361–373.

Singleton, Andrew, and JaneMaree Maher. "The 'New Man' Is in the House: Young Men, Social Change, and Housework." *Journal of Men's Studies* 12 (2004): 227–240.

Smith, Glendon, and Hilary Winchester. "Negotiating Space: Alternative Masculinities at the Work/Home Boundary." *Australian Geographer* 29, no. 3 (1998): 327–339.

Sommers, Christina. "No Country for Burly Men." *Weekly Standard*, June 29, 2009, http:// www.aei.org/article/100658.

Sullivan, Oriel. "The Division of Domestic Labour: Twenty Years of Change?" *Sociology* 34, no. 3 (2000): 437–456.

Whitehead, Stephen. *Men and Masculinities*. Cambridge: Polity, 2002.

CHAPTER 4

Enacting a Postcapitalist Politics through the Sites and Practices of Life's Work

OONA MORROW AND KELLY DOMBROSKI

Feminist, environmentalist, and social justice critiques of capitalism show us how much we need to "construct non-capitalistic ways to reproduce our life" (De Angelis 2012, xii). A postcapitalist politics (Gibson-Graham 2006b) attempts to do just that through uncovering and enacting economic possibility in a diverse array of spaces and practices, where capitalist social relations are just one set among many. In this chapter, we bring together thinking on social reproduction and community economies to help us imagine a postcapitalist politics of life's work. We do so by exploring practices of life's work as they occur in homes, workplaces, and community spaces. These practices of provisioning, caring, and income generating can reproduce capitalist social relations, but they also "hold the possibility for altering, undermining and undoing these relations" (Mitchell, Marston, and Katz 2003, 433).

How, then, can we imagine and enact a postcapitalist politics of social change through the practices and spaces of life's work? For Mitchell, Marston, and Katz the possibility of confounding reproduction and making something else becomes more concrete when glimmers of possibility in life's work are both consciously appropriated and reworked into new modes of practice (2003, 433). In this chapter, we use our research in Boston, Massachusetts (United States), and Xining, Qinghai (People's Republic of China [PRC]), to explore a postcapitalist politics that comes through recognizing and proliferating possibilities, intentionally appropriating them, and reworking modes of practice. Through these cases, we go on to argue that this occurs when life's workers negotiate surplus and necessity through caring, provisioning, and income-generating activities.

The paper unfolds in four parts. In the first section we discuss the politics of life's work and how a postcapitalist countertopography might enhance this project. In the second section we develop a framework for refracting the binaries of social reproduction and production through the lens of diverse economies. In the third section we introduce our case studies and describe the diverse economies and spatialities of life's work. And in the fourth section we analyze how the possibilities we have identified in life's work are being appropriated and negotiated in Xining and Boston.

Gathering and the Politics of Life's Work

Cindi Katz (2001a) has described the politics of social reproduction as having a "mushy constituency" that is dispersed across a variety of sites and practices. Gathering household and care practices together under the umbrella of social reproduction has served an important political purpose, highlighting the effects of capitalist production on life's workers and showing how much capitalism depends on their caring and provisioning labor. The ubiquity and necessity of social reproduction means that these practices are well positioned to transform all of the social and material relations and spaces they touch, including capitalist relations of production (Katz 2001a, 2001b). Like Katz, J. K. Gibson-Graham (2006a, 2006b) finds a politics of ubiquity appealing as it can multiply the sites and opportunities for engaging in a decentralized politics of economic transformation. Taking inspiration from second wave feminism, she writes, "A feminist spatiality embraces not only a politics of ubiquity (its global manifestation) but a politics of place (its localization in places created, strengthened, defended, or transformed). This powerful imaginary gives us the perhaps unwarranted confidence that a place-based economic politics has the potential to be globally transformative" (Gibson-Graham 2006a, xxviii).

The concept of countertopography (Katz 2001b) brings together a politics of ubiquity and a politics of place. Countertopographies provide the grounds for connecting (and enhancing) local struggles over social reproduction happening in different parts of the world, and help us to "imagine a politics that maintains the distinctiveness of a place while recognizing that it is connected analytically to other places along contour lines that represent not elevation but particular relations to a social process (e.g., globalized capitalist relations of production)" (Katz 2001b, 1229).

While the concept has been used to trace the uneven impacts of neoliberal restructuring and global capitalism on households in different parts of the world, it can also be used to map out the postcapitalist possibilities of life's work. We develop a postcapitalist countertopography of life's work in order to map the sites and practices of social reproduction *already* enrolled in the maintenance and production of noncapitalist ways of being.

Our starting point in this postcapitalist countertopography is with the glimmers of possibility that Mitchell, Marston, and Katz provide: "If it is through these practices [of life's work] that capitalism and other relations of domination and exploitation, together with their mobile subjects are produced, maintained, and remade then they hold the possibility for altering, undermining, and undoing these relations—for making new subjects. Glimmers of these possibilities spark through the minutia and magnificence of life's work and are sometimes recognized by life's workers" (2003, 433). How can we recognize, multiply, and connect these glimmers of possibility? In this chapter we draw on Gibson-Graham's diverse economies framework (2006b) to develop strategies for doing so. We recognize the precarity of life's work, but we are also interested in highlighting the possibilities for change already present in what people are doing to live well in the face of worsening ecological and economic crises. We draw on the diverse economies framework because it helps us understand how households sustain themselves (especially in times of crisis) by engaging in a diversity of capitalist, alternative, and noncapitalist economic practices (Smith 2002; Pavlovskaya 2004; Oberhauser 2005; Safri and Graham 2010; Stenning et al. 2010). And it brings our attention to the "flash points" of ethical negotiations that take place over necessity and surplus in life's work (Gibson et al. 2001; Healy 2008; Gibson-Graham, Cameron, and Healy 2013).

Community economies researchers have to some extent already established that life's work is full of economic diversity and possibility (Cameron 2000; Cameron and Gibson-Graham 2003); our task here is to explore how these possibilities might be strengthened and made more real through engaging with the ideas of social reproduction scholars (Katz 2001b; Mitchell, Marston, and Katz 2003). At the same time we ask: What shift in perspective might be necessary for theorizing life and work beyond capitalism, in a way that builds on what is already happening? How can we begin recognizing the glimmers of possibility in life's work and their contribution to an economy that is already more than capitalist?

Reframing Life's Work

Possibilities proliferate when we reframe the economy as including much more than (capitalist) production and highlight the diversity of economic practices that are necessary for sustaining lives. The diverse economies framework was developed by J. K. Gibson-Graham (2006a) as part of her feminist critique of political economy. She emphasizes that the economy is made up of diverse types of economic transactions, labor, and enterprise, only some of which are capitalist. Gibson-Graham maps out the alternative capitalist and noncapitalist transactions, labor, and enterprise *already* in our midst. She does so without situating these practices in a teleology of capitalist becoming or subsuming them into modes of production.

Rather than using the full diverse economies framework (see Gibson-Graham 2006b, 71), we have focused on the diverse category of labor to describe the practices of life's work. Within this framing capitalist social relations are reduced to waged labor, and the relationship between different kinds of labor is an open question. Instead of knowing in advance that unpaid household

TABLE 4.1. Differentiating Labor

Labor Activity	Compensation		
	Waged	Alternative Paid	Unpaid
Provisioning	Provisioning work performed for a wage	Barter, exchange, in-kind payments for provisioning. Provisioning co-operatives.	Household cooking, gardening, preserving, and DIY labor.
Income Generating	Waged or salaried job in formal workplace. Waged or salaried job in a public place. Waged or salaried job in the home.	Partially paid through in-kind payments, paying oneself a wage, paying another household member a wage, cooperative payments, and more.	Unpaid household labor that generates an income for someone else.
Caring	Care work performed for a wage in a formal workplace. Care work performed for a wage in a public place. Care work performed for a wage in the home.	Care work in exchange for something else, care work as part of a cooperative, extra care work that is only partially compensated.	Care work for one's own children or family, voluntary care work, extra care work performed in workplaces or public spaces, caring for the environment or community spaces.

Source: Authors, adapted from Gibson-Graham 2006a, 71.

labor and alternatively paid labors in the marketplace are somehow contributing to or enabling capitalist social relations, we view their relationship as a point of investigation for researchers and a point of ethical negotiation for life's workers.

In table 4.1, we rework Gibson-Graham's ideas into a diagram that illustrates how labor can be refracted through the optics of activity and compensation. We differentiate a number of important labor activities based on the ways in which they are compensated (or not). We employ the lens of compensation to differentiate between capitalist and noncapitalist activities while acknowledging that compensation is in many cases not the primary objective of these activities. The shaded examples provide a visual demonstration of how the kinds of labor associated with social reproduction can be further differentiated. While the social reproduction framing works to categorize certain activities as reproductive, the diverse economies framing labels all of these important activities as *productive labor*, whether or not they generate commodities or wages.

Admittedly, the complicated and intertwined labors of life's work may be exploitative and undesirable, even as they are producing something other than capitalism. Including all of these activities in the economy is a necessary step for enlarging the scope of noncapitalist possibility and narrowing capitalist production to one possible social relation among many others. It is this reframing that allows us to imagine life's work as (re)producing something other than capitalism and thinking through the implications (including exploitation) of those alternatives. Using this approach, what sorts of possibilities might we identify in the spaces and practices of life's work in the cities of Xining in China and Boston in the United States? In the next section we trace a postcapitalist countertopography between these places, where multiple activities of life's work are occurring in multiple places for multiple kinds of compensation.

A Postcapitalist Countertopography

As a concept, countertopography pushes us to consider the role of place in life's work (Katz 2001). Tracing the connections between spaces of caring, provisioning, and income generating in Boston and Xining, we were struck by the ways in which life's work occupied multiple spaces, including the home, the workplace, and community spaces. These accounts challenge the prognosis that blurring life and work necessarily increases precarity for women and households. While reading these places for possibility we are also inspired by the idea that "hegemony is secured—or might be frayed—in the overlapping spaces where home and work, the public and private, state and society converge" (Mitchell, Marston, and Katz 2003, 433).

SPACES OF CARING, PROVISIONING, AND EARNING IN XINING, CHINA

Between 2006 and 2012, I (Kelly) spent a total of thirteen months researching the daily lives of mothers in the city of Xining. I was interested in mapping their diverse economic practices in various spaces of work and care. I began in my own neighborhood, on the east side of the city. Outside my apartment, in the semipublic courtyard my family and I shared with some three hundred other families, I observed how grandmothers provisioned and cared for their households. Some dried chilies on large tarpaulins in public spaces; others prepared large clay jars of *paocai* pickles with the help of neighbors; still others grew herbs in small gardens they had staked out in the public courtyard. People sat outside sorting and preparing vegetables with the help of friends, knitting children's clothing, caring for toddlers and preschool children, and (sometimes) gambling over mah-jongg. In all this, grandmothers, grandfathers, and others performed productive and reproductive labor in a space that was neither public nor private.

This semipublic space enabled these individual and collective provisioning and care activities, some of which would not be possible indoors (such as drying chilies and growing herbs). The style of the courtyard is a product of a typical Chinese apartment arrangement: rows of apartments stacked six-stories-high with long, open public spaces between blocks. While the style is typically seen as "socialist," the roots of this collective style of living go back much further than communism. Traditionally, houses in China were (and are) rooms arranged around a central courtyard, with a "wing" of several rooms for each son and his family. It is in the courtyard that life—and life's work—mostly happened. The activities that occurred here included food preparation; washing of the body, dishes, clothing, and more; processing of farm produce and household commodities; and caring for children and entertaining visitors. The semipublic nature of this space of life's work and production has been preserved in a more urban and collective way through the arrangement of apartments around courtyards that are neither fully public or private. The productive and reproductive labors of the grandmothers I observed are reflected in this contemporary version of a long tradition.

Provisioning and care occurred not only in community spaces but also across the road in workplaces at an open-air marketplace. Hui Muslim butcher-mothers hung curtains in the back of their stalls, and their small ones slept there to the sounds of cleavers sharpening and customers bargaining for their cut of halal mutton or yak-beef. Other marketplace mothers sat with babies on their knees, some breast-feeding even as they directed customers to select their goods from the precariously stacked piles outside their tiny spice or dry goods shops. An elderly Tibetan couple operated a small shop for children's clothing where all the stock was laid out on two iron bedsteads every day, sometimes intermingled with a sleeping grandchild. Customers could be seen gathering around their pot-bellied stove for cups of salted tea, as the grandfather searched through piles of colorful padded long johns for the exact Disney rip-off print the customer desired.

In Xining the marketplace is also a space of life's work, where children return after school, meals are cooked, babies are raised, friends and grandparents visit, self-provisioning occurs, and income is generated. Many of the activities carried out in the marketplace are actually *nonmarket* transactions and labor. In this space, it is particularly obvious that the labor of life's work involves caring *and* provisioning *and* income-generating activities. In northwest China, mothers of young children are expected to earn an income, as they are in their "prime" years physically, and this is considered a central part of the act of mothering. Because of this, caring and providing (whether through income or direct subsistence activities) are not split or fully allocated to different people; caring and providing for children, the sick, or elderly is an act performed by multiple people for different sorts of commensurabilities. These include gifting, wages, in-kind, traditional duties, unpaid, coercive, illegal, and legal. The work is performed in love, in duty, in resignation, and in empathy—sometimes all mixed up together.

It is clear so far that the spaces of production and reproduction are intermingled and coproduced by activities of care and provisioning. The proximity of these spaces and activities creates openings where the caring needs of children and families can be negotiated alongside provisioning and income-generating activities. The glimmer of possibility that life's work offers here is that care work and even provisioning work can (and do) shape the nature of income-generating activities and spaces. This shift in perspective allows us to turn the question "how does work impact life?" on its head—and ask instead how life's workers can transform work to be more in line with the values and needs of life at any given time and place.

URBAN HOMESTEADING IN BOSTON

Urban homesteading is a sustainable lifestyle movement, largely defined by self-provisioning practices such as food preservation, urban gardening and agriculture, arts and crafts, and chicken- and beekeeping. From 2010 to 2012, I (Oona) conducted ethnographic research on the diverse economies of self-provisioning with individuals and households engaged in urban homesteading in greater Boston. Like many other U.S. and U.K. cities, landscapes of production and reproduction in Boston have been shaped by processes of capitalist industrialization that moved various kinds of provisioning and income-generating activities out of the home and into factories (Goodman and Redclift 1991; Hayes 2010). Given this context it is interesting to see a growing number of urban households in the United States bringing food production back into the household. Through self-provisioning, urban homesteaders refashion themselves as producers of household goods and services and politicize social reproduction, in ways that challenge the spatial and ideological separation of life from work that structures many U.S. cities.

The self-provisioning practices of urban homesteaders rework the spatialities of production and reproduction, blurring the boundaries between work and life in productive ways. While self-provisioning is often defined as unpaid household labor (Williams and Windebank 2003, 129), these practices are not always confined to the private home, nor are they always unpaid. For example, self-provisioning is also practiced collectively and in community spaces, and self-provisioned products are often distributed beyond the household through barter, gift, and sale. In Boston, household self-provisioning is enabled by multiple kinds of spaces within and beyond the home. These include: home and community spaces where urban homesteaders learn and share self-provisioning skills and trade goods; home and community gardens where food production is possible; public, home, and community kitchens where self-provisioning can be practiced collectively, individually, and for profit; and public and private fruit orchards, urban and rural farms, and formal and informal food distribution networks that provide the raw materials for many self-provisioning practices.

Among these spaces, home represents an important site for cultivating and exploring the glimmers of possibility in life's work. Edith is a mother, public school nurse, entrepreneur, beekeeper, and second-generation West Indian immigrant who has been self-provisioning fruit, honey, and herbal remedies for health reasons for more than thirty years. Like the mothers and grandmothers in Xining, Edith's self-provisioning enables her to blur the boundaries between production and reproduction. As a school nurse she performs caring labor for a wage at work, but also distributes homemade herbal remedies to give students the same alternative health care she provides at home.

Sam is a father and bicycling advocate who works at a nonprofit; he has recently started self-provisioning for environmental reasons. The care ethics that Sam brings to household self-provisioning also trickle out into spaces beyond the home. For example, he provisions food with others in community kitchens and organizes cooperative enterprises that socialize unpaid and reciprocally paid food-provisioning labor. Caring for home at different scales, Sam and Edith stretch the boundaries of domesticity into community and work spaces. Similar to Xining, bringing paid, unpaid, and alternatively paid labor together creates openings for the social relations of life's work to trickle out into work and community spaces.

Sam and Edith both use domestic spaces to cultivate care for family and environment through self-provisioning. Care can be described as "a species activity that includes everything we do to maintain, continue, and 'repair' our world so that we can live in it as long as possible" (Tronto 1993, 103). In different ways they bring care ethics into community and work spaces beyond the home, while enrolling other people and materialities into the activities of life's work. These shifting configurations of life's work bring production into the space of home, creating the conditions whereby social reproduction can shape production practices beyond the home. The ethical commitments that urban homesteaders invest in life's work can effect change in all of the sites and practices that this work touches.

Our postcapitalist countertopography has begun to map the connections between life's work in two parts of the globe. There is a sense of hopefulness and openness here: if life's work is being done everywhere, both in the margins and the centers of global capitalism, its very ubiquity holds the potential for transformations far beyond these two places. We can see glimmers of possibility where life's work is coming to shape spaces and practices of production, and life's workers are seemingly recognizing some of the glimmers that "spark through the minutia and magnificence of life's work" (Mitchell, Marston, and Katz 2003, 433). Recognizing glimmers is just a starting point. In the next section we explore how these glimmers of possibility can be consciously appropriated.

New Constellations: Appropriation and Negotiation

How exactly might these glimmers we have identified be consciously appropriated and strung together to produce something more than capitalist? How might we enroll them in a postcapitalist project of economic transformation? Mitchell, Marston, and Katz suggest that "to be transformative—to confound reproduction and maybe make something else—requires not only conscious appropriation of these sparks of recognition, but new modes of practice that build and rework the connections among the many spaces, actors and material social practices of life's work" (2003, 433).

These new modes of practice cannot stand alone, but must build and rework connections. To this end, our postcapitalist countertopography endeavors to trace the social and material connections between these moments of possibility, where they are being reworked within a constellation of economic difference and might be appropriated for the production of alternative collective futures. We thus return to our case studies for a second time, with a second goal in mind: to not just identify glimmers, but to show how these are being consciously appropriated and reworked into modes of practice that extend beyond the spark and beyond the individual.

While Mitchell, Marston, and Katz do not really define for us what they mean by conscious appropriation, we understand this to mean an intentional negotiation and organization of life in such a way as to enhance and foster transformation. In Boston and Xining, we use Gibson-Graham's ethical coordinates to think about the ways in which "something else" other than capitalism is being actively produced and made more real. Gibson-Graham (2006b) outlines four ethical coordinates around which a community economy might organize and negotiate: surplus, necessity, the commons, and consumption. How might surplus be distributed? What is necessary for a good life? How do we care for and use the commons? And what negotiations can be made around consumption? In the context of our case studies, we focus primarily on negotiations around surplus and necessity.

By necessity we refer to the work that is "necessary for personal, social and ecological survival" (Gibson-Graham and Roelvink 2009, 331). What is necessary for personal survival is embodied, but it is also related to a broader collective and can be negotiated in ways that account for the needs of others, including nonhumans. By surplus we refer to all of the work that is beyond what is immediately necessary for survival. In a capitalist enterprise much of the unpaid surplus that workers produce is appropriated by owners and invested in growth or taken as profits. Within traditional Marxist feminist theory women and households are understood as producing unpaid surplus in the form of domestic labor that is appropriated by their spouses (through patriarchal class relations), but also by employers (through capitalist class relations) (Dalla Costa and James 1972). Surplus can be negotiated, appropriated, and distributed differently through the individual and collective decisions of life's workers and with the help of enabling environments.

NEGOTIATING NECESSITY IN XINING

In Xining, intentional negotiations around necessity are indeed present. This is most obvious in the case of migrants who choose to come to Xining because of the possibilities of a lifestyle intermingling caring and production. In much of rural China, villages are rapidly emptying of working-age adults as they migrate thousands of kilometers to work in China's urban factories, living in workplace dormitories and leaving children and elderly people behind. But in Xining, I interviewed mothers who chose to come to Xining—situated in one of the poorest provinces in China—because of the lifestyle. Li Ping, a twenty-one-year-old mother of a young baby, migrated with her husband and his extended family before giving birth to her first child. The family opened a number of small stores in the city; they moved because "it is easy for us to earn money here." Li Ping and her husband live in a loft bed in their small wine and cigarette shop, opening the doors each day at 8 a.m. and closing at 11 p.m. They share the care of their baby for much of the day and also share household tasks, such as cooking, and business tasks, such as ordering stock and serving customers.

Is this a matter of necessity and poverty—that they must live in their shop as they earn their living? Li Ping mentions that the rent for this kind of shop on a good street is indeed very high. In one sense it is "necessary" for her to live here. But in another sense, she and her extended family have not decided to go the route of other migrant workers, where the elderly and children must stay behind as the parents migrate to cities far away to earn their income. Li Ping is particularly pleased to be able to be a daily part of her eight-month-old baby's life, reflecting that for her the best thing since becoming a mother is: "Actually, caring for my child, and also taking him out to play. Actually having time. I see his smile and I feel so happy."

Jing Yu, a forty-year-old mother of two, also migrated to Xining from a northeastern province with members of her extended family to find work. She has "left behind" her eldest son, and has not lived with him for seven years. But with her second child, a girl of four months at the time of the interview, she has decided to do things differently. Negotiating what is necessary for life with her husband, they decided to live in a small storage room at the back of a rented vegetable shop so that she could stay with her baby and breast-feed her as required. Although she could earn more by leaving her child with her in-laws and working in her previous job as a nanny to other people's children, she wanted to somehow keep her baby close by and enjoy raising and feeding her own child. Jing Yu is a cheerful and smiling presence in the couple's vegetable shop, happy to cook for friends and share her small space with other, seemingly wealthier, friends with no embarrassment. Three years later, I returned to find her much the same, although with her daughter in preschool she has more time to work in various nanny and cleaning jobs than before.

While both Jing Yu and Li Ping face inconvenience and even hardship, their decisions to negotiate what is necessary through the spaces and practices of life's work and paid work show an intentional appropriation of the glimmers of possibility that Xining offers. Rather than seeing themselves as forced into a situation of precarity, they see themselves as having resisted the left-behind migration style common all over China and chosen a migration style that better suits their desires for a particular type of mothering. While in China it is expected that a mother will earn an income, even if it means long periods of separation from her children and family, migrants such as Jing Yu and Li Ping have deliberately negotiated for something else.

Here, it seems that the spaces and activities of life's work *are* reshaping to a small degree the spaces and activities of "productive" work, in an intentional way. The fact that each of these women has made her decision in the context of an extended family, and that they are just two among many who have migrated to Xining as an alternative to factory migration, means that these intentional negotiations around necessity are also being strung together into a different sort of constellation. This constellation offers more than glimmers of possibility, but an actually occurring reality where leaving behind one's family is not viewed as a logical necessity for survival. In Xining capitalist production *does not* define everyday life, and social reproduction is in fact *shaping* the economic landscape of production and consumption. The mothers of Xining reveal—in a common-sense way—that different kinds of economies and subjectivities are possible, both now and in the future.

NEGOTIATING SURPLUS IN BOSTON

In Boston the moments of possibility in life's work are being materialized through ethical negotiations around surplus. Because surplus is what we have left over after meeting the necessities of life, decisions about how surplus ought to be appropriated or distributed are also shaped by understandings of what is necessary to personal, social, and ecological survival. Materializing glimmers of possibility through the concept of surplus helps us to trace how households in Boston are appropriating and distributing the surplus of life's work—and investing it in community and home enterprises. While surplus is often discussed in terms of value or time (the surplus value we don't even realize we're giving away while we work), the following empirical examples give a very material reading of surplus—by locating the surplus produced by life's work in objects like fruit, cake, plants, herbal remedies, and yogurt.

Edith and I are sitting beneath a grape arbor in her backyard, taking in the fruits of her labor. Bees' wings sparkle as they fly between the hive and the numerous fruit trees and bushes they pollinate, and behind us the afternoon heat infuses the air with scents from the herb garden. Edith is about to retire from her public service job and looks forward to having more time to spend in her backyard. Long before health-conscious parents worried about pesticides, genetically modified organisms, *E. coli* bacteria, or plastics contaminating their children's food, Edith planted her first apple tree and began to produce her children's baby food from scratch: "When they were small there was a real big scare with apples . . . I said, 'well I know my kids like apples so I'm going to grow them.' Now I have all this fruit," she laughs. What began as a source of food security for her household now produces surplus that is used as an alternative source of income, a gift to neighbors, and a home business. While her children were in school she used the fruit for bake sales, holiday markets, and fund-raisers. The pear tree alone yields about US$1,000 each year in pear bread that is sold to a select group of lifelong customers.

Edith started self-provisioning herbal remedies out of necessity after her first child was born with health problems. "The doctor actually had the nerve to say to me, 'Don't get attached to him, because he might die.'" Refusing to give up on her son's life she took health care into her own hands, and started making herbal remedies and keeping bees. As her children, garden, and bees have grown up and flourished together she has been able to start several home businesses selling the surplus of her life's work. For health reasons, stemming largely from necessity, Edith has increased the time she devotes to social reproduction. In combination with the unpaid labor of her children and bees her household produces a significant amount of social and material surplus that is distributed at home, at work, and in the community for various forms of commensurabilities. Edith chooses to distribute this surplus beyond the household through gift and market transactions with neighbors, church members, and a broader public of consumers. The surplus that is produced by Edith through the spaces and practices of social reproduction does not necessarily reproduce capitalism, but instead supports the community economy of her household, neighborhood, school, and church.

Sam and his family live a sustainable lifestyle that places environmental well-being at the center of life's work. For example, they have decided that driving a car is not necessary, but purchasing from local, family-owned, and cooperative enterprises is. Considering the ethics, sustainability, and pleasure of the foods they consume on a daily basis has led Sam's family to pursue a variety of self-provisioning practices at home. This was how Sam started making yogurt for his family each week, a choice that was informed by the pleasure of making things, the care ethics of sharing good food with others, the economic ethics of supporting a local dairy, and the environmental ethics of reducing plastic packaging. For Sam self-provisioning is not done out of a desire to become self-sufficient, but rather to reconfigure the social and material connections between his family and the broader social and economic networks they depend on. For this reason he decided to scale up and socialize some of his self-provisioning labor by starting a neighborhood yogurt-making co-op. Participating in a yogurt-making co-op enables Sam's family, and other members, to invest household surplus into cooperative consumption and production. As director of the co-op he gifts time and energy to maintain this zero-waste, sustainable, producer-consumer cooperative and to create spaces where surplus distribution can be negotiated cooperatively.

The decision to live a sustainable lifestyle has increased the time that Sam devotes to social reproduction and also the economic diversity of these practices. This has, in turn, multiplied the opportunities for ethical negotiations around surplus and necessity that take environmental well-being into account. Consciously appropriating the glimmers of possibility in life's work, Sam has reworked the connections between his household, neighborhood, and environment by distributing household surplus to a broader network of local, alternative, and cooperative enterprises. Sometimes Sam jokes that the various experiments his family engages in don't *really* matter and that some people might even find these daily negotiations kind of neurotic, but he can't imagine living any other way. He finds great joy in tinkering at the edges of life and work, and figuring out how to meet necessity and distribute surplus in ways that enhance the well-being of his family, community, and environment. The effect of these daily negotiations and practices should not be underestimated, as they hold the potential to (re)produce new subjectivities, habits, orientations, and economies.

In this section we have explored how surplus and necessity have been negotiated according to ethics of care for children, environment, and community. We suggest that these intentional negotiations are a kind of conscious appropriation of possibility, whereby the latent possibilities of life's work in Xining and Boston are harnessed and fashioned into new modes of practice. Between these distant places we have found some commonalities. The negotiations by mothers in Xining over what kinds of environments can support their lifestyle suggest that lifestyle politics are by no means exclusive to (mostly middle-class) urban home-steaders in Boston. The lifestyle politics of life's work might even be strengthened by seemingly unrelated negotiations around surplus and necessity happening in different parts of the world. The decisions made by Sam to distribute household surplus to local shops and cooperative and community enterprises in Boston, and marketplace mothers in Xining deciding to become shopkeepers, could be read as a shared objection to migrant factory work. Figuring out how to live well with less in Xining might also provide surprising inspiration for households trying to live sustainably in Boston. Actions in both of these places contribute to strengthening a community economy that can support ethical negotiations around life's work.

Conclusion

In this chapter we have begun to flesh out a postcapitalist countertopography of life's work. Inspired by the openness to economic possibility evident in the work of J. K. Gibson-Graham (2006) and others in the Community Economies Collective, we sought to bring this approach into conversation with the concern for politicizing life's work evident in the work of Mitchell, Marston, and Katz (2003). Our key theoretical strategy has been to refract the concept of social reproduction through the lens of diverse economies in order to render social reproduction different from itself, and render production as much more than capitalist. This has enabled us to multiply the "glimmers of possibility" identified by Mitchell, Marston, and Katz through multiplying the nodes of decision making. At these nodes of decision making, we considered how we might identify and clarify the ethical choices (Gibson-Graham and Roelvink 2009, 330) involved in meeting necessity and appropriating and mobilizing the (surplus) possibilities of life's work.

In our case studies based in Xining and Boston, we showed how possibilities are produced, appropriated, and negotiated through entanglements with place. It is in these material contexts that we sketched a postcapitalist countertopography that drew these seemingly ephemeral glimmers together into a constellation of economic difference. The countertopography of life's work in Xining and Boston drew global interconnections between seemingly disparate struggles over surplus and necessity.

What did this sort of approach help us to achieve? For one, it evoked the ubiquity of life's work globally. While our two case studies are hardly a globally representative sample, connecting a place considered at the very margins of "the global economy" with a place considered pretty close to the center of it is one way to highlight the range of places where life's work—and surplus and necessity—are being negotiated in ways that can potentially produce something *other* than capitalism. It is this approach that adds the postcapitalist descriptor to our countertopography of life's work. A postcapitalist countertopography of life's work is a concept that can potentially go further in this field. By enrolling Katz's countertopographical method into a politics of possibility, we have demonstrated a way to *proliferate* the possibilities for different kinds of noncapitalist futures, and show how life's work might shape production in friendlier ways, rather than reproducing exploitation.

We were inspired to move away from the critical stance that "tends to confirm what we already know: that the world is full of devastation and oppression, and that transformation is an unlikely if not hopeless project," and toward an "open and reparative stance that refuses to know too much, that makes space for hope and possibility" (Gibson-Graham and Roelvink 2010, 324). When applied to thinking about life's work, multiplying possibilities for producing something other than capitalism has involved, for us, moving away from a perspective where life's work is always reflecting, reproducing, and enabling capitalist domination. We have attempted to show how we might instead value "the ways in which meanings and institutions can be at loose ends with each other" and where "the richest junctures weren't the ones where everything means the same thing" (Sedgwick 1994, 5). By allowing life's work and capitalism to be at loose ends with each other, we were able to identify the rich junctures where an ethics of care can enable negotiations around surplus and necessity, where something else can happen.

NOTES

The research on Urban Homesteading in Boston was supported by National Science Foundation Grant BCS 1234241. Any opinions, findings, and conclusions or recommendations expressed in this material are those of the authors and do not necessarily reflect the views of the National Science Foundation. This chapter was prepared with support from the Julie Graham Community Economies Research Fund. Thanks to the participants in the 2013 Community Economies Theory and Writing Retreat, Bolsena, Italy, July 2013, and to Katherine Gibson, Deborah G. Martin, and Jenny Cameron for providing helpful comments on earlier versions.

1. There are divisions in terms of age and life-stage, however. Mothers normally care for babies for three months to three years, depending on their other work. Grandmothers and grandfathers typically take over care work after this. This is considered a traditional responsibility of the paternal grandmother, although in actuality the arrangements are quite diverse.

REFERENCES

Cameron, Jenny. "Domesticating Class: Femininity, Heterosexuality, and Household Politics." In *Class and Its Others*, edited by J. K. Gibson-Graham, Stephen A. Resnick, and Richard D. Wolff, 47–68. Minneapolis: University of Minnesota Press, 2000.

Cameron, Jenny, and J. K. Gibson-Graham. "Feminising the Economy: Metaphors, Strategies, Politics." *Gender, Place and Culture* 10, no. 2 (2003): 145–157.

Dalla Costa, Mariarose, and Selma James. *The Power of Women and the Subversion of the Community*. London: Falling Wall Press, 1972.

De Angelis, Massimo. "Preface: Care Work and the Commons." *Commoner* 15 (2012): xii–xv.

Gibson-Graham, J. K. "Surplus Possibilities: Post-Development and Community Economies." *Singapore Journal of Tropical Geography* 26, no. 1 (2005): 4–26.

———. *The End of Capitalism (As We Knew It)*. 2nd ed., with new introduction. 1996; Minneapolis: University of Minnesota Press, 2006a.

———. *A Postcapitalist Politics*. Minneapolis: University of Minnesota Press, 2006b.

Gibson-Graham, J. K., Jenny Cameron, and Stephen Healy. *Take Back the Economy*. Minneapolis: University of Minnesota Press, 2013.

Gibson-Graham, J. K., and Gerda Roelvink. "An Economic Ethics for the Anthropocene." *Antipode* 41, s. 1 (2009): 320–346.

Gibson, Katherine, Lisa Law, and Deirdre Mckay. "Beyond Heroes and Victims: Filipina Contract Migrants, Economic Activism and Class Transformation." *International Feminist Journal of Politics* 3, no. 3 (2001): 365–386.

Goodman, David, and Michael Redclift. *Refashioning Nature: Food, Ecology, and Culture*. New York: Routledge, 1991.

Hayes, Shannon. *Radical Homemakers: Reclaiming Domesticity from a Consumer Culture*. Richmondville, N.Y.: Left to Write Press, 2010.

Healy, Stephen. "Caring for Ethics and the Politics of Health Care Reform in the United States." *Gender, Place and Culture* 15, no. 3 (2008): 267–284.

Katz, Cindi. "Vagabond Capitalism and the Necessity of Social Reproduction." *Antipode* 33, no. 4 (2001a): 709–728.

———. "On the Grounds of Globalization: A Topography for Feminist Political Engagement." *Signs* 26, no. 4 (2001b): 1213–1234.

Mitchell, Katharyne, Sallie A. Marston, and Cindi Katz. "Introduction: Life's Work: An Introduction, Review and Critique." *Antipode* 35, no. 3 (2003): 415–442.

Oberhauser, Ann M. "Scaling Gender and Diverse Economies: Perspectives from Appalachia and South Africa." *Antipode* 37, no. 5 (2005): 863–874.

Pavlovskaya, Marianna. "Other Transitions: Multiple Economies of Moscow Households in the 1990s." *Annals of the Association of American Geographers* 94, no. 2 (2004): 329–351.

Safri, Malinha, and Julie Graham. "The Global Household: Toward a Feminist Postcapitalist International Political Economy." *Signs* 36, no. 1 (2010): 99–125.

Sedgwick, Eve K. *Tendencies*. New York: Routledge, 1994.

Smith, Adrian. "Culture/Economy and Spaces of Economic Practice: Positioning House-holds in Post-Communism." *Transactions of the Institute of British Geographers* 27, no. 2 (2002): 232–250.

Stenning, Alison, Adrian Smith, Alena Rochovská, and Dariusz Świątek. "Credit, Debt, and Everyday Financial Practices: Low-Income Households in Two Postsocialist Cities." *Economic Geography* 86, no. 2 (2010): 119–145.

Tronto, Jean. *Moral Boundaries: A Political Argument for an Ethic of Care*. New York: Routledge, 1993.

Williams, Colin C., and James Windebank. "Alternative Employment Spaces." In *Alternative Economic Spaces*, edited by Roger Lee, Andrew Leyshon, and Colin C. Williams. Thousand Oaks, Calif.: Sage, 2003.

PART THREE

Bodies and Barriers

CHAPTER 5

Whose Lives, Which Work?

Class Discrepancies in Life's Work

BARBARA ELLEN SMITH AND JAMIE WINDERS

In 1989 in Morristown, a small town in east Tennessee, workers received notice that the General Electric plant where they worked was to close. Shortly thereafter, they learned that the factory was re-opening in an adjacent Tennessee county. If the workers wanted to keep their jobs, albeit at reduced wages and benefits, they had to re-apply through a temporary labor supply agency (Weinbaum 2003).

Ten years later, in Memphis, Tennessee, Latino immigrant workers also applied for jobs through temporary agencies. In this case, the agencies funneled immigrant workers into the sprawling warehouses and just-in-time labor of Memphis's distribution sector, anchored by the FedEx Corporation. The length and timing of their workdays often varied at the last minute, depending on the volume of orders from global markets. In the context of this frenetic work environment, employer "requests" for overtime were, in truth, mandatory commands. One Latina working in logistics reported that after working overtime late into the night, she was unsure where to find her young daughter and who, if anyone, was caring for the child (Smith, Mendoza, and Ciscel 2005).

During the same time period, faculty at universities across the U.S. and elsewhere increasingly utilized information and communication technologies to work at any hour and from most any place—including homes, hotel rooms, offices, even cars. For such academic professionals, work-related obligations and preoccupations steadily seeped into all spaces and activities of life, as it became possible to work anywhere, anytime. The line between being "at work" and being "at home" blurred and, in many cases, seemed to dissolve altogether.

In 2011, unauthorized Latino immigrants in Alabama, displaced economically by the Great Recession and marginalized socially by the nation's harshest anti-immigrant state law at the time, remained unemployed but too fearful of deportation to venture out of their homes to seek jobs, take children to school (where students' legal status was to be monitored), or participate in public community activities. Some felt virtually incarcerated in their houses, unable to work and fearful to live publicly. For these workers, the line between "work" and "life" had not blurred but, instead, become dangerous to cross, as seeking work potentially jeopardized the right to live in Alabama in the first place (Winders 2014).

How can feminist scholars and activists analyze and contest these transformations in the space-times of work and home for different kinds of workers? What is the conceptual status of life's work when home is where *some* people carry out the duties of both paid employment and unpaid labor for kin and community, while others move frantically between inflexible employer demands in their place-bound jobs and the unpredictable needs of children and households? How can feminist political organizing address the sometimes-unbearable pressures of these divergent, class-specific manifestations of "flexibility" in both production and social reproduction, in both work and home and all the spaces within and between?

The theoretical legacy of Marxist feminism has long sought to analyze the relationship between wage labor under capitalism and the activities, such as child care and food preparation, necessary to sustain families and households yet historically unpaid or in the domain of low-wage, racialized domestic "help" (Glenn 1992). This chapter draws on that legacy in an effort to assess the adequacy of recent claims that the distinction between work and life is increasingly permeable and blurring (e.g., Hochschild 1997; Schieman and Glavin 2008), as the spaces of work and home merge into what Katharyne Mitchell, Sallie Marston, and Cindi Katz (2003) call "life's work." Insofar as feminist theorists have long argued that the conceptual separation of wage labor and domestic labor, along with associated binaries such as market/nonmarket, public/private, and male/female, is confounded by far messier economic and social realities, the notion that the boundaries between "work" and "home" are blurry is not new. Nonetheless, contemporary arguments about this blurring have a distinct, if not always articulated, *spatial* referent: that is, the observation that the actual sites of work are no longer fixed, but portable and fluid. Under this model, work is understood to be so fully incorporated, materially and cognitively, into personhood that, as Mitchell, Marston, and Katz write, "the domain of work and the domains of home and leisure are indistinguishable from each other—and for many *this is the contemporary 'habitus'"* (2003, 417, emphasis in original).

This chapter argues that this spatial imaginary of a contemporary habitus in which work and home seem indistinguishable, if not overlapping entirely, is based upon a particular, and to date unacknowledged, class specificity. Drawing on our own scholarship on working-class lives in the contemporary American South, we point to a series of different, much less fluid realities of life's work that, we suggest, demand political and theoretical attention from feminist scholars.

As our opening vignettes intimate and as the rest of this chapter illustrates in detail, the claim that the line between work and the rest of life is blurring or dissolving may not hold across the class spectrum, particularly when other axes of inequality, such as legal status and race, are taken seriously. Indeed, in contrast to earlier Marxist feminist scholars, who theorized class distinctions between households and tended to focus on the working class (e.g., "Women's Labor" 1973; Vogel 1983), recent scholarship has often centered on highly trained professionals whose conditions of employment, while sometimes insecure, are more subject to their own control (see Schieman and Glavin 2008; Blair-Loy 2009). Insofar as findings from such investigations have been generalized as theoretical claims about how work and life relate in the contemporary moment, the brutal insecurities facing many working-class people have been largely concealed, and the conceptual tools needed to analyze their precarious circumstances have not been developed.

We thus argue for the *preservation* of a conceptual distinction between wage labor and the (sometimes) unwaged work of household maintenance and continuity and, in particular, for more sustained examination of the highly variable, class-specific configurations of this nexus between production and social reproduction. To make this argument, we first engage briefly with Mitchell, Marston, and Katz's formulation of life's work, as well as with related scholarly discussions of social reproduction. We then illustrate our assertions regarding the theoretical significance and implications of class, and its articulation with other systems of inequality, through our ongoing research on immigration and work in the American South. In a discussion of factory workers in the rural South, coal mining communities in central Appalachia, and undocumented immigrants in Alabama and Georgia, we examine how deindustrialization and increasingly flexible production practices, neoliberal rollbacks of public institutions and regulatory protections, and related rollouts of state surveillance and punishment directed at immigrants influence the nexus of production and social reproduction and its increasingly precarious manifestation in the lives of many working-class women and men. The groups we discuss here in some ways represent distinctive populations in their exposure to the vagaries of global capitalism and related environmental and social exploitation; nonetheless, their deployment as hyperflexible labor and the neoliberal indifference, if not legally codified hostility, toward their social maintenance and intergenerational continuity may gesture toward an ominous "new normal" with far-reaching ramifications. The conclusion draws attention to the class specificity of policies promoting "work-life balance" as an antidote to the pressures of life's work and argues for the importance of quite different political demands that would contest the increasing precariousness of working-class life.

The Tangled Legacy of Life's Work

In their now-classic article, Mitchell, Marston, and Katz (2003, 417) took on the conceptual separation of production and reproduction, arguing that the division between the production of value "at work" and the reproduction of labor power "at home" was a "particularly unwieldy" way of understanding these two aspects of daily life in the contemporary moment. Instead, they suggested, a close look at "the everyday practices of widely disparate subjects" showed a growing "obfuscation" of the line between work and nonwork (ibid.). As a result of this blurring, a new kind of subject was being interpellated—namely, a "life's worker"—and new kinds of questions were being raised about how individuals understand themselves "as workers, consumers, students, parents, migrants, and lovers" (ibid., 418).

Much of Mitchell, Marston, and Katz's contribution to our understanding of the relationship between production and social reproduction focused on this question of subjectivity and their argument that, for many contemporary subjects, "work—even nonstop work—is what makes you a person; it is what gives you value as a modern, rational agent" (2003, 429). They also addressed, however, how the sociospatial contexts of those involved in life's work were "shaped and constrained by the state in contemporary capitalist society" (ibid.) and, in many cases, increasingly privatized in an era of neoliberalism. Thus, for Mitchell, Marston, and Katz, understanding the nature of life's work meant understanding new forms of subjectivity associated with the activities of work, as well as new forms of state involvement in that process of subject formation.

Mitchell, Marston, and Katz's formulation of life's work in the early 2000s appeared at a propitious moment when numerous feminist scholars were seeking to document, theorize, and analyze the consequences of neoliberal assaults on public social provisions and protections (see Bakker and Gill 2003; Bezanson and Luxton 2006). Earlier theorists' preoccupation with domestic labor in the household appeared too narrow in the face of neoliberalism's widespread social, political, and ideological transformations, and feminist scholars increasingly began to frame their investigations through the more expansive, and variously defined, concept of social reproduction. For example, Kate Bezanson (2006; this volume) analyzes the implications of neoliberal policy initiatives in Canada for the practices and viability of social reproduction, which she defined as "the daily and generational reproduction of the working population" (2006, 4). Bakker and Gill delineate a broader definition that includes not only biological reproduction of the species and "ongoing reproduction of the commodity labor power" but also the "institutions, processes and social relations associated with the *creation and maintenance* of communities" (2003, 18, emphasis in the original). These and other authors influenced by the Marxist feminist tradition resonate with our argument here in that they maintain a theoretical distinction between production and social reproduction and focus attention primarily on lower-income households.

However, diverse efforts to theorize and examine the changing nature of social reproduction have gradually yielded a concept so variable and, in some cases, all-encompassing in definition as to become an analytic almost empty of meaning. While this breadth has enabled scholars to raise new questions about the politics emanating from a range of daily activities, analyzing social reproduction as what Katz (2008, 18) describes as "the broad material social practices and forces associated with sustaining production and social life in all its variations" becomes an impossible task. The same is true of Mitchell, Marston, and Katz's assertion that "social reproduction is about how we live" (2003, 416). The vagueness of the related concept, life's work, while justified in part through its role in wider feminist deconstructions of related binaries, leaves us wanting in thinking through the many ways that paid labor and social reproduction remain spatially and temporally distinct arenas for those who are not highly educated and/or able to telecommute. Adding to the confusion, slippage between the concepts of social reproduction and life's work has led many scholars to forgo one of Mitchell, Marston, and Katz's central arguments—the collapsing distinctions between work and life, hence "life's work"—and to use these terms synonymously and interchangeably. We argue here for clarification of existing formulations and far more extensive investigation of the particularities and precariousness of life's work for those at the lower end of the class spectrum.

For many working-class individuals, households, and communities, the line between work and life is not necessarily falling away but, instead, is constantly negotiated and made manifest in both spatial and temporal terms. As wages drop and employment becomes more flexible and fleeting, working-class people are often forced to stretch their labor geographies and fragment the space-times of paid work as they take on multiple jobs wherever, whenever. Simultaneously, the withdrawal of state supports, such as housing subsidies, makes social reproduction more challenging, as household members must pay more to meet their social needs and as the literal sites of social reproduction previously maintained and/or subsidized by the state—schools, clinics, post offices—are consolidated, if not closed, particularly in rural areas (Bezanson 2006; Smith forthcoming).

In such contexts, the line between work and life becomes sharpened, not blurred, as people are forced to navigate different, sometimes conflicting, geographies and temporalities embedded in the social organization of employment, intergenerational household maintenance, and working-class community life. Among other implications, attention to these instances where the line between work and life is heightened enables us to clarify in theoretical terms the extreme precariousness and contradictions experienced by working-class people as products of multiple, unsustainable pressures on the nexus of necessary social and economic labor.[1] We argue, in short, that to understand the realities of life's work across the class spectrum and to grasp its inflections by race, legal status, and other factors, we need a more flexible understanding of the *multiple* forms the nexus between production and social reproduction can take—a nexus dependent on *whose* lives and *which* work are at stake.

Precarious Life in the American South

FLEXIBLE PRODUCTION IN THE (DE)INDUSTRIALIZED NEW SOUTH

In the late-nineteenth century, on the heels of the U.S. Civil War and postwar Reconstruction, southern political and economic elites, along with social reformers, were eager to "modernize" the region. They invested in a much-ballyhooed "New South" of bustling towns, manufacturing centers, and an expanded infrastructure of roads and rails. However, economic and social relations in this New South tended to recapitulate the concentrated wealth, tight political control, paternalism, and racially divided labor of the Old South's plantation system (Billings 1979; Wright 1996).

In an era of national industrial expansion, when increasing numbers of European immigrants alleviated northern employers' labor shortages, southern employers in the New South were able to rely on a seemingly limitless population of impoverished rural whites (women, men, and children), whom they recruited to work in labor-intensive manufacturing industries such as textiles (Woodward 1971; Wright 1996). In the new factories and associated company towns, employers pursued policies of paternalistic exploitation and fierce anti-unionism, and workers faced low wages and new strictures around the pace and nature of work (McLaurin 1971). Soon, the cost advantages of a low-wage, nonunion workforce centered in the South undermined older hubs of manufacturing, such as New England, making the South the low-wage haven for labor-intensive industries in the United States (Cobb 1984).

In textiles, the premier New South industry, workers (virtually all of whom were white) elaborated a close-knit community life through overlapping bonds of race, family, workplace, church, and other social institutions (Hall et al. 1987; Anderson and Schulman 1999). One account of social relations in the company town of Kannapolis, North Carolina, emphasized its spatial elements: "The [workers'] houses surrounded the mill in a circle, a spatial organization that facilitated travel to work and close supervision at all times. All the mills were located within a twenty-mile radius of one another, and the CEO's office was only a few steps away from Plant Number 1, allowing extremely close supervision. Power relations . . . were also reflected in the spatial organization of the county: workers lived in the unincorporated town of Kannapolis, while owners and managers lived in the nearby town of Concord, the county seat" (Anderson and Schulman 1999, 93). The dense sociospatial organization of factory and town facilitated a tight web of social interconnections among coworkers and their families and the personal exercise of paternalistic authority by owners and bosses.

Although successive generations of white southerners made their livings and reproduced their social lives in the shadow of textile mills, furniture factories, and other manufacturing sites, by the 1970s deindustrialization, automation, and flexible production practices were disrupting this southern variant of Fordism. Bluestone and Harrison (1982, 10, emphasis in original) noted, "the odds of a southern manufacturing plant shutting down were actually a little *higher* than for establishments in the North." For labor-intensive southern industries facing new global competition, the imperative to cut labor costs required either flight to locations outside the United States or new production practices at home. These economic pressures, combined with organizational restructuring via mergers and acquisitions, spelled the end of old-style southern paternalism toward white working-class men and women and the demise of the dense, if repressive, social relations of the company towns.

In 1982, for example, surviving members of the Cannon family sold their interest in Fieldcrest Cannon mills, based largely in North Carolina, to David Murdock, a corporate raider from California, who proceeded to close some mills, automate others, and raid the company's pension fund (Anderson and Schulman 1999, 94). Layoffs and declining job opportunities in Fieldcrest Cannon's original company town of Kannapolis prompted some former textile workers to seek employment in nearby Charlotte, a southern city that began to boom as a center of banking and finance around the same time (Graves 2001). Wives, husbands, and neighbors who once worked together in the mills began commuting to work in opposite directions on the interstate. Their more fleeting job opportunities and stretched daily geographies sharpened and complicated the interface between work and life—not blurring or merging the boundaries between these space-times, but creating frenetic contradictions between the demands of employers and the demands of children, schools, and life outside of work (Anderson and Schulman 1999).

For rural southern manufacturing workers more generally, the consequences of deindustrialization and flexible production have included job loss and unemployment (Gaventa, Smith, and Willingham 1991; MDC 2002) and increased contingency in the terms of employment itself (Weinbaum 2003). To be sure, in select locations across the rural South, there are growth sectors—such as poultry processing and tourism—but hourly workers in such industries face the same distinct, potentially conflicting space-times of work and home. Furthermore, their relatively low wages and, in the case of tourism, part-time and seasonal schedules can encourage holding multiple jobs and accepting overtime (Smith 1989; Marrow 2011), both of which intensify tensions between obligations to employers and to families and households. In sum, across much of the rural American South, recent trends in the structure and sectoral composition of employment have not blurred but magnified distinctions between the space-times of work and life. As one textile worker bitterly commented of her employer's new scheduling requirements with long shifts on variable days of the week, "You destroyed my family life with the twelve-hour shift" (Anderson and Schulman 1999, 102).

NEOLIBERAL ENVIRONMENTS OF THE MOUNTAIN SOUTH

The mountains of central Appalachia, especially southern West Virginia, contain some of the highest-quality bituminous coal in the world. Since the inception of coal production in the late nineteenth century, communities in these mountains have also been sites of some of the fiercest struggles over labor and life within the American South (Corbin 1983). Such contestations have occurred over the conditions of mining employment, the repressive strategies of employers and their representatives in company towns, the technologies of coal production itself, and the environmental effects of different forms of mining (Montrie 2002; Burns 2007). Although similar to the textile industry's mill villages in their dense and overlapping social relations, bipolar class structure, and repressive surveillance, the company towns of the central Appalachian coal industry became crucibles of interracial solidarity and successful trade unionism. If a historical legacy of militant resistance is any predictor of future mobilizations, one would expect central Appalachia today to be teeming with class struggle.

That is not the case. Neoliberal state policies, combined with transformations in labor-management relations in the coal industry, have produced drastic reductions in public space, social solidarity, and miners' bargaining leverage (McNeil 2011; Smith forthcoming). Although bituminous coal mining in central Appalachia currently exhibits trends that are similar to developments in the manufacturing sector of the rural South (Burns 2007), our focus here is not on such shifts in the nature of work. Rather, we briefly examine the stark impacts of neoliberal state policies on public space, social reproduction, and the prospects for community life.

In the rural Appalachian coalfields, public space takes form primarily through public institutions—above all, the local post office and public school—which are key sites in the production and maintenance of place-based communities.

Neoliberal commitments to government budget cuts, privatization, and the presumed efficiencies and economies of scale represented by for-profit business models have produced extreme shrinkage of public space. Simultaneously, the rollout of state power to protect nonunion coal operations and punish the United Mine Workers of America (UMWA) for miners' militant actions during strikes has facilitated deunionization and a concomitant breakdown of social solidarity. Further, the weakening and outright withdrawal of regulatory protections regarding the environmental effects of mining practices such as mountaintop removal (which levels mountains, destroys watersheds, and renders nearby communities unlivable) have all but foreclosed prospects for alternative forms of survival. Simply put, the ecological and social spaces for community life are under attack in central Appalachia.

The eight major coal-producing counties of southern West Virginia, for example, have experienced these trends in nightmarish proportions. Between 1980 and 2010, the U.S. Postal Service closed, or slated for closure, more than half of the post offices in these counties (Smith forthcoming). These rural post offices not only name the communities where they are located but also serve as important gathering spaces for the circulation of news and information as well as mail. Similarly, public schools represent collective gathering spaces where all in the community may come together for athletic competitions, children's performances, and other events. During the 1990s, the state and county boards of education closed at least seventy-six schools in this eight-county area of southern West Virginia; for two counties, consolidation meant the loss of more than 40 percent of their schools in a single decade (Eyre and Finn 2002; Reeves 2004). Given the mountainous topography, such closures not only spell the loss of public space but also require people to spend longer periods of time each day in transit to and from socially necessary activities. For example, hour-long bus rides, one-way to school each day, are not uncommon (Eyre and Finn 2002).

Beginning in the late 1970s and accelerating during the 1980s, the UMWA also began to collapse in the face of an aggressive anti-union campaign spearheaded by A. T. Massey Coal Company and backed by the power of state police and federal district courts (Brisbin 2002; McNeil 2011). As local union halls closed, not only did coal communities lose a critical space of working-class solidarity and activism, but the process of deunionization, wherein miners had to choose whether or not to work nonunion, produced bitter division within and among families and communities (Bell 2009). Today, working-class residents of southern West Virginia are locked in a civil war with one another, far more divided over the economic and environmental implications of mountaintop-removal mining than they are unified by trade unionism or a common vision for the future of their communities.

The experiences of coal mining communities in central Appalachia deepen our assessment of the pressures on and fractures between the space-times of work and home for working-class people in the rural American South. The neoliberal drive to close and consolidate public institutions is relocating the spaces of social reproduction at a significant remove from these working-class households, while related processes of deunionization and environmental destruction are undermining their place-based communities and prospects for social solidarity. Residents must travel increasingly long distances in order to carry out the daily functions of social reproduction—mailing a letter, attending school, meeting with a child's teacher. Here, too, the boundaries between work and home are not collapsing but becoming sharper and more difficult to navigate as residents must stretch their geographies of daily life and, by doing so, reinforce the decline of their increasingly divided communities.

THE NUEVO SOUTH

As parts of the rural South were experiencing deindustrialization and new demands of flexible labor, and as parts of Appalachia were struggling with the loss of space for community life, elsewhere in the South, especially its cities and small towns with meat-processing plants or agricultural ties, new groups of men and then women were coming to the region. Beginning in the 1990s, Latino immigrants, many of whom were undocumented, began to settle in the South, drawn by aggressive recruitment and year-round employment opportunities in rural industries like meat processing; by southern cities' need for cheap labor in construction, landscaping, and hospitality services; and by immigrants' own desires to escape political unrest, economic insecurities, and other factors in cities and towns across the United States and Latin America.[2] Although there were initial signs that Latino men and women might be welcomed in rural and urban locales, any semblance of hospitality melted away in the mid-2000s, when anti-immigrant movements flared in many southern states and when the South, somewhat ironically, began to set the template for what became yet another national movement of immigrant exclusion in the first decade of the new millennium (Winders 2007; Bauer 2009; McKanders 2010).

Efforts to exclude immigrants from southern locales in the late 2000s took a number of forms, from specific state legislation and local ordinances directed at immigrant lives and livelihoods to a general sense of unwelcome from long-term residents noted by immigrants in cities like Nashville, Tennessee (Winders 2013). Beginning in the late 1990s but really taking hold in the mid-2000s, southern state and local ordinances related to immigration started to focus on restricting both the sites of paid employment—closing day-labor sites and conducting workplace immigration raids—and the spaces of social reproduction associated with immigrant residents. Such laws tried to eliminate undocumented immigrants' access to state services; to make it illegal to rent to, house, harbor, or transport undocumented immigrants; and to restrict driver's license access, making the completion of daily tasks all but impossible (Winders 2007, 2014). Perhaps most profoundly, the 287(g) program—a 1996 federal law that enabled local police to act as federal immigration officers and detain undocumented immigrants—spread across the South in the 2000s (Coleman 2007, 2009; Armenta 2012).[3] In response, undocumented immigrants and their families in many southern locales hunkered down, taking back roads to avoid road stops (often placed near immigrant neighborhoods), expressing reluctance to volunteer at local organizations, avoiding public spaces, and advising one another not to travel in groups (Winders 2013). The 287(g) program and associated state and local policies brought public life for many immigrants to a halt.

In 2011 new legislation emerged in Alabama and Georgia, surpassing even Arizona's infamous 2010 anti-immigrant law, S.B. 1070.[4] Alabama's H.B. 56 would have, among other provisions, made it illegal to transport, harbor, or rent to undocumented residents; required public schools to track students' immigration status; and given police the right to stop people suspected of being undocumented. Such laws, as their supporters note, were designed "to intentionally make life very, very difficult and insecure for people who hire illegal immigrants, the illegals themselves, and the anti-enforcement politicians" (Newkirk 2011). Although such punitive legislation was legally contested and implementation of it was delayed by the courts, its effects came into view almost immediately: labor shortages in Alabama's and Georgia's agricultural sector, as undocumented residents and their families (some of whom were documented) left the state; immigrants afraid to leave their homes or send their children to school; local churches with drops in attendance at Mass and cancellation of activities over concerns that attendees would be detained by police roadblocks on their way to and from gatherings.

These assaults on immigrants' lives and livelihoods were further exacerbated by the Great Recession. Before the recession, some immigrant workers in rural industries like textiles and furniture production already reported uncertainty about the duration of their jobs (Marrow 2011). During the recession, Hispanic families were the hardest hit (Tavernise 2011), experiencing extreme "economic vulnerability" and, we would add, social insecurity.[5] In southern cities, day labor, a precarious option even in the best of times, has been common for immigrant workers—typically as a gateway into more lucrative employment in fields like construction. During the recession, however, that flow reversed, as the South's (and the nation's) construction industry bottomed out and as immigrants working in home construction, repair, and even yard maintenance returned, along with some native-born workers, to day labor and jobs that now lasted hours, not days.

As the need for cheap labor in places from Charlotte to New Orleans dried up, so, too, did a desire for an immigrant presence. For immigrant workers who could find employment, even getting paid was uncertain, with upward of 40 percent of immigrant workers reporting wage theft in a 2009 regional survey (Bauer 2009). Workplace immigration raids in the mid-2000s also had profound impacts on immigrant workers and their attempts to make and find a place in local communities. In North Carolina in 2006, raids at the world's largest pork-processing plant led to the eventual departure of 1,500 Latino workers (Fink 2009). In Georgia, door-to-door raids by Immigration and Customs Enforcement agents reportedly tore apart "the fabric of the community" itself (Bauer 2009, 44). As the social and economic welcome mat was rolled up for immigrants, the line between work and life became dangerous to cross.

After the 2012 presidential elections and the growing recognition of the power of the Hispanic vote in the United States, the tenor of both national and regional conversations concerning immigration changed, at least for a brief period. Talk of comprehensive immigration reform at the federal level became more than talk for the first time in decades, although its successful passage now seems uncertain and a discourse of border security continues to challenge a focus on humane immigration policies. Even in the South, the fervor surrounding immigration has cooled in many states, and recent survey data suggest that across the United States, the majority of residents support a path to citizenship for undocumented immigrants (Hesson 2013). The politics of immigration in the United States remains complex, but the anti-immigrant rhetoric that defined the 2000s and 2010s may be shifting.

Even so, the struggle continues over whether, where, and how immigrants will find social and political footing in southern locales and eventual social acceptance. Much of the South remains home to ongoing battles over what, if any, rights immigrants, particularly undocumented immigrants, should have and whether immigrant social and economic life will be possible. Thus, even as *national* discourse surrounding immigration may tip toward a more humane approach, across the South the lingering effects of the harsh laws put forward in the early 2010s remain, keeping the line between not only production and social reproduction, but also temporary presence and social belonging, sharp and sometimes treacherous for immigrants. Collectively, these efforts illustrate our broader arguments that precarious life is the product of multiple unsustainable pressures on the nexus of necessary social and economic labor and that the line between work and life, production and social reproduction, is growing sharper for many working-class individuals.

Conclusion

The political, economic, and social reconfigurations outlined in this chapter raise a number of questions for those motivated to understand life's work across the spectrum of social diversity and to pursue strategies that might lessen the burdens on life's workers. These burdens, we argue, are particularly acute in the context of working-class households and communities, where extreme precariousness is increasingly normalized. When systemic trends toward flexible production and neoliberalism require workers to travel farther and longer to find and sustain employment; reduce the number of schools, post offices, and other public institutions; and make the daily tasks of survival more time-consuming and exhausting, where and when do working-class women and men create collective life, social solidarity, and political agency? What political demands and mobilizations might address the fierce tensions experienced by workers caught between employer-mandated flexibility and the neoliberal state's erosion of labor rights, immigrant rights, public institutions, and, thus, working-class households' capacity to maintain and care for their members?

These questions clearly stretch beyond the limits of this chapter, if not beyond the limits of how we currently understand the often-dire consequences of the contemporary political-economic moment. They are important to consider, however, because they point to the conceptual and political limits of how we theorize and seek to change the relationship between production and social reproduction. When our model is one of a blurring of these two realms, of being able to work and live in the same spaces and times, we lack a way to account for the lived realities of, and stymied politics for, many working-class individuals for whom the line between work and nonwork, production and reproduction, increasingly takes them across multiple workplaces to earn their weekly paycheck and across multiple counties to complete the basic requirements for family life. At the same time, such a model cannot account for the challenges faced by working-class immigrants so fearful of detection and deportation that they do not leave their homes at all. To understand these configurations of life's work, we need a more robust accounting of the nexus between production and social reproduction, one that pays close attention to the implications of social class.

We are particularly concerned about the relative invisibility of political demands and employment policies that might begin to alleviate the fractured space-times of work and life in many working-class households. Instead, the normative aim of work-life balance and the associated call for family-friendly employment policies, both of which are commensurate with life's work conceptualized as a blurring line between paid employment and other spaces of social life, appear increasingly dominant (Gornick and Meyers 2003; Hill, Jackson, and Martinengo 2006). The development of such family-friendly policies as flextime, telecommuting, and stopping the tenure clock for academic faculty is, of course, welcome when such policies have the sincere aim of alleviating the conflicting pressures of work and home. But insofar as such innovations have come to constitute the universe of imagined solutions to the conflicting demands of life's work, they limit attention to the quite different and more severe pressures on working-class households. For workers cobbling together a livelihood across multiple low-wage jobs, the prospect that their employers might offer family-friendly policies is at best distant, if not preposterous. Gaining a higher minimum wage and expanded labor rights is far more relevant. For immigrant workers so disempowered in relation to their employers that they do not even receive payment for the work they perform, enforcement of prohibitions against wage theft is a more urgent need than work-life balance.

In sum, we need new investigations and clarified conceptual tools to theorize, with the goal of intervening in, the spatial, political, and temporal dynamics of the class-specific nexus between production and social reproduction. Treating this nexus as blurring for all workers is politically disabling under the "new normal" of widespread economic insecurity, neoliberal revanchism, and anti-immigrant rhetoric. Much is at stake in this contemporary moment and in our efforts to understand its class-specific manifestations in immigrant and working-class lives.

NOTES

1. We are developing this theoretical formulation of a nexus of necessary labor in a work in progress.

2. For work on this theme, see Winders (2013) and Marrow (2011).

3. In late 2012, the 287(g) program was ended when the federal government opted not to renew agreements with state or local agencies. The main focus of 287(g) largely continued through the Secure Communities initiative until November 2014 when it, too, was terminated.

4. Examples in this paragraph are drawn from Winders (2014).

5. Because much of the net worth of Hispanics (two-thirds in 2005) comes from home equity, when the housing market collapsed, so did Hispanic wealth (Tavernise 2011).

REFERENCES

Anderson, Cynthia, and Michael Schulman. "Social Change in Southern Textiles." In *Neither Separate nor Equal: Women, Race, and Class in the South*, edited by Barbara Ellen Smith, 91–108. Philadelphia: Temple University Press, 1999.

Armenta, Amada. "From Sheriff's Deputies to Immigration Officers: Screening Immigrant Status in a Tennessee Jail." *Law and Policy* 34, no. 2 (2012): 191–210.

Bakker, Isabella, and Stephen Gill, eds. *Power, Production and Social Reproduction: Human In/security in the Global Economy.* New York: Palgrave Macmillan, 2003.

Bauer, Mary. *Under Siege: Life for Low-Income Latinos in the South.* Montgomery, Ala.: A Report by the Southern Poverty Law Center, 2009.

Bell, Shannon. "'There Ain't No Bond Like There Used to Be': The Destruction of Social Capital in the West Virginia Coalfields." *Sociological Forum* 24, no. 3 (2009): 631–657.

Bezanson, Kate. *Gender, the State, and Social Reproduction: Household Insecurities in Neo-Liberal Times.* Toronto: University of Toronto Press, 2006.

Bezanson, Kate, and Meg Luxton, eds. *Social Reproduction: Feminist Political Economy Challenges Neo-Liberalism.* Montreal: McGill-Queen's University Press, 2006.

Billings, Dwight. *Planters and the Making of a "New South": Class, Politics, and Development in North Carolina, 1865–1900.* Chapel Hill: University of North Carolina Press, 1979.

Blair-Loy, Mary. "Work without End? Schedule Flexibility and Work-to-Family Conflict among Stockbrokers." *Work and Occupations* 36, no. 4 (2009): 279–317.

Bluestone, Barry, and Bennett Harrison. *The Deindustrialization of America.* New York: Basic, 1982.

Brisbin, Richard. *A Strike Like No Other Strike: Law and Resistance during the Pittston Coal Strike of 1989–1990.* Baltimore: Johns Hopkins University Press, 2002.

Burns, Shirley Stewart. *Bringing Down the Mountains: The Impact of Mountaintop Removal on Southern West Virginia Communities.* Morgantown: West Virginia University Press, 2007.

Cobb, James C. *Industrialization and Southern Society, 1877–1984.* Lexington: University Press of Kentucky, 1984.

Coclanis, Peter, and Louis Kyriakoudes. "Selling Which South? Economic Change in Rural and Small-Town North Carolina in an Era of Globalization." *Southern Cultures* 13, no. 4 (2007): 86–102.

Coleman, Mathew. "Immigration Geopolitics beyond the Mexico-U.S. Border." *Antipode* 39, no. 1 (2007): 54–76.

———. "What Counts as the Politics and Practice of Security, and Where? Devolution and Immigrant Insecurity after 9/11." *Annals of the Association of American Geographers* 99, no. 5 (2009): 904–913.

Corbin, David. *Life, Work and Rebellion in the Southern West Virginia Coalfields.* Champaign-Urbana: University of Illinois Press, 1983.

Eyre, Eric, and Scott Finn. "Closing Costs: School Closings, Lax Oversight Lead to Record Long Bus Rides." *Charleston (W.Va.) Gazette*, August 25, 2002, 1C.

Fink, Leon. "New People of the Newest South: Prospects for the Post-1980 Immigrants." *Journal of Southern History* 75, no. 3 (2009): 739–750.

Gaventa, John, Barbara Ellen Smith, and Alex Willingham, eds. *Communities in Economic Crisis: Appalachian and the South.* Philadelphia: Temple University Press, 1991.

Glenn, Evelyn Nakano. "From Servitude to Service Work: Historical Continuities in the Racial Division of Women's Work." *Signs* 18, no. 1 (1992): 1–43.

Gornick, Janet, and Marcia Meyers. *Families That Work*. New York: Russell Sage, 2003.

Graves, William. "Charlotte's Role as a Financial Center: Looking beyond Assets." *Southeastern Geographer* 41, no. 2 (2001): 230–245.

Hall, Jacquelyn D., James Leloudis, Robert Korstad, Mary Murphy, Lu Ann Jones, and Christopher B. Daly. *Like a Family: The Making of a Southern Cotton Mill World*. Chapel Hill: University of North Carolina Press, 1987.

Hesson, Ted. "Brookings Survey: Over Six in Ten Americans Back Citizenship." *ABC News*, March 21, 2013.

Hill, Jeffrey, Andre'a Jackson, and Giuseppe Martinengo. "Twenty Years of Work and Family at International Business Machines Corporation." *American Behavioral Scientist* 49, no. 9 (2006): 1165–1183.

Hochschild, Arlie. *The Time Bind*. New York: Henry Holt, 1997.

Katz, Cindi. "Bad Elements: Katrina and the Scoured Landscape of Social Reproduction." *Gender, Place and Culture* 15, no. 1 (2008): 15–29.

Marrow, Helen. *New Destination Dreaming: Immigration, Race, and Legal Status in the Rural American South*. Stanford: Stanford University Press, 2011.

McKanders, Karla Mari. "Sustaining Tiered Personhood: Jim Crow and Anti-Immigrant Laws." *Harvard Journal on Racial and Ethnic Justice* 26 (2010): 163–210.

McLaurin, Melton. *Paternalism and Protest*. Westport, Ct.: Greenwood Publishing, 1971.

McNeil, Bryan. *Combating Mountaintop Removal: New Directions in the Fight against Big Coal*. Champaign-Urbana: University of Illinois Press, 2011.

MDC, Inc. *State of the South 2002: Shadows in the Sunbelt Revisited*. Chapel Hill, N.C.: n.p., 2002.

Mitchell, Katharyne, Sallie Marston, and Cindi Katz. "Introduction: Life's Work: An Introduction, Review and Critique." *Antipode* 35, no. 3 (2003): 415–442.

Montrie, Chad. *To Save the Land and People: A History of Opposition to Surface Coal Mining in Appalachia*. Chapel Hill: University of North Carolina Press, 2002.

Newkirk, Margaret. "Georgia Enlists Citizens to Battle Illegal Aliens." *Bloomberg Businessweek*, July 28, 2011, http://www.businessweek.com/magazine/georgia-enlists-citizens-to-battle-illegal-aliens-07282011.html. Accessed January 18, 2015.

Reeves, Cynthia. *A Decade of Consolidation: Where Are the Savings?* Charleston: Challenge West Virginia, 2004.

Schieman, Scott, and Paul Glavin. "Trouble at the Border? Gender, Flexibility at Work, and the Work-Home Interface." *Social Problems* 55, no. 4 (2008): 590–611.

Smith, Barbara Ellen. "Another Place Is Possible? Labor Geography, Spatial Dispossession, and Gendered Resistance in Central Appalachia." *Annals of the Association of American Geographers*. Forthcoming.

Smith, Barbara Ellen, Marcela Mendoza, and David Ciscel. "The World on Time: Flexible Labor, New Immigrants and Global Logistics." In *The American South in a Global World*, edited by James L. Peacock, Harry Watson, and Carrie Matthews, 23–38. Chapel Hill: University of North Carolina Press, 2005.

Smith, Michal. *Behind the Glitter: The Impact of Tourism on Women in the Southeast*. Lexington, Ky.: Southeast Women's Employment Coalition, 1989.

Stewart, Lynn. "Louisiana Subjects: Power, Space and the Slave Body." *Ecumene* 2, no. 3 (1995): 227–245.

Tavernise, Sabrina. "Recession Study Finds Hispanics Hit the Hardest." *New York Times*, July 26, 2011. http://www.nytimes.com/2011/07/26/us/26hispanics.html. Accessed January 18, 2015.

Vogel, Lise. *Marxism and the Oppression of Women*. New Brunswick, N.J.: Rutgers University Press, 1983.

Weinbaum, Eve. *To Move a Mountain: Fighting the Global Economy in Appalachia*. New York: New Press, 2003.

Winders. Jamie. "Bringing Back the (B)order: Post-9/11 Politics of Immigration, Borders, and Belonging in the Contemporary U.S. South." *Antipode* 39, no. 5 (2007): 920–942.

———. *Nashville in the New Millennium: Immigrant Settlement, Urban Transformation, and Social Belonging*. New York: Russell Sage, 2013.

———. "Criminalizing Settlement: The Politics of Immigration in the American South." In *Oxford Handbook on Race, Ethnicity, Immigration, and Crime,* edited by Sandra Bucerius and Michael Tonry. New York: Oxford University Press, 2014, 600–627.

"Women's Labor." *Radical America* 7, nos. 4–5 (1973): 1–192.

Woodward, C. Vann. *Origins of the New South, 1877–1913*. Baton Rouge: Louisiana State University Press, 1971.

Wright, Gavin. *Old South, New South: Revolutions in the Southern Economy since the Civil War*. Baton Rouge: Louisiana State University Press, 1996 [1986].

CHAPTER 6

Reproduction . . . Amplified

Life's Work for African American Women in Milwaukee

BRENDA PARKER

> My barriers have been abuse, housing, employment, and education. I think
> just basic life is a barrier.
> —KAREN, Interviewee, African American low-income mother

Karen's sentences were similar to many others I have heard as poor African American women in Milwaukee described their life's work to me—heavy, intense, and desperate. In this chapter I describe dimensions of life's work for the nineteen low-income African American women that I interviewed from 2004 to 2008 in Milwaukee, Wisconsin, during a dizzying decade of neoliberal policy. I interpret my interviews through the academic lenses of social reproduction, black and antiracist feminism, and the categories and voices of mothers. The concept of social reproduction is one way to explore the nonproductive labor, practices, and social relations that surround and sustain households, cities, and human life in general. These include, but are not limited to, caring for and clothing children, providing education and health care, and creating community networks. Appropriately, Katz (2001, 711) has described social reproduction as "the messy, fleshy indeterminate material components of human life."

Marx framed social reproduction as the backdrop processes that produce laborers and enable capitalist production, a perspective that still reverberates through much political economic analysis, especially with regard to contemporary neoliberalism. Engagement with social reproduction has helped feminists displace hierarchical assumptions and the primacy of production in much academic work and raise critical question of value (Dalla Costa and James 1972; Mitchell, Marston, and Katz 2004; Brodie 2007; Meehan and Strauss, this volume). Feminists have highlighted the multiple forms of power, structures, and processes—within, "outside," and connected to capitalism—that shape the social reproduction of life and communities (e.g., Gibson-Graham 1996; Acker 2006; Katz 2008). In particular, antiracist and black feminists help make visible ways that the capitalist system, the state, and all forms of reproductive and provisioning activity are dialectically constructed in and through the multiply situated social actions of race, gender, sexuality, and class (e.g., hooks 2000; Hill Collins 2000a, 2000b; Kobayashi 2004; Acker 2006).

Recent feminist work calls for an integrative, empirical, comprehensive, and contemporary analysis of social reproduction, also labeled "life's work" (Mitchell, Marston, and Katz 2004; Luxton and Bezanson 2006; Bakker 2007; Meehan and Strauss, this volume). In their introduction to this volume, Meehan and Strauss ask how social reproduction studies might come into conversation with literatures related to embodiment; multiple forms of materiality (including human/nonhuman); and the complex forms of economic life and provisioning that occur in households and communities. Furthermore, they remind us that social reproduction theories have sometimes "been blind to the nitty gritty of material life" (Meehan and Strauss, this volume).

It is with the above critiques and analytical spirit that I explore social reproduction and neoliberalism in Milwaukee in this chapter. From 2004 to 2008, I met these women after meetings, in coffee shops, and at homes and informal social events. They were part of a larger research project that was devoted to understanding and theorizing the broader dynamics of race, poverty, gender, and urban neoliberalism (Parker forthcoming).

Using a broad feminist materialism approach, I asked women about not only their paid and unpaid labor but also the embodied experiences, emotions, and subjectivities surrounding their households and work. In essence, with the interviews, I began on the ground with the nitty-gritty of life's work, rather than viewing it from above or in isolation. Using feminist concepts of relationality and extended case methodology, I also tried to draw connections between daily life and surrounding processes and theoretical understandings (e.g., McDowell 2006; Burawoy 2009). My interviewees spoke to me about power; inequality; their challenges, fears, and frustrations; and areas of joy and autonomy in their labor and lives.

Informed by but unharnessed from dichotomous Marxist concepts, this chapter zeroes in on the theme of *amplification*. Amplification refers to the intensity of racialized women's work, life, and bodily experiences—laborious days where the tasks of work and love are never done and rarely rewarded. It also focuses on the emotional and bodily intensity of precarious and marginalized lives often in or on the verge of loss, whether of income, security, children, brothers, health, or life without prison bars. Critically, there is also an amplification of the gulf between white women's experiences and black women's experiences under neoliberalism as well as between desire and reality. My interviewees' desires as women, mothers, and community members are often so distanced from the actualities of their lives, yet as I describe, they carry on various material and spiritual practices in spite of it.

TABLE 6.1. Racialized Poverty in Milwaukee, Wisconsin, 1990–2012

	1990	2000	2012
Median Household Income	$24,018	$32,216	$33,122
Poverty Rate (Black / African American)	34%	33%	41%
Poverty Rate (Hispanic)	N/A	26%	35%
Poverty Rate (White)	11%	10%	11%
Child Poverty Rate	43%	38%	43%

Source: U.S. Census Bureau 2012.

Race, Gender, and Neoliberalism in Milwaukee

Located in the Midwest, in the shadows of Chicago, Milwaukee may appear as an innocuous place on the map. However, its blend of ordinary and extraordinary characteristics made it a critical place to explore neoliberalism and social reproduction. By "ordinary," I mean that Milwaukee's experience parallels many other cities in its political-economic shift from industrial- to service-sector employment, in its medium size, and in its diverse ethnic and racial population. Milwaukee also has a rich history of activism with regard to gender, race, and workers' rights.

By "extraordinary," I mean that Milwaukee has a history of experimental and edgy urban politics. The city implemented neoliberal policies like welfare reform, school vouchers, and service privatization earlier than most cities and in a more extreme form under an ideologue mayor. Milwaukee, and Wisconsin more broadly, is home to some of the most conservative foundations and strictest workfare programs in the country.

Milwaukee is a city of tremendous inequality (see table 6.1). It is often ranked the most racially segregated city in the United States; it has the eighth-highest poverty rate in the country; and the poverty rate for African Americans is three times that of whites, as is the infant mortality rate. One 2003 study found over 3,000 Milwaukee families living with no state or employment income, getting by with only food stamps. In a stingy and punitive welfare-to-work climate, a 2009 study found that only 26 percent of poor households were receiving benefits (Williams and Hegewisch 2011).

My interviewees are part of this ordinary and extraordinary picture. I came to know most of them through their participation in a poverty support network for low-income women; others were their friends and family members. Like 45 percent of African American women in Milwaukee, my research subjects were poor and had been their entire lives. Many had connections to paid work, the welfare-to-work program, and various support networks, albeit contingent or temporary. They spoke in angry or hushed tones about the traumas that shaped their lives, from homelessness to violence to the loss of a child. When placed in the context of U.S. neoliberalism, Milwaukee and my interviewees make it possible to explore the core and the outer edges (if they exist) of raced and gendered neoliberalism as well as social reproduction among the truly marginalized. In other words, the people and the place resonate beyond their space and time.

Unequal Labors: African American Women in the United States

> No other group in America has so had their identity socialized out of existence as have black women. . . . When black people are talked about the focus tends to be on black men; and when women are talked about the focus tends to be on white women.
> —BELL HOOKS, *Ain't I a Woman?*

Despite a history of black feminist scholarship in this area, much of the social reproduction and neoliberalism literature has been relatively quiet on issues of race. Historically, African American women have participated in the labor force at much higher rates— but always in lower-wage and lower-status jobs—than white women. Furthermore, poverty rates for African American women are higher than any other group in the United States. Even among similarly educated and full-time female workers, far more African American women are in poverty than white women (Jones 2009). Black women have historically experienced multiple moves in and out of labor markets. Recessions and labor market changes are harshest for African American men and low-skilled African American women—the latter never experienced the relatively high-wage industrial jobs that some men found (Trotter 1985; Gilmore 2007; Jones 2009). Furthermore, employment-related racism and disparities persist. For example, a recent study showed that Milwaukee employers were more willing to employ white felons than African Americans without criminal records (Pager 2003). Wage discrepancies and employment rates between African American and white workers remain stark and gendered, with black female workers in the Milwaukee region earning only 56 percent of white male earners in 2009 (Williams and Hegewisch 2011).

For black women, care and mothering work has been different than for many white women in the United States, in multiple ways. First, it has almost always been balanced with forced or paid labor (Hill Collins 2000a; Gilmore 2007; Jones 2009). Second, it has been controlled and characterized by whites, producing stereotypes such as the black "mammy" or "welfare queen." Third, the labor of black mothers and their children has rarely received the generous support of the state. Instead, welfare payments, urban renewal, child protection services, domestic violence services, and various forms of state "aid" have been profoundly shaped by sexist and racist assumptions (Roberts 1993; 2008a; Quadagno 1994; McCluskey 2003; Jones 2009; Alexander 2010; Richie 2012).

Mothering for African American women also takes place in a broader context of racism. Nurturing children involves shielding them and preparing them for unequal treatment at school, at work, and within the criminal justice system (Hill Collins 2000a; Gilmore 2007; Jones 2009; Alexander 2010; Sue 2010). Other unique features of black motherhood include the tendency of African American women to be "other mothers" to nonbiological children, to engage in community care, and to use the role of motherhood as a symbol of power and a basis for political activism (Hill Collins 2000a). Beth Richie (2012) notes that black mothers shoulder uneven demands for community care and social life maintenance. In part, this emerges from a faulty analysis that black women have it "easier" than black men and are therefore blamed for failings in black neighborhoods. Thus, the contradictions for black women and mothers are substantive and should not be simplified into myths of the "black supermother" (Jones 2009). "African-American communities value motherhood, but Black mothers' ability to cope with intersecting oppressions of race, class, gender, sexuality, and nation should not be confused with transcending the injustices characterizing these oppressions" (Hill Collins 2000a, 87). These intersecting oppressions and the complexities surrounding social reproduction for black women in neoliberal times are eminently clear in the voices of my interviewees.

Life's Work in Milwaukee: Always Amplified

> I have a teenager, my oldest turned fourteen today. I have a daughter that is twelve and I have a three-year-old little boy. Working, I can say that I work eighteen hours a day, being at work and then at home.
>
> —AUDRA, Interviewee, African American mother

How do my interviewees experience their labor, both paid and unpaid? How do their various forms of work (productive and reproductive, if these can be separated) affect each other? And how do these women's experiences square with extant research?[1]

First, women described the intensity of their multiple labors, a finding echoed in feminist studies of neoliberalism and by black feminists and historians (Hill Collins 2000a; Nagar et al. 2002; Brodie 2007; Bezanson and Luxton 2006; Jones 2009). Interviewees cared for up to six children of varying ages and labored up to twenty hours a day. Commonly, their children had special needs, ranging from attention-deficit hyperactivity disorder (ADHD) to diabetes to asthma. Most interviewees also cared for other family members or children and conducted paid work for temporary agencies, restaurants, or informal labor like sex work and/or plasma donations. There was periodic volunteer work and navigation of state and "shadow state" provisioning options, such as traveling to food pantries and churches; meeting with social workers, teachers, and food stamp offices; and the endless waiting at agencies and health clinics: "Yesterday, I got up at 5:00. I left Jerome at my sister's place to get the bus (laughs). I mean the bus*es*. If it all works out, I get to work at nine. . . . I don't eat lunch. I can't afford it. . . . It's dark when I pick up the baby, 7:00 usually" (Cheryl, Interviewee, African American mother).

In a few cases, paid labor appeared to provide independence and welcome relief for women, a finding that echoes some research and aligns with neoliberal rhetoric about autonomy and work. In fact, scholars have argued that women's workforce involvement is a domain in which feminist politics and neoliberal policies have perhaps treacherously coincided (Fraser 2009). A few of my interviewees found personal value and respite in paid labor: "Work is a, like I said, it's a place of refuge for me. . . . I can focus on what I need to do at work and get it done, and then, you know, look forward to that afternoon or that evening with my kids. . . . I love them true enough but, you know, I don't want to feel like I'm stressed [at home] to have to deal with them. . . . So, I'm that type of parent where if you have homework, let's talk about what you did at school today" (Tamara, Interviewee, African American mother and activist).

However, most interviewees described a different reality, one that that was paradoxically insecure and controlled. These women's labors were filtered through both the low-wage neoliberal economy and the state, which plays a critical role in differentially mediating, supporting, and unhinging social reproduction, particularly through Wisconsin's welfare-to-work program Wisconsin Works (w-2). Among the most work-focused in the nation, it provides some health and child care but requires these women to engage in thirty hours of work per week to receive assistance. Under Wisconsin law, they could be paid below minimum wage under the auspices of job training, providing a low-wage workforce to international, profitable companies such as Manpower.

The program was crafted and pursued avidly by conservative think tanks, politicians, and even Milwaukee's mayor, who argued in 1996 that "abolishing welfare is key to the health of cities." Although Wisconsin's welfare reforms were distinctive and especially austere, they aligned with neoliberal politics and philosophies, including "autonomy," new paternalism (the idea that citizenship rights should be contingent on the performance of responsibilities), service delivery privatization, flexibilization, and the control of labor supply (Peck 2001; Mead 2004; Collins and Mayer 2010). To discourage "dependence upon the state," participants were only offered services that they specifically requested, and strict term limits and lifetime limits on assistance were put in place (Mead 2004; Courtney and Dworsky 2006; Collins and Mayer 2010). In legislative debates that I witnessed, a twelve-week work exception for mothers of newborns was described as an excessively generous feature that would "condone the very problem of irresponsibility we are trying to resolve" (author's field notes).

Women in the w-2 program, including my interviewees, were sanctioned pay for late or missed work:

> They've got a very short window for excuses. If they would say, okay, I've got your doctor's statement. You'll get your hour paid for the time you were here, which I think is $5.15 an hour, but they won't include time on the bus or whatever. And they don't accept my excuse, then I don't get paid. Or let's say I have a sick child. And maybe I can't take him to the doctor, but I can stay home with the child. And I don't come back with an excuse, that's a whole day of pay I lose. That means food for my kids. (Kimberly, Interviewee, African American mother)

Such sanctions in Wisconsin are doled out more frequently for women of color than white women (Mulligan-Hansel and Fendt 2003; Wisconsin Legislative Audit Bureau 2005; Courtney and Dworsky 2006). The threat of sanctions forced my interviewees to make difficult decisions, such as forgoing a job or pay to take a child to the doctor or, conversely, leaving a child in the car while they worked.

Furthermore, the specter of sanctions or referrals to Child Protective Services had a disciplinary and isolating effect on mothers. Twenty-five percent of w-2 participants had children removed from their homes, including two of my interviewees. As Dorothy Roberts (2008a) points out, black children are more likely to be taken into foster care, in part because of cultural standards and because the state is more willing to intrude on the autonomy of black mothers. Ironically, foster parents who took in children received more state funds to care for the children than did w-2 participants (Courtney and Dworkin 2006; Roberts 2008; Collins and Mayer 2010). For these reasons, as one activist attests below, fear loomed large among my interviewees and hindered activism:

> Women were very upfront. They were there, the energy, the anger, the speech, the—everything. They had their voice. . . . However once Pay for Performance came into play, women backed off because it was an extraordinarily punitive thing and they were very afraid because they were being sanctioned like crazy. And also they were concerned that the little they had, and the most precious thing they had, namely their children, could be forfeited if they became too public and too adversarial. So they backed off and they backed off so badly that we can barely get them into the public arena. (Mary, Interviewee, white female activist)

Even without sanctions the low-wage temporary employment, which comprised 42 percent of w-2 placements and was a main source of work for my interviewees, was particularly precarious. My interviewees that participated in w-2 indicated that they had little input in their work sites and tasks, a finding echoed by academics and advocates (Collins and Mayer 2010). First, workers had no control over their tasks or work environment. Mistreatment and ambiguous dismissal was common, and discrimination and stereotyping was persistent in these industries (Peck and Theodore 2001). Second, like a double-edged sword, transportation was often provided by the agency. This made temporary work an attractive option for the w-2 program and for women who had limited transportation. However, it was often a form of wage dispossession and impinged on mothering labor:

> Whenever you work temp agencies this is how you do it. If the job pays $8 an hour, they charge you $8 a day in transportation. . . . But if they have to pick you up, say your kid gets sick, from the working scene, they're going to charge you $30 for that one pickup. It isn't because it cost them $30 to come get you. It's because they're mad that they're losing money because you're not on the clock now. . . . So if somebody calls you to say your kid is sick, you want to know exactly how sick that child is before you leave. They've got to be damn near dying for me to leave. And that's not right. (Lori, Interviewee, African American mother and activist)

To these women, combining paid work and motherhood was a Faustian bargain that usually ended badly. Women could rarely meet their children's needs given their unstable, low-wage working arrangements. Yet the financial support of the state or employer was one of a few ways to provision for their children.

While w-2 policy language reified "working" poor mothers, employers were suspicious of my interviewees' moral and maternal commitments. One interviewee described an experience where she had to miss work to take her daughter to physical therapy: "It's like he didn't understand even with my doctor's excuse. . . . I mean some employers—he acted like I was just, you know, purposely not coming to work, and that's hard. That's very, very hard" (Jara, Interviewee, African American mother). Nine women lost jobs because their employer did not believe them or they needed to take off work to care for sick children.

In other words, they were caught in traps of racial and gendered differentiation. The state interpellated them as "responsible, good mothers" if they worked at inflexible, low-wage jobs. Yet most media and policy discourses still valorize stay-at-home white mothers; and mothers face discrimination when compared to nonmothers (Williams 2000; Douglas and Michaels 2005; Correll, Benard, and Paik 2007; Williams and Boushey 2010). Overtly racialized and gendered discrimination, "microaggressions" in the workplace, and media stereotypes of poor racialized mothers deepen the problem (Fraser and Gordon 1994; Clawson and Trice 2000; Jones 2009; Sue 2010). Regarding w-2, one study reported that "more than 4 years after they sought help, most of these applicants were no better off, and, in many cases, they were worse off than when they sought assistance" (Courtney and Dworsky 2006).

Black women's paid and unpaid labors were negatively enmeshed with the state in other ways, particularly with regard to the criminal justice system. One interviewee described the toll of incarceration and violence on women in her community: "We got to be supporting each other 'cause there is some women out here right now that I do know that are struggling with the fact of loneliness and not having a daddy for their child or their daddy may be locked up. Their daddy might be dead" (Audra, Interviewee, African American mother and activist). Prisons featured prominently in the life's work of my interviewees. Only one had been incarcerated, but friends, brothers, children, sisters, and fathers of their children had. In Milwaukee, 50 percent of African American men aged 30–44 have been incarcerated, compared to approximately 5 percent of white men and 5 percent of Hispanic men (University of Wisconsin–Milwaukee Center for Employment and Training 2011). Women were often temporarily "housing" prison returnees: providing bail or financial support or otherwise negotiating the criminal justice system. Additionally, certain state benefits like low-income housing are restricted if felons live in households, so my interviewees were wary and watchful. They could not tell employers they needed work to go to court with their sons or daughters, and could rarely advocate for them within the penal system.

Incarceration does not just affect black men. Black women are increasingly sent to jail or prison, where they may be subject to violence (Richie 2012). Approximately two-thirds of incarcerated women are mothers, and one in every thirty women admitted into correctional facilities is pregnant (Glaze and Maruschak 2008; Maruschak 2008). The incarceration of fathers and mothers has profound consequences for social reproduction and bodies that are not fully understood. For example, in most states, women can be shackled during labor and childbirth, and the kinds of separations, violences, and penal experiences surrounding incarceration permeate and stunt the physical and emotional well-being and social reproduction of entire families (Women's Prison Association 2011). Upon leaving prison, the paid and unpaid labors of women and men are deeply affected through, for example, diminished employment opportunities, increased poverty, stigma, and lack of access to state resources and citizenship rights (Alexander 2010).

Overall, then, the paid and unpaid labors of my interviewees and engagements with the state were occasionally liberating but mostly punitive, grueling, and insecure. However, many of these experiences were not *new*. My interviewees viewed themselves as *always, already* workers, as *always, already* unsupported, differentiated, and/or penalized by employers and the state, primarily because of their status as racialized, low-income women. With various words, they described their complex maternal labors as "work." This work, they argued, had only ever had fleeting or fickle support from the state. While interviewees did talk about poverty, rarely did unprompted reflections on capitalism and labor markets enter into our discussions. Rather, on a spectrum of material-discursive power relations, they pointed mostly to racism and its evolving and insidious forms, including mass incarceration.

Poverty, Provisioning, and Survival Strategies

Amid these amplified unpaid and paid labors and encounters with the racialized state, how did my interviewees get by? Among other strategies, my interviewees often lumped their lives and labors together. Interviewees took their babies with them while they drove a bus for work; they made calls and appointments if they had access to phones. Some women worked for wages in their own home as child care providers while caring for their own elderly mothers or children. Some mothers worked in community service jobs such as thrift stores, and their children joined them there to do homework.

Women and families also lived together as a means of survival and as a way of pooling labor and resources. Not uncommonly, two or three families lived together in a one- or two-bedroom apartment. There, women watched each other's children while one person "provisioned" the household through paid labor; informal activities such as prostitution, blood or plasma donation, and drug sales; or visits to social service agencies or churches. Women described this kind of bundled living and labor as difficult: "It just creates—not only do you have more people going to into mental institutions [after living in shared households], because just imagine—just me dealing with my dad and he's over there, imagine if I had him in my house all day. I already live with my sister and take care of my niece who also has a handicap and then let's say I've got to take Cindy and her kid" (Tamara, Interviewee, African American mother and activist).

While these kinds of bundled arrangements were all too familiar for interviewees, their comments show both the ways that reproductive work is deeply bound up with other labors and how individual, household, and community labors are integrated. This may be especially true for African American women, who conduct so much "community mothering" and are often seen as responsible for the well-being of communities (Hill Collins 2000a; Richie 2012). The quotes from interviewees also hint at the extreme stress produced by these kinds of arrangements—stress that sometimes resulted in homelessness for families.

MANAGING MATERIALLY

While households and bodies have been understood as key spaces of social reproduction, feminist materialism (of different varieties) highlights different material
conditions of social reproduction; the integration of social reproduction, production, and consumption; and also the possibility of understanding a wide range
of material assemblages involved in life's work. As Meehan and Strauss observe
in the introduction to this volume, "human bodies are not the only producers of
life's work." Indeed, the material world consists of all types of laboring bodies and
objects—collectively called "webs" (Rocheleau 2008), "hybridities" (Whatmore
2002), and "assemblages" (Robbins and Marks 2010; see also Marks, this volume).

The women I interviewed survived daily life by consuming cheaply and managing materially, with implications for broader social relations and theoretical
understanding. First, my interviewees tried to spend as little money as possible
and to purchase goods as cheaply as they could. Often they forwent material
needs, like shoes and coats, for themselves as mothers. They also relied heavily
on the shadow state for food, personal supplies, clothing, and housing assistance.
They were clearly not alone: even in the period of economic expansion before
these interviews were conducted, emergency service needs in the city had increased by up to 94 percent (Fendt, Mulligan-Hansel, and White 2001).

For provisioning, my interviewees turned frequently to discount stores like
Walmart as a source of cheap food and, on rare occasions, for new clothes for
their children. In this way, as is true for households of all incomes now, poor
racialized women in U.S. cities have been able to buttress their household provisioning and reproductive capacities in part through the expansion of globalized
corporations, supply chains, and poor, racialized labor in other parts of the
world. In fact, from my interviewees' perspective, one of the most important and
beneficial shifts in their capacity to "get by" and "provide" for children was the
continual cheapening of goods and new possibilities for consumption.

The women I interviewed relied on not just cheap goods but a broad range of
provisioning spaces and materialities beyond the household. Automobiles and
buses were of particular importance, not just as sources of frustration and lack
but also as a place where care work took place and was enabled. More than one
interviewee reported having lived in a car for a short period of time, and one
reported leaving her children in the car while she went to work, a choice that
troubled her immensely: "Just this once, you leave your child in the car so you
can go to work. Your promise you will never do it again" (Karen, Interviewee,
African American mother).

Another woman was thrilled to have found paid work as a bus driver. She
would bring her infant son to work with her, and he would ride the bus all day

long with her. Also, mothers carried out other care tasks on public transportation, where they sometimes spent over two hours per day. On buses, they slept, held children, and supervised homework.

Cell phones, too, helped in the labor of these women. When available or affordable, they provided a rare form of security and "crisis management" amid the fragmentation and chaos of life's work: "And I got to call the teacher, and then my sister because she's got to watch the kids because my babysitter isn't showing up. You know, it's always something. This phone saves me. It saves me" (Interview, Brenda, African American mother and activist).

Embodied Social Reproduction

The materiality of social reproduction includes bodies as well as things. In recent years, feminist and antiracist feminist scholarship has explored bodies and embodiment as a critical component of life experience, but this scholarship has limited interface with social reproduction studies (Meehan and Strauss, this volume). My interviews have made clear that, however one theorizes social reproduction and life's work, the experience is deeply embodied. In the lives of the low-income African American women whom I studied, material-discursive power relations are enacted and resisted in and through bodies in ways that cannot be fully explored here. For example, nearly all of my interviewees were victims of abuse, assault, and trauma carried out by family members, boyfriends, pimps, strangers, or police officers.

Gendered and racialized violence is common. Twenty-five percent of black women are abused by a partner; and black women are killed by intimate partners at four times the rate of white women. Moreover black women who are young, who do not live with their intimate partner, who reside in low-income urban areas, and who rely on government assistance are particularly vulnerable to physical and emotional abuse (Richie 2012). This kind of trauma affects the body in immediate and direct ways (e.g., broken bones). Crucially, it also systemically produces poor physical and emotional health and behaviors (e.g., panic attacks, autoimmune disease, substance abuse) that seeps into paid and unpaid labor (Reading 2006). Women who have been raped by a household member are, for example, ten times more likely than average to abuse illegal substances or alcohol (Richie 2012).

In addition, studies have shown how poor, racialized bodies experience injustice, discrimination, and related poor health. For example, perceptions of racial discrimination have been correlated with higher blood pressure, anxiety, depression, and lower birthrate for pregnant mothers (Collins et al. 2004; Williams, Neighbors, and Jackson 2008). Health problems such as diabetes and obesity are high among inner-city African American populations, as is mortality more generally. Furthermore, poor and racialized communities are unevenly subject to environmental toxins at work and at home, such as pollution from coal plants or lead in old buildings—the latter true for many of my interviewees. The dynamics and complexities of such bodily experiences and inequalities are not well understood, although discrimination and unequal access to resources seem to be part of the story. Also, bodies are interactive—sick people that are living in stressful situations can make one another sick, and the same bodies that are at home doing labor are out there doing labor, paid or unpaid.

My research subjects' labors, lives, and bodies were haunted by illness and death. Many of the women whom I interviewed lived with significant pain and disease. Arthritis, diabetes, breast cancer, and a host of other health problems plagued them. One woman moved only with a walker, slowly and methodically. She could not navigate stairs nor pick up her crying three-year-old. Another woman had post-traumatic stress syndrome from childhood abuse and suffered severe panic attacks: "I take medicine but when it happen there is nothing I can do. I can't even leave the house sometimes. My kids have seen it. I can't keep a job, either" (Mildred, Interviewee, African American mother). Studies suggest that the poor health of my interviewees was reflected in the overall population of w-2 participants, 40 percent of whom reported mental health problems and 20 percent of whom said they had a disability (Courtney and Dworsky 2006).

Many of my interviewees were also mothers to ill children. In Milwaukee and elsewhere, poor children have significantly more health problems than nonpoor children. They have higher rates of asthma, developmental delays, and lead poisoning, for example. They also have higher rates of hospital admissions, disability days, and death rates (Wood 2003; Milwaukee Center for Urban Health 2010). Interviewees also talked of the physical and emotional labor involved in caring for sick children—physically subduing tantrums in emotionally impaired children; living with fear of forgetting an important medical device; and visiting hospitals, health clinics, and schools whenever possible. Ultimately, women often forwent important medications and treatment for themselves and their children. They did this because they were overwhelmed with responsibilities, health care facilities were limited, and they lacked time and financial resources.

The women also had to deal far too often with the loss due to death of someone they loved. In fact, morbidity and violence loomed large. The trauma and depression that accompanied the loss of children and family members shortened and impaired my interviewees' lives. Morbidity was linked in some cases to illnesses described above, but also to direct violence. Interviewees had witnessed violence as children and been abused as children and women. They knew young infants that had died and had relatives and children that had been subject to gang and other neighborhood violence.

The direct and discursive experiences of neoliberalism, racism, violence, sexism, poverty, abandonment, and death are burdens literally "carried" in the bodies of my research subjects. In some cases, this happens through brutal violence and indifference. In other cases, the chronic stress of trauma, racism, and poverty, coupled with insufficient supports, state violence, and austerity, produces subtle and cumulative bodily burdens. Babies are born with low birthweights and related health problems; children and mothers are depressed and untreated; poor ventilation leads to asthma; and immune systems are depressed and lead to stroke, diabetes, cancer, and other chronic diseases (Conroy, Sandel, and Zuckerman 2010). In places where state support for social reproduction is eroding, bodies have become broken.

Conclusion

I began this chapter with the theme of amplification. Drawing upon qualitative interviews and academic literature, I have described amplifications that reverberate from racialized difference in Milwaukee: where poor black women are more likely to experience poverty, die from intimate violence, lose children to death or illness, and suffer severe health problems than are white women. But to amplify also means to make louder. In this chapter, I sought to make audible the voices and experiences of my interviewees and their labors, including sources of support and moments of hope. I do so not just to disseminate data, but with a broader concern and question of how we might foster empathy and a sense of justice around life's work for all bodies and the survival and thriving capacity of all communities.

Social reproduction as a concept gives us a language by which we can connect to the common, repetitious tasks and the associated emotions that make all of us human and vulnerable. While this awareness of shared vulnerability and labor is not sufficient grounds for ethical action, as Judith Butler (2006) has argued, it is, nonetheless, a contrasting language of possibility amid the anomie of profit-driven capitalism. As others have posited, social reproduction might serve as a theme for disparate activist and policy efforts tailored to address a wide range of inequalities and relations. For this to be true, however, we need to keep returning to, understanding, and challenging the multiple forms of differentiation and violence that shape social reproduction.

With this in mind, I turn finally to a third meaning of "amplify"—to expand or intensify understanding through deeper analysis. It is critical to bring social reproduction literatures more fully into conversation with black feminist theories and antiracist feminist analysis, and to build on the history of black feminist and antiracist voices within the social reproduction tradition. In doing so, we can more fully understand specific, situated crises surrounding social reproduction. For example, it is now understood that poor women bear triple burdens of intensified reproduction, production, and community work under neoliberalism (Nagar et al. 2002).

But I want to suggest that we have insufficiently theorized the daily and differentiated forms of state engagement with social reproduction. This chapter illustrates the more specific nature of these burdens for low-income African American women in Milwaukee, situating them institutionally and historically, outlining inequities, and hinting at possibilities for feminist intervention. We must further explore the state's myriad contemporary and historical entanglements with social reproduction and associated rationales such as the relationships among political economies, institutional racism, legal systems, incarceration, violence, surplus masculinities, and securities (Bonds 2007; Gilmore 2007; Roberts 2008; Alexander 2010; Cowen and Siciliano 2011; Richie 2012). Furthermore, violence and power relations come in labyrinthine and subtle shades. Research demonstrates how racism, family abuse, and trauma, for example, tenaciously take hold on children's bodies. This means that political-economic "path dependencies" do not operate in isolation and are not the only ones of concern. We need carefully traced explorations of the multiple and compounding material-discursive power relations that situate life's work.

NOTE

1. All names of interviewees, children, and family members have been changed to protect identities.

REFERENCES

Acker, Joan. "Inequality Regimes: Gender, Class, and Race in Organizations." *Gender and Society* 20, no. 4 (2006): 441–464.

Alexander, Michelle. *The New Jim Crow: Mass Incarceration in the Age of Colorblindness.* New York: New Press, 2010.

American Civil Liberties Union (ACLU). *The War on Marijuana in Black and White.* New York: ACLU, 2013.

Bakker, Isabella. "Social Reproduction and the Constitution of a Gendered Political Economy." *New Political Economy* 12, no. 4 (2007): 541–556.

Bezanson, Kate, and Meg Luxton. *Social Reproduction: Feminist Political Economy Challenges Neo-Liberalism.* Montreal: McGill-Queen's University Press, 2006.

Brodie, Janine M. "Reforming Social Justice in Neoliberal Times." *Studies in Social Justice* 1, no. 2 (2007): 93–107.Burawoy, Michael. *The Extended Case Method: Four Countries,*

Four Decades, Four Great Transformations, and One Theoretical Tradition. Berkeley: University of California Press, 2009.

Butler, Judith. *Precarious Life: The Powers of Mourning and Violence.* New York: Verso, 2006.

Clawson, Rosalee A., and Rakuya Trice. "Poverty as We Know It: Media Portrayals of the Poor." *Public Opinion Quarterly* 64, no. 1 (2000): 53–64.

Collins, James W., Richard J. David, Arden Handler, Stephen Wall, and Steven Andes. "Very Low Birthweight in African American Infants: The Role of Maternal Exposure to Interpersonal Racial Discrimination." *American Journal of Public Health* 9, no. 12 (2004): 2132–2138.

Collins, Jane L., and Victoria Mayer. *Both Hands Tied: Welfare Reform and the Race to the Bottom in the Low-Wage Labor Market.* Chicago: University of Chicago Press, 2010.

Conroy, Kathleen, Megan Sandel, and Barry Zuckerman. "Poverty Grown Up: How Childhood Socioeconomic Status Impacts Adult Health." *Journal of Developmental and Behavioral Pediatrics* 31, no. 2 (2010): 154–160.

Correll, Shelley J., Stephen Benard, and In Paik. "Getting a Job: Is There a Motherhood Penalty?" *American Journal of Sociology* 112, no. 5 (2007): 1297–1338.

Courtney, Mark E., and Amy Dworsky. *Findings from the Milwaukee TANF Applicant Study.* Chicago: Report by the Chapin Hall Center for Children at the University of Chicago, 2006.

Cowen, Deborah, and Amy Siciliano. "Surplus Masculinities and Security." *Antipode* 43, no. 5 (2011): 1516–1541.

Dalla Costa, Mariarose, and Selma James. *The Power of Women and the Subversion of the Community.* London: Falling Wall Press, 1972.

Douglas, Susan, and Meredith Michaels. *The Mommy Myth: The Idealization of Motherhood and How It Has Undermined All Women.* New York: Free Press, 2005.

Fendt, Pamela S., Kathleen Mulligan-Hansel, and Marcus A. White. *Passing the Buck: w-2 and Emergency Services in Milwaukee County.* Milwaukee: Institute for Wisconsin's Future, 2001.

Fraser, Nancy. "Feminism, Capitalism and the Cunning of History." *New Left Review* 56 (2009): 97–117.

Fraser, Nancy, and Linda Gordon. "A Genealogy of Dependency: Tracing a Keyword of the U.S. Welfare State." *Signs* 19, no. 2 (1994): 309–336.

Gibson-Graham, J. K. "Querying Globalization." *Rethinking Marxism: A Journal of Economics, Culture and Society* 9, no. 1 (1996): 1–27.

Gilmore, Ruth Wilson. *Golden Gulag: Prisons, Surplus, Crisis, and Opposition in Globalizing California.* Berkeley: University of California Press, 2007.

Glaze, Lauren E., and Laura M. Maruschak. *Parents in Prison and Their Minor Children.* Washington, D.C.: Bureau of Justice Statistics, 2008.

Hildebrandt, Eugenie, and Patricia Stevens. "Impoverished Women with Children and No Welfare Benefits: The Urgency of Researching Failures of the Temporary Assistance for Needy Families Program." *American Journal of Public Health* 99, no. 5 (2009): 793–801.

Hill Collins, Patricia. *Black Feminist Thought: Knowledge, Power and the Politics of Empowerment.* New York: Routledge, 2000a.

———. "Gender, Black Feminism, and Black Political Economy." *Annals of the American Academy of Political and Social Science* 568, no. 1 (2000b): 41–53.

hooks, bell. *Ain't I a Woman: Black Women and Feminism*. Vol. 3. Boston: South End Press, 1981.

———. *Talking Back: Thinking Feminist, Thinking Black*. Boston: South End Press, 1989.

Jones. Jacqueline. *Labor of Love, Labor of Sorrow: Black Women, Work, and the Family from Slavery to the Present*. 2nd rev. ed. New York: Basic Books, 2009.

Katz, Cindi. "Vagabond Capitalism and the Necessity of Social Reproduction." *Antipode* 33, no. 4 (2001): 709–728.

———. "Bad Elements: Katrina and the Scoured Landscape of Social Reproduction." *Gender, Place and Culture: A Journal of Feminist Geography* 15, no. 1 (2008): 15–29.

Kobayashi, Audrey. "Anti-Racist Feminism in Geography: An Agenda for Social Action." In *The Companion to Feminist Geography*, edited by Lise Nelson and Joni Seager, 32–40. London and New York: Routledge, 2004.

Maruschak, Laura. *Medical Problems of Prisoners*. Washington, D.C.: Bureau of Justice Statistics, 2008.

McCluskey, Martha T. "Efficiency and Social Citizenship: Challenging the Neoliberal Attack on the Welfare State." *Indiana Law Journal* 78 (2003): 783–864.

McDowell, Linda. "Reconfigurations of Gender and Class Relations: Class Differences, Class Condescension and the Changing Place of Class Relations." *Antipode* 38, no. 4 (2006): 825–850.

Mead, Lawrence M. *Government Matters: Welfare Reform in Wisconsin*. Princeton, N.J.: Princeton University Press, 2004.

Milwaukee Center for Urban Health. *Milwaukee Health Report 2010: Health Disparities in Milwaukee by Socioeconomic Status*. Milwaukee: Milwaukee Center for Urban Health, 2010: http://www.cuph.org/mhr/2010-milwaukee-health-report.pdf.

Mitchell, Katharyne, Sallie A. Marston, and Cindi Katz, eds. *Life's Work: Geographies of Social Reproduction*. Chichester, U.K.: John Wiley, 2004.

Mulligan-Hansel, Kathleen, and Pamela S. Fendt. *Unfair Sanctions: Does W-2 Punish People of Color?* Milwaukee: Institute for Wisconsin's Future and the University of Wisconsin-Milwaukee Center for Economic Development, 2003. http://www4.uwm.edu/ced/publications/race_report.pdf

Nagar, Richa, Victoria Lawson, Linda McDowell, and Susan Hanson. "Locating Globalization: Feminist (Re)readings of the Spaces and Subjects of Globalization." *Economic Geography* 78, no. 3 (2002): 257–284.

Pager, Devah. "The Mark of a Criminal Record." *American Journal of Sociology* 108, no. 5 (2003): 935–975.

Parker, Brenda. "Material Matters: Gender and the City." *Geography Compass* 5, no. 6 (2011): 433–447.

———. *Gendering Urban Neoliberalism*. Athens: University of Georgia Press. Forthcoming.

Peck, Jamie. *Workfare States*. New York: Guilford Press 2001.

Peck, Jamie, and Nik Theodore. "Contingent Chicago: Restructuring the Spaces of Temporary Labor." *International Journal of Urban and Regional Research* 25, no. 3 (2001): 471–496.

Quadagno, Mildred J. *The Color of Welfare: How Racism Undermined the War on Poverty.* Oxford: Oxford University Press, 1994.

Reading, Richard. "The Enduring Effects of Abuse and Related Adverse Experiences in Childhood: A Convergence of Evidence from Neurobiology and Epidemiology." *Child: Care, Health and Development* 32, no. 2 (2006): 253–256.

Richie, Beth E. *Arrested Justice: Black Women, Violence, and America's Prison Nation.* New York: New York University Press, 2012.

Robbins, Paul, and Brian Marks. "Assemblage Geographies." In *The Sage Handbook of Social Geographies*, edited by Susan J. Smith, Rachel Pain, Sallie A. Marston, and John Paul Jones III, 176–194. Thousand Oaks, Calif.: Sage, 2010.

Roberts, Dorothy E. "Racism and Patriarchy in the Meaning of Motherhood." *American University Journal of Gender, Social Policy and the Law* (1993): 1.

———. "Shattered Bonds: The Color of Child Welfare." *Children and Youth Services Review* 24, no. 11 (2002): 877–880.

———. "The Racial Geography of Child Welfare: Toward a New Research Paradigm." *Child Welfare* 87, no. 2 (2008a): 125–150.

———. "The Racial Geography of State Child Protection." In *New Landscapes of Inequality: Neoliberalism and the Erosion of Democracy in America*, edited by Jane Lou Collins, Micaela di Leonardo, and Brett Williams. Santa Fe: School for Advanced Research, 2008b.

Rocheleau, Dianne E. "Political Ecology in the Key of Policy: From Chains of Explanation to Webs of Relation." Geoforum 39, no. 2 (2008): 716–727.Sue, Derald Wing. *Microaggressions in Everyday Life: Race, Gender, and Sexual Orientation.* Hoboken, N.J.: John Wiley, 2010.

Trotter, Joe W. *Black Milwaukee: The Making of an Industrial Proletariat, 1915–1945.* Chicago: University of Illinois Press, 1985.

University of Wisconsin–Milwaukee Center for Employment and Training. *Milwaukee Drilldown, November 2011.* Prepared for the Milwaukee Area Workforce Investment Board, Inc. Milwaukee, Wisconsin.

Whatmore, Sarah. *Hybrid Geographies: Natures Cultures Spaces.* Thousand Oaks, Calif.: SAGE, 2002.

Williams, Claudia, and Ariane Hegewisch. *Women, Poverty, and Economic Insecurity in Wisconsin and the Milwaukee–Waukesha–West Allis MSA.* Report Number R347. Washington, D.C.: Institute for Women's Policy Research Briefing Paper, 2011.

Williams, David R., Harold W. Neighbors, and James S. Jackson. "Racial Ethnic Discrimination and Health: Findings from Community Studies." *American Journal of Public Health* 98, no. 2 (2008): s29–s37.

Williams, Joan. *Unbending Gender: Why Family and Work Conflict and What to Do about It.* New York: Oxford University Press, 2000.

Williams, Joan, and Heather Boushey. *The Three Faces of Work-Family Conflict: The Poor, the Professionals, and the Missing Middle.* A report published by the UC Hastings Work Life Law Center and the Center for American Progress, Washington DC, 2010.

Wisconsin Department of Workforce Development. "Wisconsin Works (w-2) Overview." 2006. Retrieved from: dwd.wisconsin.gov/w2/wisworks.htm.

Wisconsin Legislative Audit Bureau. "An Evaluation of Wisconsin Works (w-2) Program." April 2005.

Wisconsin Women's Council and Women's Fund of Greater Milwaukee. *The Status of Women in Milwaukee County.* A report produced by the Wisconsin's Women's Council and Women's Fund of Greater Milwaukee, 2006.

Women's Prison Association, Institute on Women and Criminal Justice. *Shackling Brief.* New York: Women's Prison Association, 2011.

Wood, David. "Effect of Family and Child Poverty on Health Outcomes in the United States." *Pediatrics* 112, no. 3 (2003): 707–711.

PART FOUR

Working Materialities

CHAPTER 7

Dirty Work in the City

Garbage and the Crisis of Social Reproduction in Dakar

ROSALIND FREDERICKS

Each and every day in Dakar, Senegal, the city's population struggles to purge their homes and streets of messy remains accumulated the day before. The process involves an intricate web of cleaning and waste-disposal labors—"dirty work"—essential to the management and image of the city but shouldered by different people with differential rewards. The dirty work inevitably begins in the home with women's fastidious efforts to sanitize the domestic space. Sweeping and cleaning fit squarely within women's duties as household managers in Senegal, and as such, dealing with waste in the home is naturalized as intrinsically women's work. Household waste management is a thorny task: the uncompromising Senegalese heat, high percentage of organic waste, and lack of adequate storage in most Dakar homes make keeping trash from getting stinky and dangerous a complicated challenge.[1]

Once eliminated from the home, the disposal of garbage is even more vexing. In place of expensive trash receptacles, garbage is usually disposed of in small plastic bags or rice sacks or dumped loose from open plastic containers. When the municipal trash collection system is working smoothly and operating closer to the affluent city center, household women need simply transport their garbage to the arriving garbage truck as announced by the incessant honking of its driver. In the best of times, the truck comes every day. However, faced with gaps in collection, women often resort to more creative and onerous disposal strategies. Once the garbage has been evacuated from the home, the municipal trash labor force is charged with keeping the city streets clean and transporting the garbage for proper disposal at the city's fifty-year-old dump (*Mbeubeuss*) on the outskirts of the city. City sweepers clean neighborhood streets and collectors ensure proper loading of the garbage truck. Insufficient materials, poor working conditions, and politicization of the sector can render the trashworkers' jobs grueling and precarious. When the system works smoothly, the city can be quite tidy; when it collapses, one cannot ignore the stench of a city drowning in its own waste.

Municipal services in Senegal's capital city, Dakar, have been a crucible of conflict surrounding new governance agendas unleashed in the wake of structural adjustment. The contradictions of urban restructuring have manifested, in particular, through shifting geographies of responsibility and reward for doing the city's dirty work over the last three decades. Indeed, the labor of urban garbage management has been the subject of intense institutional volatility and the linchpin of a number of fierce political contests at neighborhood, city, and state levels.[2] Far from simply indicating technical failure, garbage "crises" instead profoundly illuminate the unevenness of development and its associated rhetorics of control and dirty labor burdens.

In Africa, as worldwide, urban public services crystallize the contradictions surrounding neoliberal reform and have been a key arena of struggle in the era of austerity (Mcdonald and Ruiters 2004; Bond and McInnes 2006; Foley 2010). In Senegal, neoliberal reform began with the country's first structural adjustment loan in 1979 and proceeded in fits and starts over the following decades, often through hybrid strategies of state centralization with strategic manipulation of privatization policies (Fredericks 2013). During these three decades of reform, structural adjustment has eroded urban public services and the government's role as the "employer state," with deep implications for urban politics. The large budget of the city's garbage collection system—more than 10 billion CFA in 2012 (USD $20.8 million)—and the size of the trash labor force (1,500–2,000 "surface technicians") has made the sector a primary target for reform and an important labor arena to control.[3] Owing to the symbolic power of ordering the capital (or dirtying it, for that matter), the labor of garbage collection has emerged as a particularly sticky subject for the state and households alike. Caught in the grip of a series of trash crises, the spaces of the city have oscillated between remarkably orderly and dangerously insalubrious, periodically subjecting certain residents to the noxious consequences of waste, pollution, and disease.[4]

This chapter considers how new formulas for managing the city's garbage collection have reconfigured the relations of social reproduction. Specifically, it explores the highly contested battle to flexibilize the sphere of "formal" municipal trash labor through a turn to "participatory" garbage collection, which taps and respatializes the household labor of cleaning. These dynamics highlight the fluidity between the realms of production and reproduction and confirm what Bakker and Gill (2003, 18) have described as "new patterns of exploitation and control of labor in the production-reproduction relationship" accompanying neoliberal reform.

One of the key dimensions of struggles around trash collection labor has been the status of workers and their remuneration as either formal laborers or "participants." In Senegal, like elsewhere, neoliberal reform has been underpinned by a turn to "participatory" or "community-based" development strategies often predicated on free or low-paid labor in exchange for the promise of "empowerment." In spite of lofty claims, critical scholarship has exposed discourses of participation in neoliberal development as, at worst, a cloak for exploitation (Cooke and Kothari 2001). Social reproduction is a useful lens through which we may consider the way that so-called formal and participatory labors are dialectically constituted. It is widely understood that the categorical distinction between the realms of production and reproduction determines the nature and value of work through constructing labor taking place in the home to reproduce and maintain laboring bodies as "nonwork" or work with no value (Mitchell, Marston, and Katz 2004). The restructuring of state welfare services ushered in with neoliberal reform is often accomplished through flexibilizing formal labor and reconfiguring the fabric of activities comprising life's work through rhetorics of participation. Exploring the interpenetration of formal and participatory work thus allows for a consideration of the way that labor is ascribed value or how political economic projects become inscribed in material spaces through differentially disciplining laboring bodies.

The flexibilization of labor in neoliberal contexts has often functioned, in particular, through devaluing women's work, rendering it progressively precarious and disposable (Bakker and Gill 2003; Wright 2006; Fakier and Cock 2009). Due to their marginalized positions within social hierarchies, children and youth have also been key objects of restructuring and its associated burdens (Katz 2004). Waste management is a particularly nefarious sphere in which the crisis of social reproduction can be felt, especially for marginalized populations. Research in diverse settings has highlighted how cheap waste management solutions are primary arenas within neoliberal contexts through which gender, class, age, and other lines of difference are instrumentalized to disproportionately subject marginalized populations to dirty labor burdens, often through the vehicle of participation (Ali, Olley, and Cotton 1998; Beall, Crankshaw, and Parnell 2000; Miraftab 2004; Samson 2008). Those working in waste thus end up "trashed" in a double sense, owing to the negative stigma of the work itself alongside the degradation of working conditions.

In line with the larger project of this volume, this chapter draws from an understanding of social reproduction that emphasizes the key role of discourses of identity in mobilizing new formulas of work and their rewards. The chapter draws on two moments in the history of trash politics in Dakar to emphasize how the stigmas and burdens of cheap waste management solutions and increasingly precarious arrangements for managing household garbage in Dakar have been disproportionately borne by youth and women. It explores how the two moments were interconnected through assessment of shifting priorities and possibilities for new development agendas.

The chapter is also keenly concerned with the materiality of the labor process and with exploring the intersections between materiality, identity, and state power. Throughout the analysis, I consider how different labor arrangements have been inscribed within competing state projects and the complex ways that new formulas of social reproduction may unleash power struggles within the state. Garbage management is an essential foundation of producing a modern, orderly city and, as a highly visible and arduous labor, cleaning work functions as a performance of state legitimacy (see Fredericks 2013). As a result, controlling and enforcing the labor of garbage management has been a key element of ordering the city—its communities and individuals—in the neoliberal era of flexibilized labor and self-management. Building on growing scholarship on waste (see Hawkins and Muecke 2003; Whitson 2011; Moore 2012), my analysis highlights the centrality of waste's materiality in the exercise of social subordination and state power. The sociospatial ordering of people and places is deeply wrapped up with the visceral symbolism carried by garbage and the important ways that it intersects with human labor—or the literal emplacement of burdens of dirt and disease onto specific bodies and geographies.

And yet, if the state's role in managing garbage is a process of taming the city and disciplining its residents, then it is also about the possibilities for disrupting those power relations through a politics of disorder (see Moore 2009). The chapter concludes on a hopeful note by detailing the politics of social reproduction waged by women and youth over the last few years as they deploy the power of disorder to subvert ordering paradigms. In this way, ordinary *Dakarois* have forced the state to reckon with the disproportionate burdens it had outsourced to households and workers and have creatively and effectively resisted the devaluation of their labor.

Dakar's New Trash Collectors

A major political crisis shook Dakar in 1988. As the dire social consequences of structural adjustment and overall economic crisis deepened and unemployment skyrocketed, young Dakarois took to the streets, protesting the failures of the educational system and rallying their support for the opposition presidential candidate in the year's elections. In the wake of the disputed electoral results in which the incumbent Socialist Party president won amid controversy, youth rioted in the streets and the government declared a state of emergency. Garbage piled up and putrefied in city streets and public spaces, as the political crisis was manifested through the garbage sector. Soon after, the now-famous *Set/Setal* ("Be Clean/Make Clean") social movement was spawned that would inspire the next chapter in the city's waste management (ENDA 1991; Diouf 1996). *Set/Setal* involved the localized activities of Dakar youth to cleanse and beautify their own neighborhoods in reaction to the increasing filth of the city and widespread disillusionment with their policymakers. Incubated in local youth groups, young people began to organize their own system of neighborhood waste management across the city.

Although little recognized in the literature on *Set/Setal* (ENDA 1991; Diouf 1996), young women were active participants in the movement. Joining in the neighborhood effort, young women left their houses on the days scheduled for cleanup events—just like their brothers—and went to work improving the city. Because of their household waste management duties, young women were not only well equipped to help with the cleaning of the neighborhood but also keenly motivated to be part of the solution to the garbage crisis. The fact that they were seen as the cleaners in their households legitimized their place in cleaning with their male compatriots.

Prior to 1988, trash collection was fairly regularized: the trashworkers, who were mainly adult men from outside of Dakar, had salaries and were unionized. However, the system had collapsed under the budgetary constraints of austerity and mismanagement. By the early 1990s, the *Set/Setal* youth's cleaning activities had become indispensable in filling the gaps left by the flailing trash collection company. Dakar's Socialist Party mayor, Mamadou Diop, fired the sector's workers and incorporated youth volunteers (including many women) into a citywide "participatory" trash system. This dramatic reconfiguration represented a shrewd political calculation by Mayor Diop that helped him to cope with shrinking budgets, flexibilize the labor force, and shore up political support (Fredericks 2013). The participatory trash sector thus brought these young men and women activists in as new political clients and the fresh face of the nation and its orderly development.

Though initially composed of volunteers and self-organized, the youth trash sector was soon managed by a new World Bank–funded public works agency coordinated by the municipality. The Public Works and Employment Agency (AGETIP) was formed in 1989 with the goal of generating a significant number of mainly manual and temporary jobs for unemployed youth. As a kinder, gentler approach to neoliberal development, the agency aimed to channel youth's energies and satisfy certain basic needs that had eroded with adjustment policies (World Bank 1997). The youth were responsible for street sweeping and trash collection in their own residential neighborhoods and, on average, earned the day-laborer rate of 30,000 CFA/month (around US$60 today). They lacked all protections and benefits and experienced extended periods with no compensation at all.

New Skills, New Burdens

The new scaled-back, participatory trash collection system served to off-load the burden of cleaning the city onto neighborhood youth, with little reward. In absconding in providing basic urban services at regular rates of remuneration, it made youth and their families shoulder the responsibility for satisfying their households' social reproductive needs. With reduced service, household women were forced to resort to less-than-optimal strategies to eliminate the waste and protect their families from pollution, including reducing, burying, dumping, or paying (often exorbitant) private horse-cart operators to dump their garbage out of sight. As a result, the poorest neighborhoods often became the most encumbered by garbage and its insidious dangers.

The language of participation was central to the reconfiguration of the sector. Mayor Diop promoted the *Set/Setal*-based trash system with pride, as the ultimate moment of participatory citizenship during his tenure at the helm of what he described as the "construction of a democratic urbanism" (Diop n.d.). The system did, indeed, gain him some notoriety, as *Set/Setal* youth were an invited delegation at the 1994 Global Forum held in Manchester on the theme of cities and sustainable development (Whittaker 1995). Youth were cast as do-gooders who were building their communities and acquiring skills that would allow them to become better professionals and citizens. Their position as social juniors, moreover, was used as an indicator that they were not yet deserving of full compensation because it was assumed they were too young to be their family's main breadwinner. In fact, although they were young (many may have even been under eighteen years of age), their meager salaries were increasingly relied upon by their families in the context of economic crisis. The vast majority of my respondents felt that Mayor Diop's new system was unfairly exploitative. One of my respondents reflected on the period in the following words: "Mayor Diop treated us like we were just doing this for fun, but while I was very committed to the cause, I also needed the money! I am the eldest son and was the only person in my household working at the time."[5]

Worldwide, waste labor is intensely stigmatizing, owing to the powerful symbolic associations around impurity. In Dakar, young men recalled being initially embarrassed about working in trash. Worried that they would be seen by their girlfriends, parents, and communities in general, they covered their faces so as not to be recognized, and some refused to work in their own neighborhoods (Fredericks 2009). The turn to young people for the labor of garbage management meant that this group— already seen as social juniors—had to contend with not only poor salaries and few protections but also all of the negative associations of dirty labor. However, the implications of working in the new municipal trash system were different for women than men. In certain respects, joining Mayor Diop's trash system was perceived by women and their neighbors as a natural evolution for women, and in other ways, it was deeply radicalizing. Though their connection to waste was seen as natural, cleaning activities in the public space as part of the youth movement positioned these women as workers because being paid for these duties was new (Fredericks 2009). Some of the pioneers of the *Set/Setal* movement and its transition into organized trash collection of the women workers were even nicknamed *Les Amazones*. In most zones, early on, women trashworkers did exactly the same tasks as the men, including climbing, riding, and filling the trash trucks, and many found these new roles radically new and even empowering (Fredericks 2009). In contrast with the young men, women had no qualms about visibility; they were often the first to climb onto the trucks and refused to hide their identities. For these women, the professionalization of *Set/Setal* enhanced the value of their labor due to its lack of gender differentiation: they did the same tasks as men *and* were paid for them. Once they were cleaning in the city streets, they were grouped into the category of youth and their labor was masculinized (Fredericks 2009). As detailed below, a later experiment with participation in the garbage sector on the outskirts of the city was to have very different gendered implications.

"Municipal Housekeepers" in Dakar's Periphery

From the mid-1990s to the early 2000s, two key developments emerged in the trash sector.[6] First, the municipal workers (youth brought in after *Set/Setal*) unionized in 2000 and began demanding the regularization of their labor, and nongovernmental organization (NGO) initiated participatory development projects appeared in the city's periphery. The second moment to be considered here is one of Dakar's first NGO-inspired participatory waste management projects, which was spearheaded in the Tonghor neighborhood of the Yoff district of Dakar in the early 2000s by one of Senegal's best-known NGOs, Environmental Development Action in the Third World (ENDA).[7] Tonghor is among Dakar's Lebou neighborhoods (the Lebou people are one of Senegal's nine ethnic groups), which represent some of the self-proclaimed "traditional" Lebou fishing villages that have occupied the Cape Verde peninsula for over five hundred years but that are now absorbed into the rapidly growing capital city (Sylla 1992). In certain areas, of which Yoff is an important example, the Lebou have retained a powerful customary authority base, which overlaps and competes with the municipal authority. Most of the residents of Tonghor are Lebou, though there are long-term populations of poor migrants and a more recent influx of wealthier city folks.

The Lebou neighborhoods are plagued with sanitation problems due to their location on the periphery of the city and their traditional village plan, combined with a fierce politics of land and resistance to change by the local customary authorities. These challenges were part of the justification for choosing Lebou neighborhoods as the main sites of the participatory waste management projects spearheaded by ENDA in the 1990s and early 2000s in the context of the wider turn toward NGOs' community-based strategies of urban public service provision (Gaye and Diallo 1997; Soumaré 2002; Simone 2003). These projects have been a central thrust of ENDA's activities to improve Dakar's urban environment and have earned the organization some notoriety in international development circles (see UNESCO n.d.).

ENDA launched the pilot community-based trash project in Tonghor in 2001 in collaboration with the neighborhood's main community association, the Tonghor Management Committee (CGT). Seed funding came from French and Canadian development funds, and the project was to be maintained through household contributions (a user fee). The project involved a door-to-door horse-drawn cart "precollection" system targeting over six thousand residents that would (in principle) connect up with the city's trash system (ENDA 1999). Prior to this system, women disposed of their household garbage through dumping it onto the beach or by the road to be collected by the city's garbage trucks, but during the project's tenure, the municipal garbage trucks that had previously collected the neighborhood's garbage ceased to enter into Tonghor. The project ushered in a more intimate system in which select women would collect their neighbors' garbage using what was considered the more appropriate, "traditional" method of horse-drawn carts.

The project feasibility study performed by a local community-based organization for ENDA emphasized the importance of local participation (ENDA 1999). The CGT created a pilot committee and appointed a young male member as its volunteer coordinator. The most important element of community participation consisted of the six women chosen as "animators" (*animatrices*) of the project—who served as the liaison between the households and the three (male) horse-cart drivers. Though originally from Yoff, the horse-cart operators were locally based men of the Sereer ethnic group who owned their own horse carts. Two *animatrices* accompanied each horse-cart driver to collect the garbage from the homes and load it onto the cart. Originally completely volunteer-based, these women received a small "token" of 15,000 CFA/month (USD $30) for a few months until community contributions waned and they received next to nothing. The drivers were hired on for their labors. The *animatrices* were also charged with community outreach to educate neighborhood women on how to properly store, separate, and dispose of their garbage. A key element of the education campaign entailed discouraging women from dumping on the beach or burying their garbage. In the face of persistent recourse to the beach, an ordinance was eventually enacted that prohibited all beach dumping and fined all perpetrators. This effectively forced neighborhood residents to use the fee-based horse-cart system through placing the *animatrices* in the role of policing their participation.

The village elders explicitly chose the *animatrices* from respected but poor Lebou households, because these women were seen as good representatives of the village who could make use of such an "opportunity." For their part, the women felt no choice but to participate out of an obligation to their elders, an honest desire to contribute to neighborhood cleanliness, and a desperate hope that one day their participation would bear fruit. Three of the women were divorced or widowed heads of households, and three were over fifty years of age. Importantly, two of the *animatrices* were seen as particularly well suited for the job: they had been deeply implicated in the *Set/Setal* movement and had worked for the municipality as paid trash collectors in an earlier phase of trash management. Both had been fired from the formal trash collection force in a round of downsizing that had occurred just a few years before the arrival of the ENDA projects.

Dirty Participation

Several points about community-based waste management are relevant to theories and practices of life's work. The Yoff project instrumentalized gendered associations of wastework in the home as intrinsically women's work in order to idealize women as participants and thereby extend their social reproductive duties into the neighborhood space. Women's "natural" attributes, including diplomacy, nonconfrontational style, and their intimacy with the communities, as well as their altruistic choice to work for the "common interest," were celebrated as their key skills as *animatrices*.

This reconfiguration of the space of household social reproductive activities into the community space built on the notion that women should be judged according to their skills and capacities as the managers of order and cleanliness in the home. This resonates with Dipesh Chakrabarty's observation in India of how housekeeping—specifically household trash management—"is meant to express the auspicious qualities of the mistress of the household" (1991, 20). These participatory trash projects secured the cleanliness of the neighborhood as the responsibility of its female residents in a reflection of their "auspicious qualities." The notion that women in Tonghor are natural waste managers and community educators facilitated the negation of value for neighborhood trash work as "work" deserving remuneration and placed the onus of neighborhood wastework on women's skills as municipal housekeepers.

Central to the targeting of women in these projects was a repudiation of the labors they already performed in the home—that is, all of the "life's work" that the *animatrices* left behind as they went about their neighborhood trash job—as well the extension of those unpaid activities into the neighborhood. In this sense, the jobs ended up doubling their unpaid activities by extending the realm of social reproduction into the public sphere. This extension also came as a fundamental rejection of the value of women's labor in the official trash sector. Fired from municipal trash collection during a round of downsizing in the late 1990s because they were not deemed worthy of those jobs, these women were then installed into the community-based project as idealized volunteers. Though the gendered basis of the firing was justified by the notion that the women were not primary breadwinners, both *animatrices* were in fact the main breadwinners in their families (Fredericks 2009). Quite in contrast with the early experience of women municipal trashworkers, whose labors were masculinized when they entered the public space to collect garbage, the labors of women in the community-based system were devalued. Although they toiled day in, day out alongside the horse-cart drivers, the payment of these men was never in question and was never justified through a narrative of community responsibility. The drivers were clearly considered workers, whereas the women were seen as participants whose labor was rendered an empowering duty undeserving of compensation.

Like for the youth-based system, the insidious power of these projects drew from the negative associations with the materiality of waste and cleanliness. Joining with the symbolic violence of being associated with waste was the arduous physicality of that labor process for the *animatrices*. Provisioned with only minimal equipment, if any at all, the *animatrices* did this work with their bare hands. By the end of a workday, they were literally filthy, forced to parade through their neighborhood wearing the smelly remains of other people's waste. In an Islamic society where cleanliness of the body is of utmost importance in terms of spiritual and community standing, this is no small burden. Neither was the vulnerability to disease that came of this risky exposure for people with little or no access to health care. Despite their most fastidious attempts at staying clean, the work often led to infection and disease. Thus, in contrast with the mechanized garbage truck, the intimate technology of the door-to-door horse-cart system introduced an entirely different relationship between collector and garbage and new forms of subjection to waste management's symbolic and material discipline. The deployment of gender stereotypes in these projects thus entrenched women's connection to waste, dirt, and disorder through literally weighing them down and marking them with the mess of waste. This underscores the importance of the "fleshy, messy" (Katz 2001) aspects of the crisis of social reproduction or the way it operates through the burdens of labor's materiality.

The new user fee for trash collection also dramatically reconfigured the financial burden of waste management for neighborhood women and transformed the value and treatment of the garbage within the home. Fines imposed on those who continued dumping on the beach acted to criminalize those who attempted to opt out of the program. Charging for the amount of garbage discarded in effect brought women deeper into the management of their waste alongside their neighborly *animatrices* through incentivizing strategies to reduce waste, including storing, burying, and attempts to dump garbage off the radar of local officials. Given their role in managing household cleanliness and associated expenses, women shouldered this burden, often with difficulty: the user fee often precipitated intense conflicts between husbands and wives (Fredericks 2012). For the *animatrices*, the program placed them as the taxman, supposedly drawing on their intimacies in the community, but in truth locating them on difficult terrain with regard to their neighbors as some of the community's most marginalized members.

It is also important to note the role that these projects played in producing a certain kind of community. The selection of the Lebou neighborhoods, first and foremost, among other sanitation-challenged periurban communities, was explicitly made on ethnic terms. Promotional literature on the ENDA projects often highlighted the historic legacy of Dakar's "traditional neighborhoods" and hailed the Lebou as a proud, independent people for whom community-driven development is a natural and long-standing truth. Dovetailing with the charismatic appeal of the project's ethnic identity is the work that it performed for the Lebou elite to assert their autonomy from the local state—its competitor for power and authority over the Yoff community (Fredericks 2012). In practice, the community activated by the project was exclusively Lebou, despite the fact some of the other areas populated by immigrants are considered the dirtiest and most garbage-challenged areas in Tonghor. Because autochthonous claims in Yoff are defined by ethnicity, claims to manage Yoff "traditionally" yoke ethnicity with tradition. Engaging their women in neighborhood trash collection offered a productive opportunity for the Lebou to solidify their tenacious hold on their neighborhood through the symbolic ordering of the neighborhood by these Lebou "municipal housekeepers." Extending the domestic waste management activities of Lebou women into the space of the neighborhood thus acted to entrench Lebou authority over the neighborhood in their competition with the local municipal authorities through the performance of self-management.

While these community-based garbage projects have been hailed by ENDA and their international audience as "best practices," the project's shelf life was short. After less than a year of operation, the Tonghor community-based trash collection project fell into shambles: many, if not most, residents refused to pay the user fee, and the overworked *animatrices* were exhausted by—and no longer compensated for—their labors. Even the horse-cart drivers were fed up with the increasingly irregular payment of their salaries. After a dispute between the municipality and the neighborhood authorities resulted in a towering mountain of garbage by the airport road in Yoff, the project was definitively canceled. Soon after, the municipal trash trucks began collecting along their usual circuit in Tonghor. Perhaps the most hopeful lesson to be drawn from the Tonghor project, then, lies in its failure—or the rejection of this model by the Tonghor community and Yoff local government.

Disorderly Politics

The crisis of social reproduction in Dakar has worked through different attempts at devaluing the labor of garbage collection through rhetorics of participation mobilized on the bodies of youth and women. Shifting priorities of development agendas—to pacify rebellious youth and bring "diplomatic" women into community-based development—led to the targeting of specific groups at different moments for their participation in ordering the city on the cheap.

However, this history is only half the story. An analysis of the most recent moment, particularly the period 2006–12, highlights the profound instability of these arrangements and the potential for their disruption and even reversal. Particularly from 2006 to 2014, the city was held hostage to garbage as government, trashworkers, and ordinary Dakarois fought it out over the rules, responsibilities, and rewards for managing the city's waste. The question of garbage labor has taken center stage in key political battles in recent elections, illuminating the high stakes of the politics of social reproduction.

A brief update on the history of the municipal trash collection force post-*Set/ Setal* is necessary here. After years of laboring without protections, the trash workers began organizing in the late 1990s and formed their trashworkers' union in 2000. Over the next twelve years, during the Abdoulaye Wade presidency of 2000–12, the sector suffered intense volatility with eight major institutional shake-ups. It is not an exaggeration to say that the management of garbage labor became been the linchpin in a vicious scramble for power between the national and municipal state during this time. Each institutional reorganization was keenly focused on reconfiguring responsibility for cleaning the city and its reward. The period from 2006 to 2012 deserves special attention. In 2006 President Wade dissolved worker protections, relegating them back into insecure working conditions mirroring the participatory era of the 1990s. In response, the workers began waging periodic massive strikes, demonstrations, sit-ins, and even hunger strikes in an effort to tap the power of dirt in the public space and tug at the heartstrings of the Dakarois. Through tirelessly educating and agitating over the radio waves, they quickly became one of the most visible and vocal labor unions in Senegal and managed to win some key concessions.

The success of the union cannot be understood without attending to the workers' savvy campaign of legitimation through which they contested the shame of working in waste and earned the support of the residents they served in Dakar. Despite the inherent stigma associated with their line of work, the trash-workers' union made major strides in redefining their profession and gaining widespread community support during this time. Though striking represents the most powerful lever they have to make their voices heard, the union has only gained traction in their struggle through accompanying their strike strategy with a public relations campaign that elides party politics and instead reclaims labor rights from a moral plane that engages, reconfigures, and challenges the symbolic weight of garbage. Stemming from this savvy platform, the union transformed a reviled profession into one that many Dakarois admit is "dignified" and even "noble" and thereby enlisted the active support of the communities they serve.[8]

One key indicator of community support was the neighborhood trash revolts that often accompanied the trash strikes. In April 2007, for instance, during one of the trashworkers' union's longest strikes, residents of whole neighborhoods across the city began dumping—externalizing—their accumulating household garbage into public spaces in concerted acts of protest. Participating residents and revolt organizers, who were mainly young men and older women, were quite proud of what they had orchestrated and enjoyed widespread support among their neighbors. They were very clear about their goals: to support the trashworkers' union battle, register their disdain for the state's "abandonment" of its citizens, and voice a larger demand for improved public services. Through refusing to be sullied by the state's negligence they felt they were fulfilling their duties as citizens. Public dumping served as an audacious challenge to the logic of flexibilized labor and the larger political system it represented.

The persistent trash strikes and trash revolts placed the question of trash labor at the center of an all-out political battle between the new mayor of Dakar, Khalifa Sall, after he was elected in 2009, and President Wade. Immediately after taking office in 2009, Mayor Sall acted decisively on the part of the trashworkers through formally hiring them on as fully contracted employees, regularizing their salaries, and providing them with social security and health services. The two political rivals then engaged in a sort of tug-of-war to control the sector, with the mayor making it a key priority of his administration to protect these gains and control the sector and the president battling these efforts tooth and nail. Though President Wade tried to reclaim the sector and eviscerate the mayor's office, he eventually lost this battle when he failed to be reelected in 2012. Just one month after taking power following what had been the country's most contentious and violent election yet, Senegal's new president, Macky Sall, made a dramatic gesture aimed at bolstering his image through supporting the regularization of the garbage sector. The union's collective bargaining agreement was finally signed in the summer of 2014.

Conclusion

Overall, the story of garbage politics over the last two decades in Dakar has illuminated the complex workings of the crisis of social reproduction and the contestation it has unleashed. Trash work crystallizes the dialectic between work in the city and "life's work" in the home through differentially positioning different residents of Dakar with regard to the burdens and rewards of cleaning. One's position within the family—as a social junior or the manager of cleanliness—shapes the formulas mobilized for cleaning the city. These Senegalese social dynamics intersected with wider development discourses influencing the priorities and targets of participation with important effects. Youth were seen as key participants, owing to their key role in electoral politics and the "dangers" they represent in the city as unemployed, unpredictable masses, whereas women were constructed as participants owing to their intrinsic connection to cleaning and their presumed diplomatic skills as community managers. Intertwined with the mobilization of identity and its contestation were the messy material dimensions of waste and cleaning.

This analysis also serves to highlight the complex multiscalar relations between community, municipal, and national institutions involved in urban governance and the ways in which new power relations become sedimented in and through those relations. New labor arrangements function for the state in different ways in specific moments as they become inscribed within state battles for power and legitimacy. Though the project of creating entrepreneurial subjects intrinsic to "participatory" development at first served as a performance of state legitimacy, eventually participation became a transparent code word for the state's relinquishment of its duties. It remains to be seen if the saga surrounding garbage labor in the city is permanently resolved, but the sector seems to signal a wider turn away from the neoliberal labor policies ushered in with structural adjustment in Senegal.

NOTES

1. Certain passages of this chapter include revised material from two previously published pieces (Fredericks 2012, 2013). The research is based on ethnographic fieldwork

in Dakar primarily conducted during 2006–8, with several follow-up visits between 2009 and 2014. The author is indebted to Ndeye Bineta Ndoye and Ndeye Sophie Coly for assistance with the transcription and translation of interviews conducted in Wolof or French. The author is grateful for feedback from the volume's editors. She would also like to thank those workers, officials, and residents of Dakar who generously shared their points of view. All names have been omitted to protect the respondents' identities. All French to English translation is provided by the author. Any mistakes that remain in the text are exclusively the author's responsibility.

2. His study considered only household waste management (*ordures ménagères*) and not hazardous, building, or medical waste. The study focused on the formal municipal collection system, and not on the vast system of informal recycling in the city or the management of the dump, *Mbeubeuss*. For more info on *Mbeubeuss*, see Cissé (2012).

3. This is a professional categorization used to include the collectors (*éboueurs*) and sweepers (*balayeurs*) in the formal garbage management system.

4. For instance, a cholera outbreak in 2005 was directly connected to crisis in the garbage collection system (N. Diouf 2005).

5. Personal interview, surface technician, Niary Tali, Dakar, June 29, 2007.

6. This title is drawn from Miraftab (2004).

7. ENDA (Environnement et Développement du Tiers Monde) is an international non-profit organization founded in 1972 and based in Dakar.

8. Based on in-depth surveys conducted in 2007–8 with residents in two Dakar neighborhoods.

REFERENCES

Ali, Mansoor, Jane Olley, and Andrew Cotton. "Agents of Change: The Case of Karachi City's Waste Management." *Third World Planning Review* 20, no. 33 (1998): 255–266.

Bakker, Isabella, and and Stephen Gill, eds. *Power, Production and Social Reproduction: Human In/security in the Global Political Economy*. New York: Palgrave Macmillan, 2003.

Beall, Jo, Owen Crankshaw, and Susan Parnell. "Victims, Villains and Fixers: The Urban Environment and Johannesburg's Poor." *Journal of Southern African Studies* 26, no. 4 (2000): 833–855.

Bond, Patrick, and Peter McInnes. "Decommodifying Electricity in Postapartheid Johannesburg." In *Contesting Neoliberalism: Urban Frontiers*, edited by Helga Leitner, Jamie Peck, and Eric Sheppard, 157–178. New York: Guilford, 2006.

Chakrabarty, Dipesh. "Open Space/Public Place: Garbage, Modernity, and India." *South Asia* 14, no. 1 (1991): 15–31.

Cissé, Oumar. *Les Décharges d'Ordures en Afrique: Mbeubeuss à Dakar au Sénégal*. Paris: Karthala, 2012.

Cooke, Bill, and Uma Kothari. *Participation: The New Tyranny?* London: Zed, 2001.

Diouf, Mamadou. "Urban Youth and Senegalese Politics: Dakar 1988–1994." *Public Culture* 8 (1996): 225–249.

———. *Propos d'un Maire: Mon Combat Pour Dakar*. n.d.

Diouf, Nafi. "Cholera Epidemic Spreads in Senegal, Infecting Dozens." *Associated Press Worldstream*, April 5, 2005.

ENDA. *Set Setal, Des Murs Qui Parlent: Nouvelle Culture Urbaine à Dakar*. Dakar: ENDA Tiers Monde, 1991.

———. *Volet collecte des déchets et assainissement du quartier traditionnel de Yoff-Tonghor: Etude de faisabilité*. Dakar: Enda Tiers Monde R.U.P. République du Sénégal Commune d'Arrondissement de Yoff, 1999.

Fakier, Khayaat, and Jacklyn Cock. "A Gendered Analysis of the Crisis of Social Reproduction in Contemporary South Africa " *International Feminist Journal of Politics* 11, no. 3 (2009): 353–371.

Foley, Ellen E. *Your Pocket Is What Cures You: The Politics of Health in Senegal*. New Brunswick, N.J.: Rutgers University Press, 2010.

Fredericks, Rosalind. "Wearing the Pants: Gender and the Politics of Trash Labor in Dakar." *Hagar: Studies in Culture, Polity and Identities* 9, no. 1 (2009): 119–146.

———. "Valuing the Dirty Work: Gendered Trashwork in Participatory Dakar." In *Economies of Recycling*, edited by Catherine Alexander and Josh Reno. London: Zed, 2012.

———. "Disorderly Dakar: The Politics of Garbage in Senegal's Capital City." *Journal of Modern African Studies*, 2013.

Gaye, Malick, and Fodé Diallo. "Community Participation in the Management of the Urban Environment in Rufisque (Senegal)." *Environment and Urbanization* 9, no. 1 (1997): 9–29.

Hawkins, Gay, and Stephen Muecke, eds. *Culture and Waste: The Creation and Destruction of Value*. Lanham, Md.: Rowman & Littlefield, 2003.

Katz, Cindi. "Vagabond Capitalism and the Necessity of Social Reproduction." *Antipode* 33, no. 4 (2001): 709–714.

———. *Growing Up Global: Economic Restructuring and Children's Everyday Lives*. Minneapolis: University of Minnesota Press, 2004.

Mcdonald, David A., and Greg Ruiters. *The Age of Commodity: Water Privatization in Southern Africa*. London: Routledge, 2004.

Miraftab, Faranak. "Neoliberalism and Casualization of Public Sector Services: The Case of Waste Collection Services in Cape Town, South Africa." *International Journal of Urban and Regional Research* 28, no. 4 (2004): 874–92.

Mitchell, Katharyne, Sallie A. Marston, and Cindi Katz, eds. *Life's Work: Geographies of Social Reproduction*. Antipode Book Series. Malden, Mass.: Blackwell, 2004.

Moore, Sarah A. "The Excess of Modernity: Garbage Politics in Oaxaca, Mexico." *Professional Geographer* 61, no. 4 (2009): 426–437.

———. "Garbage Matters: Concepts in New Geographies of Waste." *Progress in Human Geography* 36, no. 6 (2012): 780–799.

Samson, Melanie. "Rescaling the State, Restructuring Social Relations: Local Government Transformation and Waste Management Privatization in Post-Apartheid Johannesburg." *International Feminist Journal of Politics* 10, no. 1 (2008): 19–39.

Simone, AbdouMaliq. "Reaching the Larger World: New Forms of Social Collaboration in Pikine, Senegal." *Africa* 73, no. 2 (2003): 226–250.

Soumaré, Mohamed. "Local Initiatives and Poverty Reduction in Urban Areas: The Example of Yeumbeul in Senegal." *International Social Science Journal* 52, no. 172 (2002): 261–266.

Sylla, Assane. *Le Peuple Lebou de la Presqu'ile du Cap-Vert*. Dakar: Les Nouvelles Editions Africaines du Senegal, 1992.

UNESCO. *Community Participation in the Management of the Urban Environment Senegal*. UNESCO, n.d. http://www.unesco.org/most/africa6.htm.

Whitson, Risa. "Negotiating Place and Value: Geographies of Waste and Scavenging in Buenos Aires." *Antipode* 43, no. 4 (2011): 1404–1433.

Whittaker, Stella, ed. *First Steps—Local Agenda 21 in Practice: Municipal Strategies for Sustainability as Presented at Global Forum 94 in Manchester*. London: HMSO, 1995.

World Bank. *Performance Audit Report (PAR) for the First and Second Public Works and Employment Projects (Agetip) (Republic of Senegal)*. Washington, D.C.: World Bank, Operations and Evaluations Department, 1997.

Wright, Melissa. *Disposable Women and Other Myths of Global Capitalism*. New York and London: Routledge, 2006.

CHAPTER 8

Making Shrimp and Unmaking Shrimpers in the Mississippi and Mekong Deltas

BRIAN MARKS

The coastal deltas of the Mississippi River in the United States and the Mekong River in Vietnam are major shrimp-producing regions. While one sector harvests wild shrimp for a domestic market and the other farms them in ponds for export, in both regions household owner-operators make up the vast majority of producers (see table 8.1).

In the 2000s the globalization of shrimp production and consumption led to a crisis of social reproduction in both deltas, but shrimpers in the Mississippi and Mekong deltas experienced that crisis in materially different ways, bearing on different circuits of social reproduction.

In Louisiana, rising fuel costs and falling shrimp prices created a cost/price squeeze on producers after 2001. Reproducing the means of production (boats) consumed a growing share of shrimpers' shrinking income devoted to reproducing household labor power. Effectively, the boat now ate first from the family table. This disinvestment from reproducing labor power induced escalating self-exploitation of household labor in the short term through lower living standards, increasing use of unpaid family labor on the boat, and greater dependence on onshore wage work. Long-term social reproduction through intergenerational succession broke down as shrimpers' children left the fishery (Marks 2012).

In Vietnam, shrimp farmers faced a crisis of reproducing remunerative environmental conditions of production. Commodity price trends first encouraged conversion from freshwater rice agriculture to saltwater shrimp aquaculture, then reversed a few years later. Most coastal Mekong delta farmers could not adjust their farming systems to follow this market reversal because soil salinization and decayed water infrastructures made reversion to freshwater production infeasible (Marks 2010).

These transformations signal a series of key questions for social reproduction. What can these crises among shrimp producers tell us about contemporary crises of social reproduction? When global economic restructuring downloads the costs of crisis into the social reproductive sector, whose reproduction pays the price, and how? If the global commodity crisis squeezing shrimp producers manifests as a crisis of reproducing not only shrimpers but also their boats and shrimp,

TABLE 8.1. Comparison: Mississippi Delta and Mekong Delta Shrimp Industries

Region	Production system	Number of producers[1] (2006)	Percentage of owner-operator producers[2]	Production[3] (metric tons, 2006)	Share of national production[4]	Percentage exported[5] (2006)
Louisiana	Wild fishery	approx. 5,700	94.6–91% (1997–2008)	63,000	37% (2009)	0%
Mekong Delta	Aquaculture	approx. 313,000	92.7% (2006)	287,000	75% (2006)	91%

Source: Author.

[1] LDWF, *Commercial License Sales*; Ministry of Agriculture and Rural Development, *Results*, 395, 435.
[2] Deseran, *Louisiana Shrimp Fishermen*, 7; Miller and Isaacs, *Economic Survey*, 26; Ministry of Agriculture and Rural Development, *Results*, 395, 435.
[3] NOAA Fisheries, *Annual Commercial Landing Statistics*; Ministry of Agriculture and Rural Development, *Results*, 328.
[4] NOAA Fisheries, *Annual Commercial Landing Statistics*.
[5] Nhuong et al., "Shrimp Industry in Vietnam."

what happens if we take those nonhumans seriously? What does it mean for social reproduction to put the nonhuman materiality of fiberglass boats, diesel engines, brackish water, and shrimp larvae into the family, as it were, of social reproduction alongside its human actors?

To answer these questions, this chapter assesses how and why social reproductive crises manifest for Louisiana shrimpers through one circuit of material social practices, reproducing their mechanical means of production, and for Mekong delta shrimp farmers through another, reproducing the biotic and abiotic environmental conditions of production.[1] The argument is that (1) reproducing the means and conditions of production are important circuits in the social reproduction of Mississippi and Mekong delta shrimp producers, interdependent with the reproduction of household labor power; and (2) the materiality of those nonhuman actors matters to shrimp producers' social reproduction, shaping the distinctive forms their social reproductive crises take.

Social Reproduction and Materiality

REPRODUCING THE MEANS OF PRODUCTION

The material social practices that constitute social reproduction (SRP) are multiple and diverse. The production of labor power is central to SRP, but reproducing the capacity to work hardly exhausts the range of material social practices through which SRP is accomplished. Reproducing the means and conditions of production are as essential to SRP as shaping up labor power for the next day's shift (Meehan and Strauss, this volume; Katz 2001).

Within the schemas of SRP, the reproduction of the means and conditions of production are, perhaps, considered analytically within the scope of SRP as it applies to society as a whole, but not so much within personal and family reproduction (Bakker and Gill 2003; Bezanson 2006; although see Katz 2001, 2004). In Marx's (1967) equations, the capitalist reproduces constant capital or means of production; proletarians reproduce labor power with their wages, which equal the socially necessary cost of reproducing themselves.

In agrarian political economy, ownership of the immediate means of production by some producers and the central role of nature in the production process have long vexed critical scholars seeking to understand class composition and exploitation. But this type of economy offers some insights into how the reproduction of the means and conditions of production can be incorporated into the analysis of SRP. Central to these insights is the form of production known variously as independent commodity production, family farming, or (as described here) household commodity production. Household commodity producers own their means of production and primarily employ family labor to produce commodities. In household commodity production, divisions between social reproduction and commodity production, adjudicated by the separation of workers from the means of production, are blurred. Distributional decisions over investing surplus are made not by capitalists for workers but among members of the family; the tenor of such household business decision-making varies from egalitarian and cooperative to hierarchical and conflictual. Intrahousehold, interpersonal social relations, often structured by gender and generation, play a crucial role in determining the employment of household labor and capital between, for example, reproducing family labor and reproducing means of production (Friedmann 1978, 1980; Whatmore 1991; Gasson and Errington 1993).

Household commodity producers reproduce themselves amid competition from capitalist firms through a variety of means. Principal among these are the flexible valuation of household labor and capital in the family enterprise and flexible deployment of household resources between, within, and outside the enterprise. The flexible use of household labor and capital is crucial in reproducing household commodity production in both the short-term, everyday reproduction of labor power and operating capital and long-term reproductive circuits like the reproduction and expansion of means of production and intergenerational succession of owner-operatorship (Goodman and Redcliff 1985; Chayanov 1991; Salamon 1992).

That social reproduction is more than the reproduction of labor power is evident in household commodity production, where workers reproduce not only themselves and their kinfolk on daily and decadal scales but also the means of production they mix with their labor power to earn a living. Their social reproduction is not just "the fleshy, messy and indeterminate stuff of everyday life" (Katz 2001, 710), through which labor power is produced, but also the greasy, grimy work of reproducing means of production. We must also consider that for household commodity producers like Louisiana shrimpers and Mekong delta shrimp farmers, whose labor and capital intimately intermingle with the environmental conditions of production, the reproduction of those environmental conditions—the soggy, scaly, and salty stuff of coastal human/environmental interaction—is a vital component of social reproduction.

ENVIRONMENTAL CONDITIONS OF PRODUCTION

Cultural and political ecologists have critically analyzed the relationship between human use of the biophysical environment and social well-being in a wide array of contexts (Robbins 2012). Some of these scholars have connected crises of environmental conditions to social reproductive crisis among resource users. Watts (1983, 351), in his explication of the links between the extraction of surplus from the peasantry, deteriorating environmental conditions of production, and the crisis of social reproduction in northern Nigeria, argues: "Environmental conditions are, then, instances of the productive process." The nonreproduction of those conditions simultaneous with the "simple reproduction squeeze" of the peasantry—exploitation keeping them at a bare subsistence level and highly vulnerable to environmental shocks—becomes immediately a crisis of social reproduction.

Katz (2004) found that children in Sudan spent more time doing social reproductive tasks like collecting firewood and water as those common-pool resources were degraded and their families' reproduction became increasingly commodified. Not only was the social reproduction of these Sudanese children devalued through the "time-space expansion" of their reproductive labor, compelled by changed environmental conditions of (re)production, but their environmental knowledge became increasingly irrelevant to earning a living in the degraded and commodified rural economy—a de-skilling that marooned them without secure livelihoods in an uncertain future adulthood. The environmental conditions of production are in intimate and reciprocal relationship with the process of agrarian production and the social reproduction of those producers, such that crisis in the reproduction of those conditions and/or that production process often translates into a crisis of social reproduction.

Making Global Shrimp

The humble shrimp punches far above its weight in political-economic terms. Globally, about 6.5 million metric tons were harvested from the sea and grown in ponds in 2009, with aquaculture contributing 52 percent of shrimp supply that year (Valderrama and Anderson 2011). Sixty percent of the world's shrimp are traded internationally. Shrimp exports totaled $10.9 billion in 2003, making shrimp the most valuable commodity in the global seafood trade (Gillett 2008). The globalization of shrimp is associated with technical innovations in production and a supply and price revolution in the international market. Between 1980 and 2003 world shrimp production more than tripled and export volume more than quadrupled, most of that increase due to exponential growth in shrimp farming (Valderrama and Anderson 2011). Greater supply, reduced production costs, and increasing concentration in seafood wholesaling and retailing (Lebel et al. 2008) caused real shrimp export prices to fall by more than half from 1980 to 2003 (Keithly and Poudel 2008).

THE LOUISIANA SHRIMP FISHERY

The commercial Louisiana shrimp fishery, located around the Mississippi River delta, dates back to the mid-nineteenth century. The introduction of motorized boats and trawl nets reduced the labor and capital intensity of production, allowing for mass owner-operatorship of boats by familial households after 1920. A durable structure of household commodity production, constituted by family operation of shrimping vessels, an open-access fishery management regime, and socially embedded market transactions between fishermen, docks, and processors, distinguishes the Louisiana shrimp industry (Marks 2012).

More than 90 percent of Louisiana shrimpers own and captain their vessels and procure much of their operating capital and labor through household economies (Deseran 1997; Marks 2005; Liese et al. 2009). Shrimping is a multigenerational livelihood for many participants, with intergenerational transitions historically accomplished through training on boats by parents and in-laws, financial assistance from family in purchasing or building boats, and sweat equity from households' and relatives' labor constructing and maintaining boats, nets, and equipment.

Louisiana made up 37 percent of U.S. shrimp production by volume in 2009 (NOAA Fisheries 2009) but occupies just 4 percent of the market share, as imports now constitute about 90 percent of U.S. consumption. Between 2000 and 2003 alone, the U.S. shrimp industry's market share fell from 17.6 percent to 11.5 percent (NMFS 2004). As imports poured in and dockside Louisiana shrimp prices plummeted from $1.74/pound in 2000 to $1.04/pound in 2004, the price of diesel—the largest operating expense of shrimp vessels—escalated from $1.44/gallon in 2000 to $2.36/gallon by 2005, peaking at nearly $4.00/gallon in 2008 (U.S. EIA 2011). Combined, these forces imposed a cost/price squeeze on shrimpers. The squeeze bit ever deeper into the surpluses Louisiana shrimpers realized during the 2000s, prompting many to leave the fishery. The number of Louisiana shrimpers fell from 9,988 in 2000 to 5,101 by 2008 as many fishermen went bankrupt, retired, or took better-paying work. Four major hurricanes between 2005 and 2008 contributed to this decline, but the magnitude of the cost/price crisis is underscored by the fact that more shrimpers left in the four years before Hurricane Katrina in 2005 than the four years after.

THE MEKONG DELTA SHRIMP INDUSTRY

Vietnam's most important shrimp producing region is the coastal zone of the Mekong delta. In 2006, the delta yielded 75 percent of Vietnam's shrimp, 91 percent of which was exported, almost all farm raised (Nhuong et al. 2006; Sinh and Phuong 2006). The Mekong delta shrimp sector's history is far briefer than Louisiana's. The provinces that became Vietnam's "shrimp mine" in the 2000s pursued a very different development path in the two decades prior. After 1975, extensive land reclamation and salinity exclusion infrastructure projects in the coastal delta converted brackish wetlands into rice fields. Within this reclaimed area farmers attained rising, but still low and unstable, rice yields, as productivity and farmer incomes continued to lag due to water and soil quality problems (Hoanh et al. 2003; Marks 2010, 122–130).

Commodity price trends helped motivate dramatic change in the coastal Mekong after 2000. Rice prices fell to historic lows in the late 1990s (USDA 1998–2008) as shrimp prices skyrocketed (Jory and Cabrera 2003). A national Vietnamese government directive in 2000 liberalized agricultural land use planning and provided a further push for shrimp in the delta. A "shrimp fever" of land conversion in 2000–2001 saw farmers transform some 280,000 hectares of freshwater fields and orchards to saltwater shrimp ponds (Binh et al. 2005). In 2006 there were roughly 290,000 household shrimp farmers producing on 500,000 hectares of the coastal Mekong delta. The majority practiced traditional extensive or improved extensive aquaculture, stocking shrimp larvae at low densities with correspondingly low capitalization requirements and yields, with a small number of intensive shrimp farmers growing high densities of shrimp using feeds, chemicals, and paddle wheel aerators that necessitated much higher capitalization (Ministry of Agriculture and Rural Development 2006; Marks 2010; Nhuong, Bailey, and Wilson 2011).

By the mid-2000s, the commodity price trends spurring the shrimp boom began to reverse. Shrimp prices fell to half their 2000 peak by 2004–2005 as rice recovered, then surpassed, its late 1990s average (USDA 1998–2008). Some farmers sought to reintroduce rice onto their fields-turned-ponds during the rainy season, but accumulated salinity and degraded infrastructure meant in all but a few places rice died from excessive salt (Tho et al. 2008). The situation only worsened in 2007–8, when rice prices doubled in six months and shrimp prices slumped to unprecedented lows. Mekong delta shrimp farmers experienced a cost/price squeeze most could not mitigate through crop diversification back toward rice growing, as the salinization of water and soil now made freshwater production impossible.

Crises in the Mississippi Delta

Me and my wife started off working together, about 35 years ago. I made the first boat, working by myself, and [then] I made another boat, a big steel hull, so I'm making like three times the money, basically. Making money but to keep your equipment up takes over half the income. We was always a family operation. My three boys worked with me, my wife, my daughter, and as we come up, if I'm making money, this one had a rough time, well I'd be over here, and vice versa. It would keep it in, like, in the family. But the circle keeps getting smaller and smaller because all of us is making less money. And one of 'em do have a job. He got out and he's got him a little job. But the other ones are still in the same circle, and we're doing like this—it's closing up. At one time this thing was bigger than a big pot, if you want to call the circle, now it's littler than your little finger. Money-wise, I'm talking about, and we're still trying to keep each other going, but the circle's getting faster and faster and littler and littler. And sooner or later, well, how little does the circle get before you get squished? (Interview, Louisiana shrimper, 2004)

The cost/price squeeze on household commodity production in the Louisiana shrimp fishery initiated a cascade of interrelated reproductive crises. Reproducing the means of production became costlier, absorbing more of households' declining incomes and eating into family consumption. The short-term reproduction of household labor was pressed by the consumption shortfall along with greater demands for unwaged labor on boats and waged labor onshore to make up for the cash-flow deficit. Falling margins and the underinvestment in and self-exploitation of family labor contributed to a crisis of long-term social reproduction—the breakdown of intergenerational succession in the fishery.

The means of production for Louisiana shrimp fishermen include the fixed capital in their boats and operating expenses consumed while shrimping. The shrimp boat's productive capacity depends on the reproduction of this constant capital. As one Louisiana shrimper remarked in a 2004 interview, "The wives sometimes don't understand the boat comes first. It's your first wife." Boats, engines, and nets frequently need minor repairs and maintenance; periodically hulls, cabins, and motors require major overhauls; and eventually the entire vessel wears out and must be replaced or upgraded.

Louisiana shrimping households historically accomplished the reproduction of boats through leveraging networks of family labor and capital augmented with bank loans. Major investments in boats are often articulated with intergenerational transfer, as sons, sons-in-law, and siblings succeed to owner-operation by inheriting or building new boats with family help. Most of the older Louisiana shrimpers (50-plus years old) whom I interviewed in 2004 and 2011 said they got their first boats between the late 1970s and early 1980s. These vessels were often paid for and built by fathers, in-laws, and extended family. Their shares in the boat, and unwaged labor as deckhands, were eventually paid off and reciprocated by the owner, who in turn helped more family members enter the business. The depth of shrimping families' cultural identification with their boats is underscored in a number of ways: the convention of naming boats after wives and children, painting on the bow the first letter of the family's name, the crucial role of the boat as a material space for social reproduction, childhoods spent on boats over the summer, formative young adult experiences learning to trawl from parents and in-laws, and Blessing of the Fleet parades and parties on deck.

With the coming of the cost/price crisis, boats became an increasingly heavy millstone weighing on household reproduction. After 2002, boat loans could no longer be paid down, deferred maintenance on boats piled up, and some vessels were repossessed. Other shrimpers reacted by downgrading to smaller boats with lower operating expenses. The hurricanes of 2005 and 2008 further compounded the crisis as many boats were destroyed or thrown ashore, unable to work, and soon repossessed. Still, as the large majority of Louisiana shrimpers held no debt on their boats (Liese et al. 2009; Miller and Isaacs 2011), financing existing fixed capital did not pose a challenge to household reproduction as the escalating operating expenses did.

Shrimpers estimated that before 2000 two-thirds of their fishing revenues went to household consumption and one-third to operating expenses; but four years later two-thirds went to running the boat. The rising price of fuel, shrimpers' single-largest operating expense, consumed 20–30 percent of total expenses in 2002 (Lafleur, Yeates, and Aysen 2005), 35–50 percent by 2008 (Liese and Travis 2010; Miller and Isaacs 2011). Combined with falling shrimp prices, rising operating costs dramatically shrank the surplus shrimpers realized from their work in the 2000s. This shortfall was essentially made up by transferring shrimping income from reproducing labor power to means of production—from groceries and house payments to diesel and ice. This is where the materiality of shrimp boats and human shrimpers matters, specifically the differing material requirements of their reproduction. The reproductive requirements of a shrimp boat are more inflexible than the labor power of its human owners. A boat without fuel or a broken engine simply stops working, while a family keeps going despite greatly reduced income from their labor and escalating intrahousehold conflicts. As before the crisis, boats and people are reproduced from a common budget derived from household commodity production: both eat off the same table, so to speak. What the cost/price squeeze did was shift the distribution of that revenue so that now the boat eats first from the family table, whereas formerly the boat's smaller reproductive requirements left a much larger consumption fund from which household labor was reproduced. Those Louisiana shrimpers who kept their boats going through the 2000s did so at the expense of underinvestment in the short- and long-term reproduction of labor power, jeopardizing the viability of household commodity production.

(UNDER)REPRODUCING LABOR POWER

The women who didn't work before, they've *had* to go back to work. It's mental stress on the women because they're trying to keep their family together, they're the ones who have to pay the bills, they see the economic problems maybe before their husbands see it coming. . . . The wives and the kids, it's been more a lifestyle change than it has anything else. Whether it's having to go back to work or having to serve beans more often or going out to eat less. . . . My husband and I have always worked as a team, but a lot of wives have had to work on boats for free instead of deckhands that never did that before. Last year this happened to a lot of people. (Interview, Louisiana shrimper's wife, 2004)

Household labor among Louisiana shrimping families was greatly restructured in the 2000s. Reproductive unpaid housework, generally done by women, was financially disinvested in to keep boats running while labor time formerly devoted to reproduction was pushed into unwaged work on shrimp boats and waged work onshore. Unwaged work on boats, primarily done by husbands and male relatives, became much less remunerative as margins fell. Shrimpers intensified the self-exploitation of household labor at sea by replacing paid deckhands with unpaid family members. Large offshore shrimping vessels, who often shrimp for weeks at a time with several deckhands, kept their hired crew; but the operators of many mid-sized and inshore boats who work shorter trips for less of the year found it feasible to either work alone or replace hired deckhands with unpaid family members, usually wives, children, or siblings, after 2000. About one-third of interviewees in 2004 reported wives working as unpaid deckhands, with about one-half of those starting after 2001.

Waged labor, often that of wives, in the onshore economy was also crucial to many Louisiana shrimping families' economic survival. Slightly more than half of interviewed shrimp fishermen and shrimpers' wives worked an onshore job in 2004, the rate of working women doubling since 2001. Families with a full-time working woman experienced smaller declines in real income after 2001 than families without onshore incomes or with only part-time, low-paid contributions. Jobs in the offshore oil field drew many fishermen and their sons out of shrimping permanently in the 2000s; unlike women's shore jobs, men's full-time oil field employment was incompatible with shrimping and was much better compensated. All these dislocations in social reproduction translated into greater intrahousehold stress and conflict, especially between husbands and wives. One shrimper's wife explained, "My husband wants to know where the money goes, but I need to be trusted. I'm not stealing from you. If you're not getting any money, you don't have any. He's very stressed, I told him he's getting paranoid and obsessed about money. He don't trust his deckhand" (Interview, 2004).

Intergenerational succession in the Louisiana shrimp fishery largely stopped in the 2000s. The majority of shrimpers interviewed in 2004 and 2011 were over fifty years old, very few younger than thirty. The aging shrimpers who remained in the fishery did so as much from a lack of education and employment alternatives as active interest in shrimping as a career. While in prior generations young people's entry to the sector was supported by relatives, the scouring of household reproduction by the crisis left few family resources remaining to foster generational succession. Shrimpers' children, observing their parents' economic condition, actively fled the sector for other occupations. Those young people who still wavered were strongly advised to not follow their parents' example. One fisherman quipped, "If I had a son who wanted to shrimp, I'd slap him behind the head."

Crises in the Mekong Delta

> SHRIMP FARMER: A long time ago, this was a freshwater area. We had
> lots of fruit trees here—bananas, coconuts, everything really. There
> was a lot of production. There were field fish back then, turtles, big
> pythons, but we don't have those anymore. They had dikes and sluice
> gates up against the river to protect against the salinity. But that's no
> more since the saltwater's come in.
> INTERVIEWER: Is there an alternative, could people do something else
> given the present situation?
> SHRIMP FARMER: (Laughing) Well, since almost nobody's making any
> money with shrimp, we could go back to rice! But there's no way to
> do that, we're stuck for good! We'd have to spend twenty years to get
> the salt out of the land, so we can't . . . . Anyhow, people were poorer
> when this was a freshwater area. In the past, the people who lived
> in the saltwater section of the district could get rich, and those who
> lived in the freshwater area were poorer—they didn't earn much
> because the price of rice was so low, much lower than shrimp. (Interview, local government official and shrimp farmer, 2008)

The crises of household commodity production among Louisiana shrimp fishermen and Mekong delta shrimp farmers derive from the same international commodity price trends. Both were experienced as crises of social reproduction, but the circuits the crisis was expressed through differed. In the coastal Mekong, the crisis manifested as an inability to reproduce environmental conditions of production supporting stable household incomes.

Devoted for decades to commodity agriculture supplying national and export markets and suffering from acid-sulfate soils, widespread destruction of coastal forests, and a lack of quality freshwater behind the salinity barriers thrown up after 1975, the coastal Mekong delta's landscape before the shrimp boom was hardly pristine, nor was it subsistence oriented. Nevertheless, the conversion from rice to shrimp farming in the early 2000s represented a major transition in those already greatly humanized and commodified conditions. Water control structures were largely abandoned, and saline water flowed freely where it had been essentially excluded for two decades. Plant and animal life died and was replaced by salt-tolerant species. Rice, coconut palms, freshwater fish, ducks, chickens, and other crops largely disappeared within a few months or years of the conversion, with only backyard kitchen gardens remaining in a landscape now devoted almost exclusively to cash-crop export production.

For all these changes, in livelihood terms the conversion to shrimp aquaculture was largely positive, especially in the early 2000s when shrimp prices remained relatively high relative to the very low prices farmers were getting for rice in the late 1990s. A Mekong delta shrimp farmer observed: "The environment has changed. Before [the conversion to shrimp], there was lots more vegetation, now there's only a few crops, it's more desolate. In terms of living, before when I was farming we spent less money but now life is better, we have a good income" (Interview, 2008).

The conversion to shrimp, by increasing household incomes, supported coastal Mekong delta producers' social reproduction even as it profoundly changed the environmental conditions of production in a way that effectively locked them into shrimp culture. Another ambiguity of the shrimp boom was the unstable reproduction of the shrimp themselves and the pond environments they lived in. Vietnamese shrimp producers suffered high mortalities in their ponds from high loads of bacterial and viral pathogens in the water and the shrimp larvae they stocked into their ponds, water and soil chemistry problems, and limited ability to treat those issues through veterinary inputs and chemical treatments to their ponds. Mostly, farmers facing disease problems simply emergency-harvested their ponds before all the shrimp died. As one farmer said, "If you can't fix 'em, catch 'em."

The low shrimp yields and frequent crop failures of many shrimp farmers were predictable, given the limited capitalization of Vietnamese household producers; their ponds' insufficient water supply and drainage, rapidly reengineered from an irrigation system designed for freshwater agriculture; and farmers' lack of experiential knowledge of this new and demanding production system. Yet this mattered little to producers at the peak of shrimp prices in the early 2000s. When the shrimp boom was transforming the face of the coastal Mekong delta in 2000–1, one kilogram of shrimp bought more than 100 kilograms of rice so that even with low yields and the obliteration of most other production possibilities, shrimp brought a much higher household income. Consequently, few producers were concerned if the soil in their fields was quickly becoming so salinized from shrimp production that rice could no longer grow if they wanted to plant it.

Rice and shrimp did manage to coexist in some districts of the coastal Mekong delta in the 2000s. Rice-shrimp rotational culture, with roughly half the year devoted to one harvest of each crop, became established in a few districts of the coastal delta after 2001, whereas shrimp monoculture became the norm in the rest. One farmer explains his process of transitioning from rice to shrimp as the rainy season ends around the Lunar New Year:

> In January I dry out the land, pull up the rice stubble, bring in water a bunch of times to wash out the acidity, and I landscape the ground. Then I spread lime to kill any pathogens. I use a net to catch any random fish that got into the pond, then I treat the water once more. After 15–20 days, I buy the shrimp larvae and stock them. I check the pH and feed the shrimp. If some change occurs in the water then I treat it with agricultural lime. After four or five months, I harvest. (Interview, rice-shrimp farmer, 2008)

Where rice-shrimp was ecologically and institutionally feasible—due to prior investments in water infrastructure to support both crops, greater farmer experience with transitioning between hydrological regimes twice a year, and better access to abundant freshwater—it did not necessarily flourish. The reason was shifting market prices. When shrimp was expensive and rice cheap, farmers technically able to grow both rice and shrimp abandoned rice and tried to grow shrimp throughout the year. As price ratios reversed in the late 2000s, the acreage of rice-shrimp surged correspondingly: in one district the area of rice-shrimp doubled or shrank by half in a single year several times, largely driven by price trends. In those coastal districts where environmental conditions no longer supported rice cropping at any point in the year, cropping systems were much more stable throughout the decade, but this environmental stability presaged greater livelihood vulnerability as commodity prices and margins turned downward and producers found themselves unable to shift production away from shrimp.

THE COST/PRICE SQUEEZE OF THE LATE 2000S

> The farmers hope input prices will fall and more importantly the selling price of shrimp's got to increase. If shrimp prices were high then high input prices would be no problem, but now it's a problem. This year, it just won't do. (Interview, Vietnamese shrimp farmer, 2008)

In 2007–8, the production economics of shrimp in the coastal Mekong delta went into deeper crisis. Input costs, after rising steadily for years, spiked even higher.

Fuel and shrimp feed prices went up, and fertilizer prices doubled between late 2007 and mid-2008. Simultaneously, the bottom fell out of the shrimp market, prices declining to less than half the heights seen in 2000–1. Rice prices doubled in 2007–8, making the rice-shrimp price ratio, once over 100-to-1, now just 20-to-1 or less. These pressures cut deeply into the margins farmers realized on growing shrimp and made rice, the crop most abandoned years before, attractive again. Farmers responded to the crisis primarily through the extensification of shrimp production, cutting down their use of inputs and stocking density. One rice-shrimp farmer said about the price situation in late 2008, "It's affected me. For example, following the procedures correctly you have to use 500 kilos of lime per hectare to prepare your pond. But these days, I've reduced it to 200–300 kilos to economize on costs."

In those few places in the coastal delta where rice crops could still be grown successfully, rice-shrimp farming saw a dramatic resurgence in 2007–8. These producers were able to (partially) mitigate the production crisis, but in most of the coastal Mekong delta this change was impossible due to salinization. In those places, going back to rice would mean years of rehabilitating the land to flush out accumulated salinity and reconstructing the salinity control infrastructure, and for all that, there was no promise that commodity prices might not reverse just as quickly again. Thus, farmers were essentially stuck with shrimp despite its delivering a fraction of the income they expected because the environmental conditions of production that they helped to change so radically, motivated by very different economic conditions, now gave them few alternatives.

Mekong delta shrimp farmers suffered a shortfall of income, and corresponding strains in the reproduction of family labor power, in 2007–8. The lack of alternative cropping options made it harder for farmers to regain that income from other forms of agricultural production, and the salinization of the environment caused subsistence resources to largely disappear years before. As the rural delta has few off-farm employment options and already had high underemployment, most shrimp farming families tightened their belts and rode out the crisis in place, reducing their investments in production and reproduction alike to survive. Farmers interviewed in 2008 considered the conversion to shrimp, overall, to have improved their family income, but they worried more about their ability to sustain that standard of living into the future.

Conclusion

As shrimp producers on both sides of the Pacific struggled through the deepening cost/price crisis of the 2000s, the Mississippi and Mekong deltas came into political conflict when U.S. shrimpers sought trade tariffs against Vietnamese shrimp imports.[2] Opining on the case, the *Wall Street Journal* argued, "Vietnamese peasants get jobs; American teenagers munch their products as they goggle at TV: This is globalization. As always with globalization, someone has a grievance. Traditional American shrimpers are hurting, because cultivated shrimp are driving down prices. It's hard to blame 'unfair' behavior by the Thais or Vietnamese, who are simply more efficient" (King 2004).

Such teleological, binary oppositions ignore the parallels between Louisiana and Mekong delta shrimp producers, parallels that suggest the problem is not Americans against Vietnamese or tradition against globalization but a shared crisis of family producers in a global market increasingly disconnected from those producers' social reproduction. The principal analytical difference between Louisiana and Mekong delta producers is not geography or efficiency, but which circuits of reproduction their common economic crisis manifests through. The crisis of household commodity production did not cause as dramatic a shift in livelihoods for Mekong delta producers as it did in Louisiana, but the persistence of Vietnamese producers' engagement with shrimp is an expression of the same reproductive crisis as Louisianians' abandonment of shrimping. Where the inability of Louisiana shrimpers to reproduce their boats and themselves threw more and more of them out of the industry, Mekong delta shrimp producers find themselves unable to cease reproducing environmental conditions of production that exclude every productive possibility but shrimp aquaculture. This understanding of Mississippi and Mekong delta shrimpers' plight helps counter the equally futile options of protectionist nationalism and free trade we are offered with a contextualized, materially nuanced "shrimpers of the world, unite!"

What does it mean to consider the "greasy, grimy" and "soggy, scaly" aspects of SRP, to connect social reproduction to the materiality of nonhumans? For one, it underpins the argument that SRP encompasses multiple interconnected circuits of material social practices. The specific materiality of those circuits matters—they may, in assembly, enact or undermine the reproduction of their constituent parts, but boats are not shrimp who, in turn, are not people. Further, no materiality asserts itself outside its historical/geographical context: social reproductive crisis might manifest elsewhere, or not at all, with a different mix of price signals, producer decisions, and material forces acting on those producers' land, water, and equipment. Taking account of the multiple material circuits of SRP can help us see the imprint of capitalist globalization in crisis, a crisis disguising and displacing itself firstly as an environmental and productive crisis that, in its differing material manifestations, expresses a common social reproductive crisis from which linked, but materially specific, translocal responses may be formulated.

NOTES

1. This research was funded through a Pre-Dissertation Grant from the Social and Behavioral Sciences Research Institute at the University of Arizona, a Fulbright-Hays Doctoral Dissertation Research Abroad grant, and Bureau of Ocean Energy Management, Regulation and Enforcement Cooperative Agreement M10AC20003. Interviews were conducted by the author in person in 2004, 2008, and 2011–13. I thank the many people in Louisiana and the Mekong delta who shared their time and information with me. *Xin cảm ơn các bạn and merci tout le monde.*

2. U.S. antidumping tariffs were imposed on Vietnam and five other countries in 2005.

REFERENCES

Be, Tran Thanh, and Le Dung. "Economic and Environmental Impacts of Rice-Shrimp Farming Systems in the Mekong Delta." In *Economy and Environment in Vietnam: Case Studies*, edited by Herminia Francisco and David Glover, 221–251. Singapore: International Development Research Centre, 1999.

Bakker, Isabella, and Stephen Gill, eds. *Power, Production and Social Reproduction: Human In/security in the Global Economy.* New York: Palgrave Macmillan, 2003.

Bezanson, Kate. *Gender, the State, and Social Reproduction: Household Insecurities in Neo-Liberal Times.* Toronto: University of Toronto Press, 2006.

Binh, Thanh, Nico Vromant, Nguyen Thanh Hung, Luc Hens, and E. K. Boon. "Land Cover Changes between 1968 and 2003 in Cai Nuoc, Ca Mau Peninsula, Vietnam." *Environment, Development and Sustainability* 7 (2005): 519–536.

Chayanov, Alexander. *The Theory of Peasant Co-operatives.* Columbus: Ohio State University Press, 1991.

Deseran, Forrest. *Louisiana Shrimp Fishermen and Local Economies: A Survey.* Baton Rouge: Louisiana Sea Grant, 1997.

Friedmann, Harriet. "Simple Commodity Production and Wage Labor in the American Plains." *Journal of Peasant Studies* 6, no. 1 (1978): 71–100.

———. "Household Production and the Natural Economy." *Journal of Peasant Studies* 7, no. 2 (1980): 158–184.

Gasson, Ruth, and Andrew Errington. *The Farm Family Business.* Wallingford, U.K.: CAB International, 1993.

Gillett, R. *Global Study of Shrimp Fisheries. FAO Fisheries Technical Paper 475.* Rome: FAO, 2008.

Goodman, David, and Michael Redclift. "Capitalism, Petty Commodity Production and the Farm Enterprise." *Sociologia Ruralis* 25 (1985): 231–247.

Hoanh, C., T. Tuong, K. Gallop, J. Gowing, S. Kam, N. Khiem, and N. Phong. "Livelihood Impacts of Water Policy Changes: Evidence from a Coastal Area of the Mekong River Delta." *Water Policy* 5 (2003) : 475–488.

Jory, Darryl, and Tomas Cabrera. "Marine Shrimp." In *Aquaculture: Farming Aquatic Animals and Plants*, edited by John Lucas and Paul Southgate, 382–419. Oxford: Blackwell, 2003.

Katz, Cindi. "Vagabond Capitalism and the Necessity of Social Reproduction." *Antipode* 33, no. 4 (2001): 708–727.

———. *Growing Up Global: Economic Restructuring and Children's Everyday Lives.* Minneapolis: University of Minnesota Press, 2004.

Keithly, Walter, and Pawan Poudel. "The Southeast U.S.A. Shrimp Industry: Issues Related to Trade and Antidumping Duties." *Marine Resource Economics* 23 (2008): 459–483.

King, Neil. "Catch of the Day: Battle over Shrimp." *Wall Street Journal*, June 11, 2004.

Lafleur, Elizabeth, Diane Yeates, and Angelina Aysen. "Estimating the Economic Impact of the Wild Shrimp, *Penaeus* sp., Fishery: A Study of Terrebonne Parish, Louisiana." *Marine Fishery Review* 67, no. 1 (2005): 28–42.

LDWF (Louisiana Department of Wildlife and Fisheries), *Commercial License Sales by Parish/State, License Year 2010*, http://www.wlf.louisiana.gov/licenses/statistics. (Accessed June 8, 2011).

Lebel, Louis, Phimphakan Lebel, Po Garden, Dao Huy Giap, Supaporn Khrutmuang, and Sachiko Nakayama. "Places, Chains, and Plates: Governing Transitions in the Shrimp Aquaculture Production–Consumption System." *Globalizations* 5, no. 2 (2008): 211–226.

Liese, Christopher, and Michael Travis. *The Annual Economic Survey of Federal Gulf Shrimp Permit Holders: Report on the Design, Implementation, and Descriptive Results for 2008.* Miami: Southeast Fisheries Science Center, 2010.

Liese, Christopher, Michael Travis, Diana Pina, and James Waters. *The Annual Economic Survey of Federal Gulf Shrimp Permit Holders: Report on the Design, Implementation, and Descriptive Results for 2006.* Miami, Fla.: Southeast Fisheries Science Center, 2009.

Marks, Brian. "Effects of Economic Restructuring on Household Commodity Production in the Louisiana Shrimp Fishery." Unpublished master's thesis, Department of Geography and Regional Development, University of Arizona, 2005.

———. "Small Fry in a Big Ocean. Change, Resilience, and Crisis in the Shrimp Industry of the Mekong Delta of Viet Nam." Unpublished PhD dissertation, School of Geography and Development, University of Arizona, 2010.

———. "The Political Economy of Household Commodity Production in the Louisiana Shrimp Fishery." *Journal of Agrarian Change* 12, nos. 2–3 (2012) : 227–251.

Marx, Karl. *Capital.* 3 vols. Edited by Frederick Engels. New York: International Publishers, 1967.

Miller, Alexander, and Jack Isaacs. *An Economic Survey of the Gulf of Mexico Inshore Shrimp Fishery: Implementation and Descriptive Results for 2008.* GSMFC Publication 195. Ocean Springs, Miss.: Gulf Coast Marine Fisheries Commission, 2011.

Ministry of Agriculture and Rural Development. *Results of the 2006 Rural, Agricultural and Fishery Census.* Hà Nội: Statistical Publishing House, 2006.

Nhuong, Tran Van, Connor Bailey, and Norbert Wilson. "Governance of Global Value Chains Impacts Shrimp Producers In Vietnam." *Global Aquaculture Advocate* November/December (2011) : 44–46.

Nhuong, Tran Van, Dinh Van Thanh, Bui Thi Thu Ha, Trinh Quang Tu, Le Van Khoi, and Tuong Phi Lai. "The Shrimp Industry in Vietnam: Status, Opportunities and Challenges." In *Shrimp Farming and Industry: Sustainability, Trade and Livelihoods*, edited by A. Atiq Rahman, AHG Quddus, Bob Pokrant, and Liaquat Ali. Dhaka, Bangladesh: BCAS and University Press Limited, 2006.

NMFS (National Marine Fisheries Service). *Fisheries of the United States, 2003*. Silver Spring, Maryland: National Oceanic and Atmospheric Administration, 2004.

NOAA Fisheries. *Annual Commercial Landing Statistics*, 2009, http://www.st.nmfs.noaa .gov/st1/commercial/landings/annual_landings.html. (Accessed June 8, 2011).

Robbins, Paul. *Political Ecology: A Critical Introduction*. Malden, Mass.: Wiley-Blackwell, 2012.

Salamon, Sonya. *Prairie Patrimony: Family, Farming, and Community in the Midwest*. Chapel Hill: University of North Carolina Press, 1992.

SEAT (Sustaining Ethical Aquaculture Trade). *Sustaining the Shrimp Value Chain in Vietnam*. Can Tho City, Vietnam: SEAT, 2009, http://seatglobal.eu/wp-content/uploads/ 2009/12/Vietnam-shrimp-english.pdf.

Sinh, Le Xuan, and Nguyen Phuong. *Value Chain Study of Shrimp Industry in Tra Vinh Province. Report for the Tra Vinh Improved Livelihoods Project of Canadian International Development Agency*. Colleges of Agriculture and Fisheries, Can Tho University, Vietnam, 2006.

Tho, Nguyen, Nico Vromant, Nguyen Hung, and Luc Hens. "Soil Salinity and Sodicity in a Shrimp Farming Coastal Area of the Mekong Delta, Vietnam." *Environmental Geology* 54 (2008): 1739–1746.

USDA Foreign Agricultural Service. *Vietnam Grain and Feed (Monthly) Rice Updates*. USDA. 1998–2008.

U.S. EIA (Energy Information Agency). *Short-Term Outlook—Real and Nominal Prices*, 2011, http://www.eia.gov/emeu/steo/realprices/index.cfm. (Accessed June 4, 2011).

Valderrama, Diego, and James Anderson. *Shrimp Production Review*. St. Louis: Global Aquaculture Alliance, 2011. www.gaalliance.org/update/GOAL11/DiegoValderrama.pdf.

Watts, Michael. "Hazards and Crisis: A Political Economy of Drought and Famine in Northern Nigeria." *Antipode* 15, no. 1 (1983): 24–34.

Whatmore, Sarah. *Farming Women: Gender, Work and Family Enterprise*. Basingstoke, U.K.: Macmillan, 1991.

CONCLUSION

Demanding Life's Work

CINDI KATZ, SALLIE A. MARSTON,
AND KATHARYNE MITCHELL

Life's work continues as we care for others and ourselves in hard times, as twenty-first-century economic, political, and environmental conditions continue to erode the stability and security of everyday life. Witness: the severe rollbacks of social welfare programs in Harper's conservative Canada (Bezanson, this volume); recent rollouts of increased state surveillance in the spaces of work, play, and love (Clark, this volume; Smith and Winders, this volume); the gritty material conditions of household trash collection (Fredericks, this volume) and shrimp production (Marks, this volume) as formal labor schemes take greater bites out of household time; or the differentiated impacts of the global economic recession for gendered and racialized bodies (Gorman-Murray, this volume; Parker, this volume), to name a few scenarios. Social reproduction, and its new frontiers of research and activism, matters more than ever. And yet, as Meehan and Strauss (this volume) have pointed out, the codependence but simultaneous distinctiveness of social reproduction and production is still not widely appreciated or adequately understood.

Consider this moment from a very well-attended session of the Association of American Geographers (AAG) national meeting in Seattle in 2011. At the podium is a renowned Marxist economic geographer reporting on Chinese industrial labor practices. At the end of his engaging presentation, one of us raises our hand and asks, "Could you tell us how social reproduction both affects and has been affected by these different forms of production?" The presenter flatly responds: "Social reproduction is production." When pushed further to acknowledge or at least speculate about the potential relevance of how labor is produced and sustained to the Chinese manufacturing case, the presenter just rephrases his previous response: "Reproduction is simply production; and yet, production is more fundamental than reproduction." This interchange is symptomatic of the willful inattention to social reproduction by critical political economy and masculinist Marxists.

For those interested in how labor is produced—how workers are able to present themselves at their sites of work—the subsuming (and therefore obscuring) of reproduction within production is problematic, both theoretically and politically. Such misrecognition prevents us from accessing the complex ways social reproduction is a *prior* condition for capitalist production—both historically, as Federici (2004) makes very clear, but also practically, as the chapters in this volume attest. As Joel Wainwright suggested in an e-mail correspondence about the AAG session mentioned above (co-organized with Geoff Mann), the eliding of social reproduction with production, or its relegation as a less fundamental concept or process than capitalist production, erases at worst and minimizes at best its central relevance to social, economic, and political life: "Social reproduction involves more than just producing living-labor that is capable of being sold. . . . [It] both is and is not the same as relations of production. More precisely: social reproduction is a necessary condition of capitalist production, *but something which exceeds it* and in ways that matter politically" (Wainwright 2013, italics added).

Because of persistent masculinist dismissals, occlusions, or possibly simple misunderstandings of the theoretical and practical relevance of social reproduction (see Katz 1996; Gibson-Graham 2006), we applaud this volume and the work it does to extend our understandings. As the pieces gathered here illuminate, social reproduction is a routine part of all lives, whether as non-capitalocentric practice, capitalist practice, or some combination of both. Simply put: there can be no production without social reproduction, as Marx parsimoniously expressed. In what follows, the three of us reflect briefly on our own work in the realm of social reproduction and how our ideas and foci have unfolded since the publication of *Life's Work*, first as a special issue of *Antipode* in 2003 and later as an edited book published by Blackwell in 2004.

Art, Learning, and Life's Work

SALLIE A. MARSTON

Politics has been central to my continuing intellectual commitment to social reproduction. This interest is refracted in the emergence and amplification of much exciting scholarship that, since the late 1980s, identifies the increasing relevance of social reproduction to production and to the politics of everyday life. Autonomist Marxists including Leopoldina Fortunati (1989), George Caffentzis (2002), and Silvia Federici (2004), as well as anarchist geographers (for an overview see the special issue of *Antipode* on anarchist geographies, November 2012), have in their own ways demonstrated not only how bodies are nourished and enabled to undertake labor through the complex practices of social reproduction but also the opportunities that reproduction provides for building alternative, noncapitalist practices that are personally dignified, premised on ethical commitments around mutual aid, and ultimately socially just.

Since the publication of *Life's Work*, I have been increasingly interested in pursuing two fundamental theoretical questions in collaboration with Keith Woodward and J. P. Jones: What is the world? How does the world work? Of course, these are huge theoretical questions, but I have been mostly concerned with how best to address them empirically. To answer these questions it seems critical to grasp how material life is arranged and how the elements of its organization—objects, bodies, doings, and sayings—coalesce in sites to produce persistence and rupture, connection and isolation, and hope and despair, especially with respect to political projects (Marston, Jones, and Woodward 2005; Woodward, Jones, and Marston 2010). In these investigations, our objective has been not to find truths or systems or causes, but instead to grasp a world composed of a multiplicity of forces and trajectories with the potential for differentiation; that is, to comprehend difference as a fundamental condition of the world and politics as an immanent process of the coming together of humans and nonhumans (Woodward, Marston, and Jones 2012).

In concert with numerous collaborators and on a variety of projects, I have looked at what is called "social reproduction" in the Marxist lexicon. I have mostly avoided using the category a priori in an effort to enable the complexity and possibilities of sites and situations to reveal themselves. The aim in so doing is to keep the unique intricacies of material practice from being obscured or held hostage by an embattled concept like social reproduction (Woodward, Jones, and Marston 2010). In my work with Woodward and Jones, our empirical question has been: What forces, trajectories, and connectivities are bound up in contemporary doings around livelihood and what is their potential for political effect? As well: How do the subjects caught up in these forces understand and articulate what is happening in their worlds?

One project that takes up this question involves artists, scientists, and community members working together to address the remediation of a polluted watercourse running through a poor neighborhood.[1] There, a New York City artist and environmental activist collaborated with an engineer, a scientist, urban planners, a local business, and a youth organization to produce a piece of "maintenance art" that cleans polluted stormwater runoff before it enters the Bronx River. The resulting work, called "WaterWash" (Ball n.d.), demonstrates that caring for the earth and engaging others in its care leads to learning and collective knowledge production that can foster environmental recuperation and social change. The participatory framework around which this collaboration is organized also engages nonhuman others: in the form of native and nonnative plants, some of which filter and cleanse water; others that attract birds and animals; and still others that promote the production of detoxifying microbes, all working together in the task of remediation. In the artwork, particular categories of expertise are both engaged and challenged, and alternative categories emerge as salient and critical to its success both aesthetically and politically (Ingram 2012). As well, the tranquility of the site enlists noncentrally involved passersby as they move along the sidewalk of a busy expressway by offering a quiet place for recovery and restoration. WaterWash links care for the environment to a politics of collaboration and mutual aid where constituencies not routinely engaged—for example a white, middle-class, middle-aged, university-educated female artist and African American and Latino youth, whose economic, educational, and social opportunities are severely limited—come together in a supportive and transformative way.

In analyzing WaterWash, Mrill Ingram (2013) situates the piece within a longer tradition of feminist environmental art aimed at making visible the means through which the quotidian work of enabling and maintaining life—both human and nonhuman—also enables production. As an art piece, WaterWash also reminds us of the role aesthetics plays in provoking certain sensibilities and eliciting responses for particular ends. The liveliness of the work and its oscillation between fantasy and ecology express how a capitalist politics of environmental exploitation and degradation, which results in toxic environments for poor people, can be challenged by a noncapitalist one that entrains young people into different ways of doing. WaterWash, as a site of aesthetic practice, environmental knowledge production, remediation, and community decision-making, provides an opportunity to think differently about the conceptual complexity of social reproduction and how its unfolding cannot be easily categorized or dismissed as implicitly secondary to production.

The second project is one I have engaged in with a faculty colleague and graduate and undergraduate student researchers. It explores the conjunction of teachers, schoolchildren, and university students in a collaborative relationship that supports caring for and learning from nonhuman living things while enhancing the potential for once-distant others to build sites of mutual aid and communal learning. The University of Arizona's (UA) Community and School Garden Program places graduate and undergraduate students in low-income schools in the Tucson Unified School District (TUSD) (Moore et al. 2012; Moore et al. 2015). Its aim is to promote collective action for social change, social and environmental justice, and a more sustainable world by training students to support the development, maintenance, and enhancement of school gardens. While school gardens have been understood to be deployed in the service of neoliberal educational reforms (Allen and Guthman 2006; Pudup 2008), our initial research suggests that to ignore the empowering effects of the gardens on the collective of individuals who make them happen would be to misunderstand the uniqueness of any site and the kinds of effects it produces (e.g., Hung 2004).

Of course, even before Althusser's (1971) critical work on ideologically driven capitalist structures—especially education—schools were also understood to be sites of radical potential (Freire 1970). In our work at eleven schools in the TUSD, we have found that gardens can operate in a meaningful way as a bulwark against the neoliberalization of educational curriculum premised on standardized testing. Gardens offer opportunities for engaged and experiential learning among young people of different ages where different kinds of knowledges converge and are mediated. For instance, while university students might bring abstract scientific understandings of plant function or soil composition to the collaboration, schoolchildren bring insights to in situ processes such as animal or insect behavior or sun/shade balances in the schoolyard, so critical to plant survival in the desert.

The collaborative maintenance of the gardens also provides a site for schoolchildren with difficult home situations to escape and partake of the benefits of alternative spaces, where their contributions are valued. Collaborating counselors and teachers attest to the fact that the daily care for nonhuman—chickens, plants, fish, worms, plants—living things by schoolchildren produces a knowledge base and a set of practices that support confidence, calm, and an existential sense of connectedness to others. We have observed that the garden—as a site for the nurturing of nonhuman living things—also promotes experience and relationships as key to learning and knowing, in contrast to the relentless competition that promotes the capitalist model of singular achievement. School gardens are too often dismissed as sites for play or auxiliary learning, but the close observation of them by the UA intern-researchers reveals those practices to have complex effects that create bonds among and between the participants—both human and nonhuman—that have profound effects. Is the school garden a site for the training of emerging neoliberal subjects? Perhaps, but it is certainly far more, as solidarity-building activities promote an ethic of care and commitment that sustains and transforms those subjects, offering them and creating alternative ways of being.

The coming together of humans and nonhumans in the form of school gardens and participatory art projects involves immanent processes that assemble bodies and objects around a dense field of practical routines and exceptional moments. In this complex web, a politics of social reproduction generates forms of cooperation and interaction premised on dignity and respect and positive knowledge-creation and exchange. This kind of social reproduction also lays a foundation for alternative, possibly noncapitalocentric, forms of production. And, although seemingly mundane and minor, these comings together constitute the worlds we make and the relations through which we live.

Precarious Time

KATHARYNE MITCHELL

Drawing on both scholarly readings and my own insights from life experiences, I have become more cognizant of the importance of time. More specifically, I've begun to consider the fragmentation of time, especially vis-à-vis the diminishing human capacity for deep attention, to be one of the most fundamental crises affecting industrial societies today. I think this crisis is connected to how we live and labor in just about every way imaginable, yet it is often set aside as a separate discussion more pertinent to media and technology studies, rather than to the larger question of social reproduction.

My theoretical and empirical orientation in this direction arose largely as a result of an activist research project I began with Sarah Elwood about five years ago. We conducted a Web-based mapping project with middle-school children to try to ascertain how spatial awareness of one's immediate surroundings might galvanize greater civic engagement (see Mitchell and Elwood 2012). There were a lot of interesting outcomes of this project, but two really helped me to reframe my thinking about social reproduction. The first was around the intertwined issues of education and collective memory, especially how ideas, understandings, and forms of care are transmitted (and also transformed) intergenerationally; the second was the role of technology in this process. It was these interests that led me to the philosophical work of Bernard Stiegler, and it was his work that galvanized my fascination with time, particularly in relation to technologies (or technics) in the contemporary period of consumer capitalism.

In essence, Stiegler (1998, 2010) argues that the accelerated development of new technologies in late capitalism is producing a profound crisis in which long-term desire and the capacity for deep attention are being lost. In their place we see increasingly short-term reactive drives and wants associated with consumerist society and technology speedup. While many theorists have warned of the multiple societal problems associated with "fast capitalism" (see Pred and Watts 1992), what Stiegler does that I find unique and important is to show how these processes are also associated with subjectivity formation. He makes the case that attentional knowledges such as techniques for the care of self and others—transmitted intergenerationally through educational processes (broadly conceptualized)— are being lost in the current era as a result of the increasing prevalence of consumption-oriented psychotechnologies (computers, games, SMS, etc.). These types of technologies impair the capacity for deep attention and the ability to maintain relationships across time, short-circuiting the links between generations and profoundly damaging the ways in which subjects are constituted intersubjectively.

There is a lot of interesting philosophical discussion in Stiegler about how the processes of subjectivity formation or "transindividuation" occur relationally, and how collective memory figures into this (Mitchell and Elwood 2013), but my main point here relates to the contemporary technological forces acting on subjectivity, or the formation of the contemporary *who*, which relates directly to *who* becoming what kind of labor. I think that this "who" is becoming radically transformed by new orientations to time, and that these transformations are both produced by and productive of the specific forms of contemporary market economies that envelop most folks living in industrialized societies.

Of course feminists have long been interested in identity and how different kinds of bodies and subjectivities are recruited in capitalist and noncapitalist activities in specific material processes and paths (see Hartmann 1979). As Meehan and Strauss have noted in the introduction, bodies are materially embedded in, and/or *excluded from*, spheres of production and social reproduction, and "enrolled in processes of value creation and accumulation in fast-changing and highly uneven ways." These insights remain vital and centrally pertinent to any analysis of value creation in the labor process. What I'm proposing here is another layer, which is that human bodies are also, *in addition*, being conscripted into a new relationship to time.

So, this focus on the changing constitution of the *who* has become, for me, *one of the most critical questions requiring our attention since the publication of* Life's Work *ten years ago.* And this, in turn, has led me to a renewed interest in the later work of Foucault and the many people studying questions of neoliberal governmentalities. Those working in this area have drawn largely on Foucault's lectures, compiled and translated in *The Birth of Biopolitics*, in which he outlines the twentieth-century expansion of market order and mechanisms of rule into more and more areas of social life (Foucault 2010). One of the key insights from this body of work has been the idea that in order to govern through the market, subjects must be formed as market actors. Thus, as Rose (2000) and others have noted, individuals and groups are recruited into advanced systems of calculation, competition, choice, and self-care that enable the enterprise society to function and expand.

Because of my interest in education, children, parents, and, more recently, philanthropy, I've been particularly attentive to how parents have been enrolled as these kinds of self-actualizing, choice-seeking subjects over the past decade or so. One of the trends that has most captured my attention in this area is the rise of parent activism around education, especially the demand for more choice and competition in public schools (primarily through the proliferation of charter schools). Manifold parent advocacy groups, such as Stand for Children and the League of Education Voters, have sprung up almost overnight to demand greater parental oversight and control over public schooling (McGuinn and Kelly 2012;

for a critical analysis see Fine and Karp 2012). While seemingly parent-initiated and -led, however, empirical work indicates that most of these supposedly "grass-roots" parent organizations are actually heavily seeded and fertilized through major grants from private philanthropies such as the Walton Family Foundation, the Broad Foundation, and the Bill and Melinda Gates Foundation (see Mitchell and Lizotte 2014). The same is true for much of the popular culture and other media reports on parents vying for more choice in schooling: the "visible" hand of venture philanthropy is very much in evidence.[2] In other words, these parents are being recruited via charity into new forms of choice-seeking, while simultaneously being formed as calculating subjects *responsibilized* vis-à-vis their own care and the care of their children.

These activist and *activated* parents are increasingly alienated from considerations of social care and collective material equality at the same time that new kinds of technologies are eroding broader social and educational links between the generations. Stiegler argues that intergenerational educational links, such as those between parents and children, are necessary for the formation of mature, responsible (not *responsibilized*) subjects, who learn the attentional knowledges necessary for the care of themselves and others, and who have the capacity for deep attention. But subjectivities are now being formed and emerging in which most parents and children—like most people more generally—are in a nearly constant state of distraction. As the editors have noted, "our worlds are increasingly on edge," and I would add, in advanced societies, this "edge" is our increasing inability to pay concentrated attention to anything. Distraction is the new ontology, and one of the last areas of the life world to be colonized is *attention*.

My research, reading, and everyday observations have indicated to me that the most critical questions that have arisen over the past decade are those related to subjectivity formation and, as the editors note, it thus remains imperative that we continue to explore a "feminist materialist politics grounded in the concept of social reproduction." But I have come to believe that we also need to investigate our changing relationship to time, focusing on the fundamental question of attention. We are in a critical moment in which the nexus of consumer capitalism and innovations in psychotechnologies are producing a social world wherein the capacity to learn and transmit systems of care and concern is being eroded. This current moment reflects a crisis in social reproduction with profound consequences for the future.

The Refuse of Social Reproduction

CINDI KATZ

The precariousness of life has become more palpable in the years since *Life's Work* appeared. I mean this in two senses: the affective insecurity spurred by the threat of terrorism; and the economic insecurity of living under the increasingly unequal and brutal conditions of globalized neoliberal capitalism. Both are made worse in times and spaces of economic and political crisis. At least in the United States, but I think more widely, the post–September 11 world and its strategically conjured threats have produced a widespread sense of affective insecurity. In this "insecurity state," Americans have acquiesced to increased policing and more and more invasive state surveillance, despite—or for some because of—its racialized nature (Sorkin 2008; see also Clark, this volume; Smith and Winders, this volume). Intertwined with the insecurities triggered by what I have called "banal terrorism" after Michael Billig's notion of "banal nationalism," the hardening of neoliberal capitalism and its associated disinvestments in the social wage have produced a sense of insecurity about the future that crosses class and locality (Billig 1995; Katz 2007). These two affective states of insecurity are linked, just as are the national security and neoliberal capitalist states. The practices of social reproduction are implicated in these altered states of being and have drawn my attention over the past decade. Part of my research has focused on the ties between home-based and homeland security. As security practices associated with social reproduction are amped up through evolving technologies such as nanny cams, Internet-monitoring software, online student management systems, ambulatory GPS tracking devices (sometimes known as "digital angels"), vehicle speed monitors, and electronic corrals enabled by cellular phone technologies, the household not only mirrors the state's practice and performance of security but simultaneously readies future subjects of the "insecurity state."

Spurred by these concerns, my work has addressed the ways insecurity about the political-economic, geopolitical, and political-ecological future has infiltrated domestic life and the arena of social reproduction but is addressed largely through "management" strategies rather than through political or social activism. Under the rubric of "childhood as spectacle," I have focused on the management of children's lives in some key sites of social reproduction, including the home, schools, public play environments, policing, and the legal system. My project frames the child as accumulation strategy, commodity, ornament, and waste, and approaches social reproduction through examining such cultural forms and practices as child protection and parental hypervigilance; school tracking and testing; play, recreation, and extracurricular activities; diagnosing and medicating children; and college admissions. My argument is that the specter of waste—of one's own child becoming waste, of time wasted, of resources squandered—haunts the everyday practices of social reproduction in insecure times and spaces, leading to the often bemoaned, but every day becoming more common, phenomena of overscheduling, child surveillance, "parental involution," and "hothouse" children.

The connection to waste—and my invocation of the child as waste—is meant to signal the profound class politics and uneven geographies of the altered practices of and investments in social reproduction. By looking at the middle-class experience of ontological insecurity in some of my recent work, my intent is both to take stock of the ways anxiety about the future has crept into the pores of the contemporary social formation even in its more privileged sites and to show how their responses affect those whose existence is historically more precarious (Katz 2012). The fraught nature of what we might think of as "social childhood" gets at the nub of this relationship. Prior to the rise of neoliberal regimes of governance, childhood was more of a matter of shared and public concern, a social investment understood to be essential to producing a differentiated labor force, common values, and with them a productive if not completely harmonious collective future. Free public schooling was the cornerstone to this part of the social wage, but so too were social housing, social welfare, free or low-cost health care, and the like. In recent years this sense of social childhood—as limited in its realization as it was in the United States—has been utterly degraded so that it has come to mean "other people's children." As the future is conjured increasingly as a zero-sum game in which the success of others can be a weight upon one's own child's advantage and advancement, "other people's children," whether close in or strangers, are seen not so much as key to a thriving collective future in which "we" all have a stake but as a threat.

The aspirations of those coming of age under these circumstances are managed through a congeries of intimate and institutional frameworks, and those who are marginalized or extruded from the promises of a productive future must be managed in other ways (see Davidson 2011; Katz 2011). The material social forms and practices of containing and managing people "excessed" from the prospects of steady work, and with it the likelihood of a viable future, include the military as well as juvenile detention and incarceration facilities, arenas of social reproduction that have not suffered the same sorts of disinvestments as those I've been detailing. This is to say nothing of other forms of structural violence or debt peonage that can waste the lives of these young people. In charting this uneven and divisive terrain of social reproduction and its failures, I am—like many of the contributors to this volume—trying to understand the effects of neoliberal capitalism in registers often disregarded by political economists despite the ways they open spaces for political organizing and action.

In addition to clarifying these concerns with security and securing the future, social reproduction has also proven to be a powerful lens for looking at crisis—political-ecological as much as political-economic—and assessing its sprawling toll in a more nuanced way. In the wake of Hurricane Katrina, for instance, I looked at the ways decades of racialized and gendered disinvestments in social reproduction created a political economic and physical landscape in New Orleans more readily devastated by the storm than would have been the case if the state's commitments to maintaining infrastructure and the social wage had not been so eroded by neoliberalism and the effects of "hostile privatism" (Lipsitz 2006). But worse was that the aftermath of the storm revealed a city, state, and federal government intent on deepening the gouges of racialized hostile privatism concentrated on issues of social reproduction, destroying much of the extant public housing and failing to compensate many renters for their losses, decimating the teachers' union and shrinking the public school system, shuttering the venerable Charity Hospital, and leaving the legal system in disarray. At times the response was so callous that it seemed intended to provoke a demographic shift in the city and the wholesale demographic collapse of poor black neighborhoods (Woods 2005; Katz 2008). Working on "the scoured landscape of social reproduction" in New Orleans, and parsing social reproduction into environmental infrastructure, health care, education, housing, and social justice, has led me to look at other cities with similar catastrophic disinvestments in these elements of social reproduction, notably Detroit and the Bronx in New York City. In each of these cities the attention to nature and the environment has been a marked aspect of their ongoing revitalization, and suggests a reshaping of the contours of public investment in urban social reproduction from social concerns to those of political ecology.

While this tendency to privilege the environmental and infrastructural over and against the social wage raises concern because it reveals how cities are being remade by and for more privileged constituencies, it does at least shine light on the production of nature as part of social reproduction, which I see as a critical question for future work. When Marx and others talk about reproducing the means of production, that necessarily includes the environmental conditions of and resources for production. Yet there has been a symptomatic silence about social reproduction in most writing on the environment and likewise about the environment in work on social reproduction—even when it's concerned with reproducing the means of production. It has long been my argument that the production of nature happens in the course of everyday life and through the material social practices of social reproduction, and that attending to environmental concerns in this fashion—as many environmental justice activists and artists do—is a way of bringing together social and environmental or political-economic and political-ecological concerns with the possibility of making them new (see Loftus 2012; Ingram 2013). Sometimes I think if I had said "sensuous labor" rather than "fleshy, messy" in one of my early definitions of social reproduction, some of the more narrow-gauge Marxists might have snapped to, and been more attentive to, social reproduction in all its fullness. For Marx "unceasing sensuous labour and creation . . . is the basis of the whole sensuous world as it now exists" (Marx and Engels 1970, 35). It is that sensuous engagement with the material world—labor and pleasure as critical practices—that simultaneously makes the world and consciousness of it and the self as being in the world. These metabolic practices through which the material world—global and intimate—is made and remade, and the laboring subject transformed, cannot be thought apart from the sensuous labor of social reproduction.

Conclusion

Social reproduction is at the heart—in every sense of the term—of the creation of surplus value and capitalist accumulation. Yet for all too many Marxists it remains a backwater for analytic consideration, as the conference exchange with which we opened can attest. Its association with the messy and fleshy aspects of things and practices is part of the problem, as is the centrality of women and people of color in many of these material social practices. Too many Marxists still like to keep their class lines clean.

But it is through the everyday practices of social reproduction—life's work— that a social formation as much as its laboring bodies and the conditions of production are made and remade, and where the toll of neoliberal governance and various forms of oppression and dispossession is experienced in visceral ways. It is these conjunctures that give life's work its political power and potential. Its practices are *critical* in the Lefebvrian sense—the chance for rupture, and with it the possibility that they could be done differently, that things, social conditions, and relationships could be otherwise is immanent to them.

These political practices are social and material, but the lack of obvious, easily accessible, centralizable locations of these practices poses a problem for collective organizing. Since social reproduction is everywhere, it is also nowhere in particular, and that seems to be a political challenge many theorists prefer to avoid. Yet in recent years, especially with the exhilarating rise of the "occupy" movements, the centrality of social reproduction to contemporary organizing has become clear, even as many of the issues it raises have been colonized by the language of "right to the city," which sounds and must feel to its adherents to be less messy and fleshy. But if "occupy" and similar movements are going to be more than flashes in the pan, more than the occupation of a delimited space by an activated community, they are going to have to develop and work out a vision for what kinds of cities and other occupied spaces anyone and everyone would want "rights" to. That sort of political project involves organizing new horizons of political action and the creation of new geographical imaginations rooted deeply in the everyday practices of social reproduction. These are the matters and matter of life's work.

NOTES

1. The project has also explored the art-science collaborative projects called "Slow Cleanup" involving artist Francis Whitehead. See Francis Whitehead, "New Landscape Paradigms for Post Carbon Cities," *Make Art With Purpose* (2011), http://www .makeartwithpurpose.net/projects.php?id=15. Another involving artist Jackie Brookner, called the "Fargo Project," can be seen on youtube. Tedx, "The Fargo Project: Jackie Brookner at TEDxFargo," last updated December 24, 2012, http://www.youtube.com/ watch?v=yplULLsVYzc.

2. See, for example, the funding behind the popular procharter school education documentary, *Waiting for Superman* (Guggenheim 2010), and the movie where two mothers take over a failing public school, *Won't Back Down* (Barnz 2012), both of which were backed by the conservative Philip Anschutz Foundation. Julie Cavanaugh, "The Truth behind *Won't Back Down*," *Huffington Post*, last updated November 25, 2011, http://www .huffingtonpost.com/julie-cavanagh/wont-back-down_b_1906434.html.

REFERENCES

Allen, Patricia, and Julie Guthman. "From 'Old School' to 'Farm-to-School': Neoliberalization from the Ground Up." *Agriculture and Human Values* 23, no. 4 (2006): 401–415.

Althusser, Louis. "Ideology and Ideological State Apparatuses (Notes Toward an Investigation)." In *Lenin and Philosophy and Other Essays*, translated by Ben Brewster, 127–186. New York: Monthly Review Press, 1971.

Ball, Lillian. "Waterwash." n.d. http://www.lillianball.com/. (Accessed September 12, 2014).

Billig, Michael. *Banal Nationalism*. London and Thousand Oaks, Calif.: Sage, 1995.

Caffentzis, George. "On the Notion of a Crisis of Social Reproduction: A Theoretical Review." *Commoner* 5 (2002): 1–22.

Davidson, Elsa. *The Burdens of Aspiration: Schools, Youth, and Success in the Divided Social Worlds of Silicon Valley*. New York: New York University Press, 2011.

Federici, Silvia. *Caliban and the Witch: Women, the Body and Primitive Accumulation*. Brooklyn, N.Y.: Autonomedia, 2004.

Fine, Michelle, and Stan Karp. *Review of Parent Power: Grass-Roots Activism and K-12 Education Reform*. Boulder, Colo.: National Education Policy Center, 2012: http:// nepc.colorado.edu/thinktank/review-parent-power.

Fortunati, Leopoldina. *The Arcane of Reproduction: Housework, Prostitution, Labor and Capital*. Brooklyn, N.Y.: Autonomedia, 1989.

Foucault, Michel. *The Birth of Biopolitics: Lectures at the College de France 1978–1979*. Basingstoke and New York: Palgrave Macmillan, 2010.

Freire, Paulo. *Pedagogy of the Oppressed*. New York: Herder and Herder, 1970.

Gibson-Graham, J. K. *A Post-Capitalist Politics*. Minneapolis: University of Minnesota Press, 2006.

———. "A Feminist Project of Belonging for the Anthropocene." *Gender, Place and Culture* 18, no. 1 (2011): 1–21.

Hartmann, Heidi. "The Unhappy Marriage of Marxism and Feminism: Towards a More Progressive Union." *Capital and Class* 3, no. 2 (1979): 1–33.

Hung, Yvonne. "East New York Farms: Youth Participation in Community Development and Urban Agriculture." *Children, Youth and Environments* 14, no. 1 (2004): 20–31.

Ingram, Mrill. "Sculpting Solutions: Art-Science Collaborations in Sustainability." *Environment* 54, no. 4 (2012): 24–34.

———. "Washing Urban Water: Diplomacy in Environmental Art in the Bronx, New York City." *Gender, Place and Culture* (2013), DOI: 10.1080/0966369X.2013.769429.

Katz, Cindi. "Towards Minor Theory." *Environment and Planning D: Society and Space* 14, no. 4 (1996): 487–499.

———. "Banal Terrorism: Spatial Fetishism and Everyday Insecurity." In *Violent Geographies: Fear, Terror, and Political Violence*, edited by Derek Gregory and Allan Pred, 349–361. New York: Routledge, 2007.

———. "Bad Elements: Katrina and the Scoured Landscape of Social Reproduction." *Gender, Place and Culture* 15, no. 1 (2008): 15–29.

———. "Accumulation, Excess, Childhood: Toward a Countertopography of Risk and Waste." *Documents d'Anàlisi Geogràfica* 57, no. 1 (2011): 47–60.

———. "Just Managing: American Middle-Class Parenthood in Insecure Times." In *The Global Middle Classes: Theorizing through Ethnography*, edited by Rachel Heiman, Carla Freeman, and Mark Liechty, 169–187. Santa Fe: SAR Press, 2012.

Lipsitz, George. "Learning from New Orleans: The Social Warrant of Hostile Privatism and Competitive Consumer Citizenship." *Cultural Anthropology* 21, no. 3 (2006): 451–468.

Loftus, Alex. *Everyday Environmentalism: Creating an Urban Political Ecology*. Minneapolis: University of Minnesota Press, 2012.

Marx, Karl, and Friedrich Engels. *The German Ideology*, with an introduction by C. J. Arthur. New York: International Publishers, 1970.

McGuinn, Patrick, and Andrew P. Kelly. *Parent Power: Grass-Roots Activism and K-12 Education Reform*. Washington, D.C.: American Enterprise Institute, 2012, http://www.aei.org/files/2012/07/31/-parent-power-grassroots-activism-and-k12-education-reform_134233335113.pdf.

Marston, Sallie A., John Paul Jones III, and Keith Woodward. "Human Geography without Scale." *Transactions of the Institute of British Geographers* 30, no. 4 (2005): 416–432.

Mitchell, Katharyne, and Sarah Elwood. "From Redlining to Benevolent Societies: The Emancipatory Power of Spatial Thinking." *Theory and Research in Social Education* 40, no. 2 (2012): 134–163.

———. "Intergenerational Mapping and the Cultural Politics of Memory." *Space and Polity* 17, no. 2 (2013): 33–55.

Mitchell, Katharyne, and Chris Lizotte. "The Grassroots and the Gift: Philanthropy, Neoliberal Morality and Activism in Education." *Foucault Studies* 18 (September 2014): 69–89.

Moore, Sarah A., Morgan Apicella, Sallie A. Marston, and Moses Thompson. "Designing Nature for Learning: School Gardens for Youth and Child Education." *Children, Youth and Environments* 22, no. 1 (2012): 250–259.

Moore, Sarah A., Jeffrey Wilson, Sarah Kelly-Richards, and Sallie A. Marston. "School Gardens as Sites for Forging Progressive Socio-Ecological Futures." *Annals of the Association of American Geographers* 105, no. 2 (2015): DOI 10.1080/00045608.2014.985627.

Pred, Allan, and Michael J. Watts. *Reworking Modernity: Capitalisms and Symbolic Discontent.* New Brunswick, N.J.: Rutgers University Press, 1992.

Pudup, M. B. "It Takes a Garden: Cultivating Citizen-Subjects in Organized Garden Projects." *Geoforum* 39, no. 3 (2008): 1228–1240.

Rose, Nikolas. *Powers of Freedom: Reframing Political Thought.* Cambridge: Cambridge University Press, 1999.

———. *The Politics of Life Itself: Biomedicine, Power, and Subjectivity in the Twenty-First Century.* Princeton: Princeton University Press, 2006.

Sorkin, Michael. *Indefensible Space: The Architecture of the National Insecurity State.* New York: Routledge, 2008.

Stiegler, Bernard. *Technics and Time: The Fault of Epimetheus,* translated by George Collins and Richard Beardsworth. Stanford: Stanford University Press, 1998.

———. *Taking Care of Youth and the Generations,* translated by Stephen Barker. Stanford: Stanford University Press, 2010.

Wainwright, Joel. Email communication, 2013.

Waiting for Superman, directed by Davis Guggenheim. U.S.: Walden Media, 2010.

Won't Back Down, directed by Daniel Barnz. U.S.: Walden Media, 2012.

Woods, Clyde. "Do You Know What It Means to Miss New Orleans? Katrina, Trap Economics, and the Rebirth of the Blues." *American Quarterly* 57, no. 4 (2005): 1005–1018.

Woodward, Keith, Sallie A. Marston, and John Paul Jones III. "On Subjectivity, Politics, and Autonomous Spaces." *Progress in Human Geography* 36, no. 1 (2012): 204–224.

Woodward, Keith, John Paul Jones III, and Sallie A. Marston. "Of Eagles and Flies: Orientations Toward the Site." *Area* 42, no. 3 (2010): 270–280.

CONTRIBUTORS

KATE BEZANSON is an associate professor and chair of the Department of Sociology at Brock University.

SUSAN BRAEDLEY is an assistant professor in the School of Social Work at Carleton University.

JESSIE H. CLARK is an assistant professor at the University of Nevada Reno.

KELLY DOMBROSKI is a lecturer in the Department of Geography at the University of Canterbury.

ROSALIND FREDERICKS is an assistant professor at New York University's Gallatin School of Individualized Study.

ANDREW GORMAN-MURRAY is a senior lecturer in geography and urban studies in the School of Social Sciences and Psychology at the University of Western Sydney.

CINDI KATZ is a professor of geography and executive officer of the Earth and Environmental Sciences Program at the Graduate Center of the City University of New York.

MEG LUXTON is a professor and former director of the Graduate Program in Gender, Feminist, and Women's Studies in the School of Gender, Sexuality, and Women's Studies at York University.

BRIAN MARKS is an assistant professor in the Department of Geography and Anthropology at Louisiana State University.

SALLIE A. MARSTON is a professor in the School of Geography and Development at the University of Arizona.

KATIE MEEHAN is an assistant professor in the Department of Geography at the University of Oregon.

KATHARYNE MITCHELL is a professor in the Department of Geography at the University of Washington.

OONA MORROW is in the PhD program in geography at Clark University and is a member of the Community Economies Collective.

BRENDA PARKER is an assistant professor in the Department of Urban Policy and Planning at the University of Illinois at Chicago.

BARBARA ELLEN SMITH is a professor of women's and gender studies in the Department of Sociology at Virginia Tech.

KENDRA STRAUSS is an assistant professor of Labour Studies and an associate member of the Department of Geography at Simon Fraser University.

JAMIE WINDERS is an associate professor in geography at the Maxwell School of Citizenship and Public Affairs at Syracuse University.

INDEX

American South: coal industry, 108–10; commutes, 107; and globalization, 107; and Latinos, 110–12; and neoliberalism, 108–10; textile industry, 106–8; unemployment, 107–8; unions, 106–8, 109

amplification, 119, 122–27

Appalachia. *See* American South

artwork, 176–77

attention, 179–81

Australia, 65–78

Boston, Mass., USA: diverse economies, 88–90; life's work, 88–90; necessity, 93–95; and surplus, 92–95

Canada: as federation, 27 (*see also* open federalism); and global recession (2008), 33, 38. *See also* Conservative Party (Canada)

child care, 35–36, 86–88, 91–92, 124, 125, 127

childhood, 182–84

coal industry, 108–10

collective memory, 179–81

Community and School Garden Program, 177–78

commutes, 107, 109

Conservative Party (Canada), 25–40; and child care, 35–36; election of, 26–27, 27–30; and family values, 30–31, 32, 34–37, 38; income splitting, 36–37; moral orientation of, 28, 29–30, 34–35, 39–40; and neoliberalism, 29–30, 32, 39–40; open federalism, 28 (*see also* open federalism); stimulus spending, 29

cooperatives, 94

countertopographies, 83–84, 86–90

criminal justice system and race, 126–27

crisis, 65, 66, 67–68

Dakar, Senegal, 139–52

diverse economies, 84–85

domestic labor: definition, x; domestic work, x, 46; and men, 67, 72, 77; scholarship on, 3–4, 8, 104. *See also* househusbands; waste management

ecology: and artwork, 176–78; hurricanes, 164; and production, 159–60; protections, 109; self-provisioning, 88–89, 94; and shrimp industry, 161–62

environment, 184

Erdoğan, Tayyip, 53

gendered citizenship, 72–74, 76

globalization, 3; and American South, 107; commodities, 128; and security, 48–49; of shrimp industry, 160, 169–70

Harper, Stephen. *See* Conservative Party (Canada)

household commodity production, 156–70; and competition with capitalists, 159; cost/price crisis, 156, 161–62, 163–64, 168; intergenerational support, 163

household labor: gender divisions, 67. *See also* househusbands

househusbands, 65–78; and employment, 72–75; financial concerns, 71–72; growing number of, 67–69; and masculinity, 72–74, 76–77; and parenting, 75; and public vs. private sphere, 76; and recession (2008), 68–69

identity scholarship, 11–12

immigrants, 111–12

International Women's Day, 53, 56

Iraq War, 53

Islam and women, 51–52

Justice and Development Party (AKP), Turkey, 49–50, 51, 53, 54, 59n3

191

GEOGRAPHIES OF JUSTICE AND SOCIAL TRANSFORMATION